Innovation and Technological Diffusion

This book deals with two key aspects of the history of steam engines, a cornerstone of the Industrial Revolution: specifically, the road that led to its discovery and the process of diffusion of the early steam engines.

The first part of the volume outlines the technological and scientific developments which took place between the sixteenth and eighteenth centuries, proving critical for the invention of this strategic technology. The most important question addressed is why England came up with this innovation first as opposed to other countries (e.g., France, Italy), which were more advanced in terms of knowledge pertinent to it. The second part of the volume traces the process of diffusion of the early steam engines, the Newcomen model, through 1773, the year prior to the first commercial application of the second generation of steam engines (the Watt model). The process of diffusion is quantified on the basis of a novel method before proceeding with a discussion of the main determinants of this process.

Kitsikopoulos pulls together a large amount of relevant evidence found in primary sources and more technically oriented literature which is often ignored by economic historians. This book will be of interest to economic historians and historians of technology.

Harry Kitsikopoulos is Clinical Professor, Department of Economics, New York University, USA.

Routledge explorations in economic history
Edited by Lars Magnusson
Uppsala University, Sweden

For a complete list of titles in this series, please visit www.routledge.com.

Innovation and Technological Diffusion

An economic history of early
steam engines

Harry Kitsikopoulos

Routledge
Taylor & Francis Group

LONDON AND NEW YORK

First published 2016 by Routledge

2 Park Square, Milton Park, Abingdon, Oxfordshire OX14 4RN
52 Vanderbilt Avenue, New York, NY 10017

Routledge is an imprint of the Taylor & Francis Group, an informa business

First issued in paperback 2019

British Library Cataloguing in Publication Data
A catalogue record for this book is available from the British Library

Library of Congress Cataloging in Publication Data
A catalog record for this book has been requested.

ISBN: 978-1-138-94811-2 (hbk)
ISBN: 978-0-367-87476-6 (pbk)

Typeset in Times New Roman
by Swales & Willis Ltd, Exeter, Devon, UK

To my two little fairies,
Karina and Klio

Contents

Figures

Tables

Preface

Steam power has been the subject of systematic analysis by economic historians since the late 1970s with the publication of Nick von Tunzelmann's *Steam power and British industrialization to 1860* (Oxford: Clarendon Press, 1978) and John W. Kanefsky's dissertation, *The diffusion of power technology in British industry 1760–1870* (Ph. D. thesis, University of Exeter, 1979). The subject witnessed renewed interest in subsequent years through the publications of Alessandro Nuvolari, either in his single-author articles or in collaboration with B. Verspagen and/or von Tunzelmann (e.g., Nuvolari, Verspagen, and von Tunzelmann, 'The early diffusion of the steam engine in Britain, 1700–1800: a reappraisal', *Cliometrica*, 5, 2011, pp. 291–321). These seminal publications went a long way in elaborating on the microeconomics of steam power diffusion as well as the impact of this technology on sectoral and aggregate growth rates. Furthermore, the introduction of steam engines particularly in collieries, the sector which accounted (by far) for the highest number of installations, was the underlying cause for the spectacular growth of British coal output during the eighteenth century, marking the transition to a radically different energy regime, described in some recent monographs by E. A. Wrigley (*Energy and the English Industrial Revolution*, Cambridge and New York: Cambridge University Press, 2010) as well as by A. Kander, P. Malanima, and P. Warde, (*Power to the People: Energy in Europe Over the Last Five Centuries*, Princeton: Princeton University Press, 2013).

Given that steam power has been dealt with by such capable historians, it would seem that another monograph on the subject would be condemned to produce diminishing returns when it comes to our knowledge on the subject. In the author's view, however, this would amount to a false assessment.

Part I of the book delves into a question which surprisingly has not drawn any rigorous study: why was England the first country to invent the steam engine as opposed to a country such as Italy which had developed a more solid tradition on scientific principles pertinent to steam power? Part I consists of two chapters which address this question. Chapter 1 presents a factual narrative of the key technological and scientific developments which took place in the early modern period culminating eventually in the invention of the Savery and Newcomen models.[1] Chapter 2 discusses critically several explanations regarding the question of "why England first?" and argues that England surged ahead in this race because of a combination of factors as opposed to any single one of them playing singlehandedly the only role.

Part II of the book deals with the microeconomics of diffusion of the first generation of steam engines which found wide commercial applicability, the Newcomen model; and it focuses on the period from 1706, when the very first engine was installed, to 1773 which was the year prior to the first commercial application of the second generation of steam engines, the Watt model. Part II is comprised of four chapters following a brief introduction which reviews the literature on technological diffusion. Chapter 3 presents a method of measuring the diffusion rate which differs in several substantial respects from previous accounts. Chapter 4 enters the explanatory part by engaging in a comparison of the cost of steam power vs. other energy sources. Chapters 5 and 6 deal with the two factors which in the author's view played the most decisive role in conditioning the diffusion of Newcomen engines. The first of these factors was the improvement of engineering skills which led both to the construction of more powerful engines with lower fuel consumption as well as to better management of them on a daily basis. The second factor acted as a constraint on the diffusion process with little signs of improvement by 1773. Specifically, the installation cost of steam engines and related appurtenances was so substantial that it necessitated the achievement of a fairly high level of output in order to render this decision economically sound. Achieving such high levels of output at the firm level, however, hinged on the strength of demand conditions which were often limited due to the fragmentation of markets imposed by poor transportation networks in several parts of the country. The Epilogue following these four chapters pulls together the entire evidence and formulates the key conclusions.

As imperative as it is to state what the book is all about, it is equally important to justify what the book is not concerned with. This study is not part of the literature on the energy transition of the eighteenth century. A substantial part of this study deals with the adoption rate of this strategic technology which acted as a precondition for the transition from sources of energy such as water and animals to coal. But it does not seek to enter the literature on this energy transition which has already received expert treatment on the part of the historians cited above. It is also not a study of the impact of steam power on the trajectory of the British Industrial Revolution simply because, as von Tunzelmann argued long ago, this contribution was minimal even by 1800, nearly a century into the diffusion path of this technology. The impact of steam power was felt well into the nineteenth century, particularly once it played a pivotal role in the transportation revolution brought by railroads and having spread within the factory system. However, Chapter 2 reviews certain configurations in a pan-European context which aligned in the most favorable way in the case of England, proving to be critical not only for the invention of steam engines but also paving the way for the Industrial Revolution.

The author perceives the contributions of this monograph in the following respects: (a) in posing questions which have not drawn any prior systematic treatment, such as England's uniqueness in coming up with this monumental invention; (b) in adopting a novel method of quantifying the diffusion of steam power;

(c) in bringing together a wealth of empirical material relevant to the factors which conditioned the diffusion process which is often lacking in the literature of early steam engines; and (d) while the study confirms, through a more systematic analysis, the relevance to the diffusion process of factors which have being stressed by the literature (e.g., the importance of engineering skills), it does downplay the importance of others (e.g., the role of the patent premium), and discusses a factor which has scarcely received any attention (the impact of market configurations).

The author is indebted to several individuals and institutions which played a decisive role in the culmination of his work. The effort started in 1998 through the award of a Smithsonian summer fellowship allowing access to the valuable collections of the Dibner Library of Rare Books. Three years later another summer fellowship granted by the NEH allowed me to return to the Dibner and to complete the task of gathering material from primary sources. I was fortunate to have my visits coincide with the times the library was headed by two individuals of exceptional professionalism, Bill Baxter and Ron Brashear.

Anonymous referees provided valuable comments while Margaret Jacob was kind enough to give me her insights on Chapter 2 during the early stages of writing. When the analysis of the empirical material started in recent years, I was fortunate to receive from Alessandro Nuvolari an electronic version of Dr. Kanefsky's database. I am grateful to the former for sharing it with me and to Dr. Kanefsky for giving me an update on his subsequent addition of entries to the database as well as providing very useful comments on Chapter 3. The econometric analysis benefited from the generous advice of several colleagues at the Economics Department of NYU: Nazgul Jenish, John Lazarev, Bruce McNevin, Konrad Menzel, and Quang Vuong. But I am most thankful to two former graduate students of my department, Lawrence Costa and Michel Dilmanian, for their very hard work and dedication to this project. Lawrence and Michel handled the revisions made to the Kanefsky database, prepared all the graphs, ran the tests and authored, either individually or jointly, the appendixes which appear in Part II of the book describing the econometric methods and results.[2] In addition, Alexandros Kaliontzakis, an undergraduate student at NYU, was kind enough to prepare the three diffusion maps of the Epilogue.

Finally, I am grateful to Mary C. McDonald, Director of Publications at the American Philosophical Society, for granting me permission to reproduce the first chapter of the book which originally appeared in the *Proceedings* of the Society; as well as to Susan Babbitt who did an amazing job in polishing the prose and the aesthetic appearance of the article. Most importantly, I was fortunate to work on this project with Emily Kindleysides, Senior Editor at Routledge, and her very helpful assistant Laura Johnson; their cheerful personalities and willingness to address my numerous questions rendered the process of preparing the manuscript as easy as it can be.

The usual disclaimer applies: while all the aforementioned individuals made valuable contributions to my effort, I am solely responsible for any remaining flaws.

Harry Kitsikopoulos
Riverdale, April 2015

Notes

1 This chapter is the only one that has been published, appearing in the *Proceedings of the American Philosophical Society*, 157, 3 (2013), pp. 304–44.
2 The econometric analysis appears in appendixes in order to make the main text more approachable to those who lack the relevant expertise.

Part I

Innovation

1 From Hero to Newcomen

The critical scientific and technological developments that led to the invention of the steam engine

Historians of all sorts have published over the years countless narratives referring to the Newcomen and Watt models, the first steam engines to have had a widespread impact, from altering the institutional structure of capitalism by solidifying the position of the factory system to boosting sectoral and aggregate growth rates as they diffused in large segments of the economy. No written account, however, has been produced during the past century or so referring to the evolution of steam devices that ultimately led to the invention of the Newcomen model.

The first fragments of knowledge on the properties of steam date back to antiquity, followed by fourteen centuries of silence on this subject. When interest resurfaced at the dawn of the early modern period there were two parallel streams of development. The first involved the construction of several devices utilizing steam power, the second a number of experiments that led to a major scientific breakthrough, the discovery of the vacuum. There is a widespread belief that until well into the nineteenth century science played little, if any, role in the process of technological innovation and that, in fact, the reverse may be true; the contribution of steam engines to the formulation of the laws of thermodynamics is often used as an example. The story that will be told in this essay proves that the invention of the steam engine constitutes a remarkable exception. It will be argued that without the discovery of the vacuum the modern steam engine would not have emerged as a historical artifact.

This is a story that revolves around the work of a limited number of individuals, virtually all of them living in Italy, France, England, and Germany. The first section of this introductory essay will focus on the period c. 1550–1640, when the ancient references to steam were rediscovered in Europe, disseminated through publications, and crystallized in a few simple devices. The second section will review the key experiments that led to the discovery of the vacuum in the period 1640–60. The third section will deal with the devices that followed this scientific breakthrough, while the fourth will focus on the last two links of this evolutionary process, the Savery and Newcomen models, the first working steam engines. The concluding section will summarize the evidence and formulate certain generalizations stemming from it.

The West rediscovers Hero of Alexandria

The first known reference to steam as a motive power was made by Hero of Alexandria (first century AD) in his work *Pneumatica.* Hero described an apparatus, called an aeolipile, consisting of a boiler filled partially with water and placed over a fire; the steam generated passed through a pipe into a globe with orifices, and as the steam escaped from the latter it caused the globe to rotate (Figure 1.1). It is not clear whether this device was put to any use, but because Hero named two of his inventions *Libations at an Altar by Fire* and *Libations Poured on an Altar, and a Serpent made to Hiss, by Fire* some have speculated that a modified version of his apparatus was used to produce mystical impressions in worshippers. A boiler hidden in the hollow figure of an idol would produce steam channeled through a pipe ending in one or two branches to the nose and/or mouth of a deity placed in a temple, the escaping steam giving the impression of a breathing figure, inspiring awe; similar mystical illusions would be created when steam escaped from the mouth of a serpent, a creature highly venerated in ancient times. Such speculation seems justified given the testimony of Greek and Roman travelers to Egypt who were impressed by such spectacles.[1]

The centuries following Hero's writings, through the early modern period, constitute a sort of Dark Ages for steam power, with at least one notable exception. A learned man named Gerbert (either a professor or a priest) installed in a church in Rheims, in the tenth century, "an hydraulic organ in which the air escaping in a surprising manner by the force of heated water, fills the cavity of

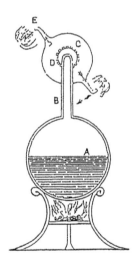

Figure 1.1 Hero's aeolipile. A fire below a boiler *A* generates steam that passes
through the pipe *B* into the globe *DC*; by escaping through the orifices of
the latter it causes its rotation.

Sources: Clark, *An Elementary Treatise*, p. 6. A similar description is given by Arago, "History of the Steam Engine," p. 5.

the interior of the instrument, and the brazen pipes emit modulated tones through the multifarious apertures".[2]

Hero's works did not draw attention for the next sixteen centuries but finally resurfaced in Italy during the Renaissance inspired by the Humanists (e.g., Petrarch, Boccaccio) through the reign of Cosimo de' Medici. Regiomontanus, a noted German astronomer, who visited Italy in 1461 with the express purpose of studying ancient Greek manuscripts, came across the *Pneumatica,* and proceeded to translate it. Regiomontanus returned to Nuremberg after six years without following up on Hero's ideas on steam; he was preoccupied with an observatory built on his behalf by a wealthy benefactor. But by the middle of the sixteenth century there was a flurry of Italian translations beginning with the Bologna edition of 1547, the Ferrara reprint of 1589, and other notable editions in 1575 and 1592; other editions of lesser note and numerous references to Hero's writings also sprang up during those years. The dissemination of these ideas moved northward. Salomon de Caus familiarized himself with Hero during a visit to Italy at the end of the century before moving back to France; and by the 1640s Hero's treatise had gone through five editions in England. Exposure to Hero's ideas generated great interest among the savants of Europe, as evidenced by the writings of Hieronymus Cardan (1557), an eminent Italian mathematician and physician; of Jacob Besson (1569), a French professor of mathematics and natural philosophy at Orleans; and of the German theologian Malthesius (1571), who described in one of his sermons a contrivance that worked with the power of steam. The second half of the sixteenth century highlights the modern rediscovery of the powers of steam and some nascent speculations about its mechanical applications, with Italy at the epicenter and the diffusion of this knowledge moving fairly quickly to France and somewhat more slowly to England and the Germanic lands. By the early seventeenth century aeolipiles were quite common, used in the melting of glass and metals, for blowing fires in houses, and improving the draft of chimneys.[3]

But the more interesting question is, when did Europeans start coming up with their own versions of steam power contrivances? In addressing this question we shall begin with the year 1543, when Blasco de Garay, a captain of the Spanish navy, claimed to have invented a machine capable of propelling large ships even in the absence of wind. The particulars of this invention are difficult to come by because our knowledge of it is based solely on a manuscript published in 1826, the latter relying exclusively on a letter sent to its author by Thomas Gonzalez, director of the royal archives of Simuncas. The Spanish King Charles V was intrigued enough to order a trial, which took place in the port of Barcelona on 17 June 1543 on board a ship of two hundred tons called *Trinity* and was witnessed by a committee of high officials from Catalonia. All we know of this apparatus is that it consisted of a copper boiler and moving wheels on either side of the ship and that the latter moved at about one league per hour, a rate very similar to that of sailing ships at the time. De Garay took the apparatus apart once the experiment was over, and the project was never followed through, although the king bestowed promotions and treasure on de Garay. It is not clear why the project was aborted, but one may speculate that the king's preoccupation with a military expedition, the fact that the apparatus was "complicated and expensive" (according to one hostile member of the committee) without providing an impetus greater than that of winds, and the fear of explosions, all played a role in this regard.[4]

De Garay's "invention" is puzzling in terms of both the timing and the place of its appearance. Spain did not have a scientific tradition regarding the powers of steam; in fact, no European country did at that time. The Barcelona experiment took place four years prior to the first Italian translation of Hero's *Pneumatica*. It is highly unlikely that de Garay succeeded in coming up with an apparatus more sophisticated than an aeolipile; the level of mechanical skills at the time would not have permitted the construction of anything resembling the steam engines of the eighteenth century. The most likely explanation is that de Garay put together two existing technologies: Hero's aeolipile, the knowledge of which would have been remarkable, but not impossible, at the time; and the notion of placing paddlewheels on the sides, something that had been used in both Roman boats and late medieval galleys.[5] In other words, de Garay came up with a fairly simple mechanism in which an aeolipile generated motion to paddlewheels in the manner depicted in Figure 1.2.

Assuming de Garay's device was an aeolipile, the very first European invention differentiating itself from Hero's ideas comes, befittingly, from a well-known

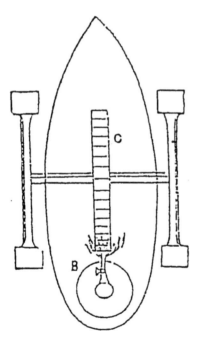

Figure 1.2 De Garay's "steamboat." The main source of power was probably an aeolipile B giving motion to a central wheel that in turn transmitted it to the paddlewheels.

Source: Clark, *An Elementary Treatise*, p. 14.

Italian mathematician and chemist, Giambattista della Porta, whose home in Naples was the focal point of local savants. Della Porta's device, described in analytical detail in a pamphlet that came out in 1601, used the power of steam to press upon the surface of water, forcing it up a pipe. Its most obvious application was in fountains (see Figure 1.3). The main question della Porta tried to address was how much steam was generated by a certain quantity of water. His methodology was somewhat flawed and his device never found any applications. In the end, it was more of a toy than a contrivance with practical mechanical applications.[6] Nevertheless, it highlights the dawn of an era that eventually led to the invention of practical steam engines, although it is significant that it comes up a half century after the subject of steam was rediscovered in Europe.

Frenchmen, following closely in the steps of Italians in showing an interest in the powers of steam, are represented by Salomon de Caus, a landscape gardener by profession who was employed in France and Italy and came to England some time in 1609–10, attracting the attention of Prince Henry, the eldest son of James I. The prince died in 1612, and when his sister married the Elector Palatine, de Caus followed them to Germany. In 1615 a publisher in Frankfurt printed his

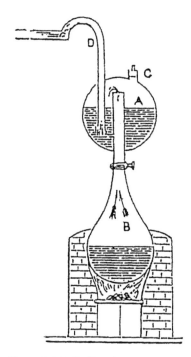

Figure 1.3 Della Porta's apparatus. In this apparatus steam rises from a boiler *B* through its neck, which ends above the surface of the water, partially filling a vessel *A*. The building pressure of steam presses upon the water, which is forced up the pipe *D*.

Source: Clark, *An Elementary Treatise*, p. 16.

celebrated book, which has an encyclopedic character covering subjects from the design of grottoes and fountains to various methods of raising water and mill-work, among others; he explicitly states that many of these designs were inspired when he was working for Prince Henry. In this book de Caus describes a little apparatus consisting of a single vessel partially filled with water. As the latter is heated at its bottom the steam generated presses upon the water, forcing it up a pipe (see Figure 1.4). This little contrivance is a simpler version of an aeolipile and of della Porta's device and is, in fact, less efficient than the latter. De Caus himself did not assign particular importance to it. He gave only a brief descrip-tion of it in the context of a large and very diverse range of topics; it seems that he treated it as an object pertinent only to fountains, as befitted his professional interests. Incidentally, he also referred to a discovery made in 1603 by another Frenchman, Florence Rivault, involving a copper ball partially filled with water that, after being heated, burst asunder with great force.[7]

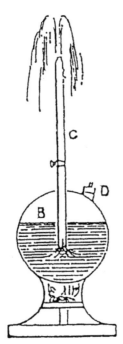

Figure 1.4 De Caus's apparatus. The device consists of a single vessel *B* partially filled with water through the valve *D,* which also acts as a regulator of steam. The vessel is heated at the bottom and steam builds up inside the vessel, pressing on the water and forcing it up the pipe *C.* De Caus's design is very inefficient because as water is replenished through *D* it cools down the boiler, wasting both time and heat in generating steam again, whereas in Porta's design cold water is forced out of a second vessel, separate from the boiler generating the steam (see fig. 3).

Source: Clark, *An Elementary Treatise*, p. 17.

Italian interest in the powers of steam continued through this period but did not lead to any technological breakthroughs. Giovanni Branca, a noted engineer, published a book in 1629 in which he depicted an aeolipile enclosed in a figurehead shooting against a wheel and causing it to revolve (see Figure 1.5). In his book Branca was copying devices invented by others, including this mechanism, and there were conceptual flaws in it; the steam partially condensed passing through the air and coming into contact with the cold surface of the wheel. Nevertheless, it is a device worth mentioning because the movement of the wheel was meant to be transmitted to other wheels through a piston moving stampers suspended over mortars.[8] In other words, this apparatus conceptualizes for the first time the possibility of harnessing the power of steam for productive purposes.

At this point it had been eighty years since the flurry of translations of Hero's work and thirty years since the first steam contrivances deriving from the aeolipile. Hero's concepts were known in England by this time, but one is struck by the complete absence of Englishmen participating in these developments. However, things were about to change in a dramatic fashion. Hero and the aeolipile were certainly known by that time, as evidenced by a reference to a device reminiscent of Branca's by Bishop John Wilkins, a polymath and founder of the Royal Society, in his *Mathematicall Magick* published in 1648. But it was David Ramsay who initiated an English tradition that eventually led to the invention of steam engines. Ramsay was a groom of the bedchamber to Prince Henry when the latter noticed and employed de Caus. It is likely that Ramsay witnessed the working of

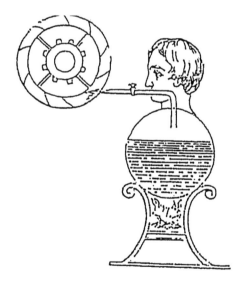

Figure 1.5 Branca's aeolipile. The steam generated in the boiler is transmitted through the pipe projecting through the figure's head to the side of a wheel. The power generated by the latter can be transmitted to other mechanisms not depicted here.

Source: Clark, *An Elementary Treatise*, pp. 17–18.

de Caus's apparatus but was not impressed with it, since there is no evidence that he dealt with steam-related matters in subsequent years. Eventually he became involved with several patents as a co-grantee, including one with Dud Dudley for the smelting of iron using pit coal. Jenkins speculated that he may have had nothing to do with any of these inventions and that his name was listed because of his known technical skills and his connections to the royal court. But then he appears as the sole petitioner for a patent in 1630 (granted the following year) referring to an engine using "fire". Ramsay included the following claims: "To Raise Water from Lowe Pitts by Fire" and "To Raise Water from Lowe Places and Mynes, and Coal Pitts, by a new Waie never yet in Use". In the terminology of later decades "fire engines" referred to steam engines; Ramsay clearly had steam power in mind. We know nothing of his device since the patent includes no analytical description and there is unanimity among historians that Ramsay's ideas did not materialize into anything concrete. But it is utterly remarkable that the very first person who attempted the construction of a steam power device on British soil (Ramsay was a Scotsman), assuming his was not an aeolipile, focused his attention on an application of paramount economic importance, i.e., mine drainage, particularly of coal mines. One may speculate that de Caus planted an idea in Ramsay's head, and that the latter focused on this problem in subsequent years through contact with people familiar with the problem of mine drainage.[9]

The extirpation of an ancient doctrine ("Nature abhors a vacuum")

During the century from the 1540s to the 1630s, Europeans became reacquainted with the lost knowledge of antiquity but contributed little to either theoretical understanding or techniques relating to steam. Beginning in the 1640s, however, there occurred key scientific breakthroughs relating to the physics of the atmosphere that were of critical importance to the eventual invention of steam engines.[10] For two millennia the celebrated Aristotelian doctrine of *horror vacui* (nature abhors a vacuum) dominated thinking among European savants; the notion of absolutely empty space was simply inconceivable. This notion came into question when the grand duke of Tuscany ordered his workers to dig a well in order to supply water for his palace. Water was found at a depth of 40 feet and a suction pipe was installed. When the pump, however, was put to work the water would not rise above 33 feet, falling 7 feet short of the top of the well. Galileo was consulted. Unable to solve the paradox, he retreated to Aristotelian logic, explaining that water rushed into the pipe as the vacuum was formed by the pump (because nature abhors a vacuum) and adding that there seems to be a limit to nature's abhorrence, this limit being 33 feet.[11]

    Galileo, as is well known, was placed under house arrest by church authorities for promoting Copernican views, but was allowed to invite a few friends to stay and work with him. One of them was Evangelista Torricelli, a brilliant scientist who had written a book on the mechanics of motion, prompting Galileo's invitation. About the time Torricelli was exposed through Galileo to the puzzle posed by the Grand Duke's well, another Italian, a mathematician by the name of Gasparo Berti, was experimenting on the same issue (c. 1641–42). Berti took a lead tube 36 feet long and fitted with a valve at the bottom, filled it with water, and partially immersed it in a water vessel. The valve was then removed and some water ran out into the vessel, but the one in the tube was stabilized at about 30 feet. Berti's experiment posed a problem identical with that of the pump in the well. But it was Torricelli who finally figured it out. Galileo had taught him that air has weight, and that led Torricelli to the conclusion that as the air was sucked out of the pipe in the well the atmosphere outside the pipe pressed on the water, forcing it to a height whose weight was identical with (i.e., counterbalanced) that of the atmosphere. Through an experiment similar to Berti's and carried out by his pupil Vincenzo Viviani in 1643, Torricelli proved the same principle by using mercury. Since the density of the latter is 14 times that of water, a pump would draw up a column of mercury to a height of one-fourteenth of that of water, i.e., 30 inches. The mercury experiments allowed him to invent the barometer. Torricelli's experiments "confirmed his hypothesis that it was not nature's intolerance of a vacuum but the weight of the atmosphere that kept the fluid suspended".[12] The *horror vacui* doctrine, lasting for two millennia, was finally thrown into the dustbin of history.

Torricelli published no account of his findings, but through correspondence with friends the news of his experiments reached Pascal in France. There was no acquaintance between the two of them, and Pascal did not get details of Torricelli's experiments. Nevertheless, he was able to produce the same results. His views on the physics of the atmosphere were first formed through an experiment involving a glass tube, open at the top and having some mercury at its base. The tube was immersed in a vessel of water and the deeper it went, the higher the mercury rose due to the higher water pressure. Pascal reasoned that the same principle applies to the atmosphere, that is, its pressure is less at high altitudes than at lower ones. To prove this principle, he asked his brother-in-law to take a barometer up a mountain near Clermont. The experiment took place on 29 September 1648, registering lower readings in the barometer tube at the top of the mountain.

Two years later the spirit of invention moved to Germany, where Otto von Guericke, the Mayor of Magdeburg and a former military engineer, engaged in some crucial experiments of his own. One of them was virtually identical with Torricelli's tube. It was exhausted of air, thus forcing the water to move up to about 30 feet. But two other experiments incorporate an element crucial to the eventual invention of modern steam engines. In the first, performed in 1654, he evacuated the air out of a fixed cylinder fitted with a piston. The latter subsequently descended under the pressure of the atmosphere despite the efforts of twenty men to keep the piston at the top of the cylinder (see Figure 1.6a). In the second experiment (1661) a similar cylinder fitted with a piston is connected over pulleys with a scale of weights; when the air is exhausted from the cylinder through a pump, the piston descends, pulling the scale upward (see Figure 1.6b). Von Guericke's experiments were crucial, but not because he discovered the vacuum and the mechanical effects of atmospheric pressure. That had been done by Torricelli and Pascal several years earlier. Instead, it was his use of a cylinder

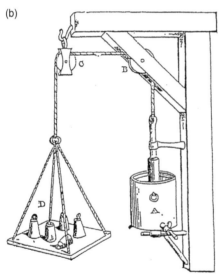

Figure 1.6 Guericke's experiments. In the 1654 experiment (1.6a), Guericke uses a sphere to pump air out of a cylinder fitted with a piston. Once the air is out the atmosphere presses on top of the piston and, despite the efforts of twenty men, the latter descends downward. In a similar experiment, performed in 1661 (1.6b), when the air is sucked out with a pump at the base of the cylinder the piston descends, pulling up the scale of weights.

Sources: Bourne, *A Treatise on the Steam Engine*, pp. 5–6; Briggs, *The Power of Steam*, p. 22.

fitted with a piston that was important. If the evacuation of air caused the descent of the piston to raise a certain weight, then it was a matter of time before someone could figure out that the same effect could be produced by condensation of steam, and that if this action was performed repeatedly a powerful device would be in place. One interesting question to ask here is whether von Guericke conceived of his experiments on his own, as Pascal did, unaware of the specifics of Torricelli's work. That may well be the case. On the other hand, there are some interesting connections among some of the aforementioned individuals. Berti's experiments were witnessed by Athanasius Kircher, a well-known scholar based in Rome with a deep interest in steam. Kircher, in turn, had a German pupil, Caspar Schott, who returned to Germany at the end of the Thirty Years' War after teaching in Italy for twenty years at the time von Guericke started his experiments. In fact, the two of them developed a correspondence. These connections reveal the type of channels through which, and the speed at which, scientific information flowed and make it clear that von Guericke was aware of, and became inspired by, the Italians' work on the physics of the atmosphere.

Schott published two books in which he referred to von Guericke's experiments, in 1657 and 1664. Robert Boyle, the son of the Earl of Cork, and subsequently a founding member of the Royal Society, became fascinated with matters of science while taking his Grand Tour in Europe, where he familiarized himself with Galileo's work. He followed von Guericke's experiments very closely and became acquainted with them very shortly after the publication of Schott's 1657 book. Boyle studied what he called the "spring and weight of the air" and published his views in 1660. What is most important, he came up with the most efficient pump of the time with the help of his able assistant Robert Hooke. Boyle was able to reproduce Pascal's experiment without having to ascend to a mountain top. He simply suspended a mercury column inside a pump. As the air was gradually taken out, the mercury of the column descended.

Lingering at, not crossing, the threshold of glory: from the Marquis of Worcester to Papin

During this twenty-year period (1640–60) these scientific developments were destined to have revolutionary effects on the development of devices utilizing steam. There was resistance to them in some quarters, in many cases driven by Descartes's rationalism, which rejected the notion of a vacuum and the usefulness of experiments (see Chapter 2). But the evidence was too powerful to negate. Nevertheless, these major scientific breakthroughs did not seem to have translated right away into radically different designs at the level of techniques. At least there is considerable doubt in the case of Edward Somerset, the Marquis of Worcester.[13] In his pamphlet entitled *Century of Inventions,* published in 1663, the marquis laid claim to a number of outlandish inventions. Of particular interest are those numbered 68 and 98–100. His description of them suggests some sort of steam-powered device, for example, "an admirable and most forcible way to drive up water by fire.".[14] But while the marquis enumerated several uses for his apparatus (mine drainage, irrigation, use at urban waterworks, elevation of the level of rivers to render them navigable), at the same time, he provided obscure and very limited information on their working mechanism. He talked, for instance, about two vessels: the first worked to the point of consuming its water when the second is utilized, thus keeping the fire constant. This description suggests the use of two boilers working in tandem to produce a "constant fountain [of] steam".[15] This is clearly a hydraulic device possibly powered by steam.

Subsequent historians have raised doubts about the marquis's claims, treating his description as wishful thinking rather than practically relevant engineering prowess. In fact, no working model has survived. In addition, despite the author's promise to publish a book giving details of the device's working mechanism accompanied with plates that would allow any skilled engineer to reconstruct it, no such published account came forward in the remaining four years of his life. And it certainly did not help that the marquis made some very outlandish claims when it comes to other inventions.[16]

Such doubts, however, seem to be unfounded. To begin with, the apparatus was witnessed by two credible observers who had no interest in the marquis's scheme nor any prior association with him. The first account belongs to Samuel Sorbière, historian to the King of France, who published in 1664 an account of his impressions during a visit to England; in 1663 Sorbière had visited Vauxhall, where the marquis had erected his invention with the help of his assistant Caspar Kaltoff. The second account was recorded in 1669, two years after the marquis's death, by the secretary of Cosimo de' Medici, Grand Duke of Tuscany. Both observers provide brief descriptions, without details, of the working mechanism of the device they witnessed. Thus there is no doubt that such a device did exist. In between these years, there is also a reference to the device by Dr. Hooke in a letter to Boyle (1667). The reference is utterly derogatory, calling the marquis's schemes "purely romantic" and adding that even Kaltoff admitted to him that the device had functioning problems. Hooke was not allowed to examine it up close, but there is no doubt he referred to a tangible object. Finally, the grant of a monopoly to the marquis by Parliament, by means of a private Act, a few months prior to the publication of *The Century* is also suggestive. It is not clear whether any witnesses were called during the process and there is no evidence that the marquis supplied a working model to the lord treasurer, as the passing of the Act required. Nevertheless, the formality of the process suggests that the members of Parliament were aware of the existence of a tangible model.[17]

But there is an even more intractable issue at hand: assuming the apparatus was real, how did it work? Most later observers are inclined to believe that the device was a double de Caus or a double della Porta engine (double because of the two "vessels"), two of the suggested versions depicted in Figures 1.7a and 1.7b. This speculation is plausible because the marquis spent the years c. 1648 to 1656 in exile in France following the fall of Charles I. His stay in France, preceding the inception of his invention, would certainly have acquainted him with the work of his two predecessors; in fact, during these years the second edition of de Caus' work was published in France. On the other hand, Robert Stuart, one of the most respected authorities on steam engines in the nineteenth century, leaves open the possibility that the device incorporated a piston. In referring to his invention, the marquis notes that "one pound raise[s] an hundred as high as the one pound falls; and the one pound being taken off, the hundred and twelve pounds shall again descend, performing the entire effect of an hundred weight."[18] Stuart speculates that the marquis may be describing here a steam engine with a piston weighing one pound attached to a lever whose other end raises 112 pounds. If that is the case, such a construction would be much simpler than the version reminiscent of de Caus's and della Porta's devices. An engine incorporating a piston is not out of the question, for from the time von Guericke's experiments became known in England, to Boyle and his circle at first, and the erection of the engine at Vauxhall there is an interval of five or six years, during which the marquis was back in England and thus could have come across the idea of a cylinder with a piston. On the other hand, there is no strong evidence that the marquis was rubbing shoulders with the narrow circle of savants who were abreast of von Guericke's experiments. Thus the more likely scenario is that his invention was a more elaborate version of de Caus's or della Porta's devices.

(a)

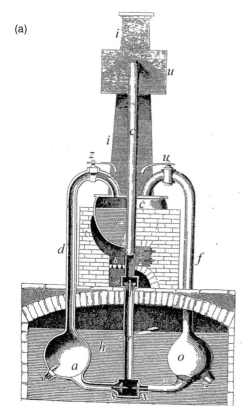

Figure 1.7 (continued)

(b)

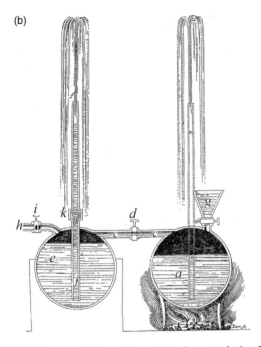

Figure 1.7 Two versions of Somerset's steam device. Figure 1.7a, visualized by Stuart, conforms very closely to a model proposed by Millington. Water is boiled in the boiler *c*, the stopcock *z* is opened, steam runs through the pipe *d* into the vessel *a*, which is partially filled with water. The steam forces the water through the valve *s* up the pipe *e* into the reservoir *u*. The stopcock *z* is then turned off and the pressure of steam in vessel *a* is eliminated, allowing water to force itself into the vessel *a* from the reservoir which it is submerged into. Exactly the same operation is repeated on the right-hand side of the apparatus, the two procedures alternating with each other. In figure 1.7b water is poured through the funnel *g* into the boiler *a*, generating steam that passes through the pipe *c*, once the stopcock *d* is opened, into the cold water vessel *e*. The steam forces the water from *e* into the eduction pipe *f*. Stopcock *d* is then closed, water is allowed into *e* through pipe *h*, stopcock *d* is opened again, and the entire cycle begins anew. See Stuart, *A Descriptive History*, pp. 14–15, 19–20.

During the last quarter of the seventeenth century developments in steam power technology became almost exclusively an Anglo-French affair. Jean de Hautefeuille, a high official of the Church with an interest in mechanics, published in 1678 several interesting ideas incorporating the notion of using gunpowder on alternate sides of the piston in order to produce a vacuum but, most significantly, achieving the latter through the condensation of steam. This was the first time the idea of using steam condensation and a piston to exert mechanical effects was expressed. Unfortunately, Hautefeuille limited himself to conceptualization; we have no evidence he crossed into the realm of experiments or came up with any

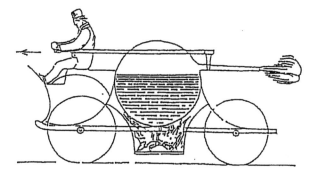

Figure 1.8 Newton's locomotive. The circular boiler is mounted on wheels, and
as the steam is forced out in one direction it propels the vehicle in the
opposite direction.

Source: Sewell, *Elementary Treatise*, p. 244.

concrete devices. His ideas, however, reflect the level of maturity attained by
that time in visualizing the crucial components of a steam engine right before its
ultimate invention.[19]

A few years later, in the 1680s, the celebrated Newton came up with the first
conceptualization of the use of steam for locomotive purposes (see Figure 1.8).
Newton's vision coincides chronologically with some attempts made by Samuel
Morland, master mechanic to the King of England, the exact nature of which is
surrounded by uncertainty. As early as 1661 we find him petitioning for a patent
regarding "an engine for the raiseing of water out of any mines or pits in greater
quantities, shorter time, and with much lesse help than has ever yet been practiced
or heard of". A warrant was issued in which there is a handwritten clarification
stating that this apparatus used "the force of Aire and Powder conjointly".[20] In
Jenkins's view this was added by King Charles II himself. He took an active
role in producing accurate descriptions of patents. A patent, however, was never
issued, most likely because Morland felt that his design was impracticable.

Twenty years or so elapsed before Morland came back in 1682 with another
device that was shown to the king. The device almost certainly utilized steam;
the state papers refer to Morland's "new invention for raising any quantity of
water to any height by the help of fire alone".[21] The king was very content, stating that "we are fully satisfied [it] is altogether new and may be of great use for
the clering of all sortes of mines."[22] Morland failed, once again, to seek a patent,
perhaps because he was sent by the king around that time to help out with some
hydraulic projects of his French counterpart at Versailles. Morland's work in
France was not successful. He fell into disgrace and faced financial difficulties
that prevented him for a while from coming back to England. After his return
little was heard of him.

While in France, Morland did seek the patronage of the French king, but it is
not clear whether it was for a special pump he invented or for a steam-powered

apparatus. The case for the latter is strengthened by two manuscripts he published, one of them in Paris in 1685. The references to steam are limited and vague, but it is stated that,

> when subjected to the laws of statics, and, by science, reduced to the measure of weight and balance, it bears its burden peaceably (like good horses) and thus may be of great use to mankind, especially for the raising of water.[23]

This statement is followed by a table of figures that show the connection between different cylinder diameters and the quantity of water capable of being raised to certain heights. His figures are remarkably close to accurate, indicating that, at the very least, he experimented with steam.

There is another piece of evidence, admittedly circumstantial, that strengthens the case that Morland came up with a tangible device. Roger North (son of Dudley North) published his diary, which shows a sketch of a steam engine. He did not attribute it explicitly to Morland, but Jenkins speculated that it was probably his since North was familiar with Morland's work through the close association of the latter with his brother Francis. North's sketch is accompanied with a description of his that makes reference to a boiler producing steam acting upon a piston in a closed cylinder and forcing it up, but it is not made clear how the piston completed the cycle by moving downward; if by condensation, this would anticipate the invention of later steam engines. The description continues by mentioning that this apparatus was connected to wheel work that could be applied to various uses. In the end, it is not clear how Morland fits in the overall prehistory of the steam engine. It is certainly plausible that he developed an interest in steam early on, since his unsuccessful 1661 device places him chronologically at the time when the Marquis of Worcester had the same preoccupations, the two of them being part of the same royal circle. Perhaps Jenkins's view is the most accurate, that is, Morland did produce some steam-powered apparatus, but there is considerable doubt that it bears a direct link to the eventual invention of more sophisticated steam engines.[24]

Morland was the last individual before the final stretch that leads to the invention of the steam engine. Those who have been mentioned so far played a role in this evolutionary process, but there may have been others we know nothing about, either because they have left no traces of their efforts or because such records have not yet been found. But one thing is certain: the final stretch evolved into a race among three individuals. Denis Papin was the most tragic of these figures.[25] Born in Blois, he graduated from the University of Angers with a degree in medicine and two years later, in 1671, was appointed curator of experiments in the French Academy following a recommendation by Huygens. Huygens, having impressed Colbert with his scientific achievements, was invited by the latter to join and become one of the founding members of the Academy in 1666. He had also attended the same university and this, along with the fact that Colbert's wife was also from Blois, may have played a role in Papin's invitation to the Academy.

Papin's experiments focused from the very beginning on methods of creating a vacuum and on the theory of pneumatics. An account of these experiments was published in 1674. Huygens shared similar interests, and in responding to Colbert's invitation he committed himself to experiments for "examining the power of common powder by enclosing a small quantity of it in a very thick iron or copper box—Examining in the same way the power of water rarefied by fire".[26] Papin's stint in the French Academy was fairly short. He left in 1675 for London where he met Lord Brouncker, president of the Royal Society, bearing a reference from Huygens. He was immediately offered employment in Boyle's laboratory, where he conducted experiments, among other things, with a double-acting air pump of his own invention, and a few years later he became a member of the Society. After a three-year stint in Venice working for a scientific society (1681–84), he returned to England, where he stayed until 1687, when he moved to Germany. France was not an option by that time, given the revocation of the Edict of Nantes (1685). Germany, on the other hand, offered the prospect of engaging in independent scientific work under the sponsorship of Karl Augustus, Elector of Hesse-Kassel, who extended the invitation to him. Germany was welcoming to Protestant refugees, Augustus had a reputation for being keen on scientific pursuits, and the invitation to Papin was accompanied with the offer of a chair at the University of Marburg.

Papin's association with Huygens was critical for his subsequent scientific achievements. Keeping his promise to Colbert, Huygens designed a rudimentary device consisting of a cylinder on the bottom of which he placed a small quantity of gunpowder, which was ignited. Huygens hoped to expel the air from the cylinder through the explosion, create a vacuum, and have the weight of the atmosphere press down the piston; however, the gaseous products left behind by the explosion led to the creation of only a partial vacuum. The piston was connected through pulleys to a weight, which was partially lifted upon the piston's descent, reminiscent of von Guericke's experiments, the main difference being that the latter created a vacuum by sucking the air out of the cylinder with an air pump. Huygens's device was constructed in 1680, at a time Papin had already moved to London, but it is probably safe to assume that the latter became aware of his mentor's experiment, because in 1687 he came up with a virtually identical device and experiment of his own, which he published in the *Acta Eruditorum* (1688). Papin, however, was not content with the results, realizing that gunpowder failed to create a perfect vacuum.

This dissatisfaction led to a conceptual breakthrough of historic importance in the discovery of steam engines, which he described in the same publication (1690):

> I tried then to succeed in another way; and as water being changed by fire has the property to becoming elastic as air, and afterwards of recondensing itself so completely by cold that it retains no appearance of this elastic power, I have thought that it would not be difficult to construct machines in which, by the means of a moderate heat and at little expense, water would create this perfect vacuum which has been fruitlessly attempted by the means of gunpowder.[27]

Papin came up with a device (described in Figure 1.9) that was entirely impracticable because condensation was time-consuming and because the direct contact of the fire with the cylinder could damage the latter. Nevertheless, his conceptualization suggested for the first time in history the use of steam and its condensation as a means of achieving mechanical effects.

As brilliant as his idea was, what happened in the next several years amounted to a complete disappointment in following through. In the form of an experiment, his device was simply a model, its main flaw being the slow condensation of steam. But Papin, at the very least, suspected that condensation may be achieved "by different constructions easy to imagine".[28] Furthermore, he suggested that his device could find a diverse number of applications, one of them being the draining of mines, which was a paramount problem at the time in England and elsewhere: in fact, he suggested converting the piston's movement into rotary motion. He even had the opportunity to engage personally in tackling this problem when he received an employment offer in the early 1690s from a Bohemian noble who encountered flooding in his mines, an offer Papin declined, citing as a reason the warfare that plagued the region and suggesting to the noble that his 1690 device was the solution to his problem.[29] His work also became better known through the publication of some of his papers in 1695, one edition printed in Kassel (where he moved the next year) in French, and one at Marburg in Latin

(a)

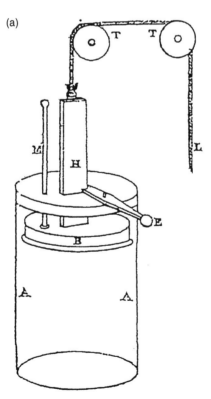

(b)

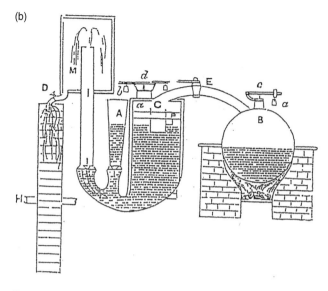

Figure 1.9 Papin's steam devices. In his 1690 device (1.9a) Papin took a small model cylinder fitted with a piston 2.5 inches in diameter. He put a small quantity of water on the metallic base and placed a fire underneath it, which produced steam and moved the piston to the top. Once there, the piston was held in that position by a latch, then the fire was removed and the steam condensed, creating a vacuum underneath the piston; once the vacuum was complete, the latch was released and the atmospheric pressure pushed the piston down. Papin calculated, without constructing it, that a cylinder of about two feet in diameter and four feet in height would raise 32,000 pounds per minute to one foot high, equivalent to one hp. In his description, Papin revealed that it took one minute to drive the piston to the top, but he never mentioned how long it took to condense the steam once he removed the fire. This point is critical in determining the number of strokes per hour the piston could complete and thus the amount of useful work it could perform. Papin's 1707 engine (1.9b) is quite different. Steam is generated from the boiler *B* to the cylinder *C* pressing down a floating piston *P*. The water, under the pressure of the piston, rises up the pipe *I* into the receiving tank *M* and from the latter into a waterwheel. Water is replenished through the funnel *A* and as it refills the cylinder *C* it forces up the piston, the process at that point being ready to begin a new cycle.

Sources: Farey, *A Treatise on the Steam Engine*, pp. 97–98; Clark, *An Elementary Treatise*, pp. 26–27.

two years later his 1690 paper was reviewed in the *Philosophical Transactions* of the Royal Society.

Papin kept experimenting and in 1698 he came up with a machine that was accidentally destroyed. This accident, along with his belief that the skills of mill-wrights at that time were not advanced enough to construct reliable cylinders, seems to have acted as a catalyst. But perhaps the most decisive event was Savery's successful completion of a working steam engine whose mechanism he saw in sketches drawn and sent to him by Leibniz during a visit of his to England in 1705. Papin must have felt that he had to move in a radically different direction with his designs. The Elector of Hesse was there, once again, to support him. This, however, was a less promising direction. In 1707 he published an account of an engine in which he abandoned the idea of using steam and the atmosphere to act upon a piston in favor of the idea of using steam to press directly upon water, thereby retreating to the days of de Caus, della Porta, and (possibly) the Marquis of Worcester (see Figure 1.9b). This engine still exhibited signs of his considerable ingenuity, such as the use of a floating piston that prevented the steam from coming into contact with cold water. But it was a device that generated less than one hp and, what was more important, incorporated outdated design principles.

Papin's new engine was received with notable indifference by the Royal Society, which failed to publish an account of it. Its members surely felt that they owed more allegiance to a fellow countryman (Savery), whose engine proved its practicality, than to a Frenchman whose long absence from England cost him valuable contacts within the Royal Society. Papin did return to England in 1708 and sent a report to the Royal Society, asking it to fund a project that would propel ships through steam power. This and a number of other proposals were ignored. At that point the end of his life was near. It was marked by obscurity. In the end, Papin's personal and professional journey was tragic. He engaged with the finest scientific minds of his time (e.g., Huygens, Boyle, Leibniz), possessed the skills of a mechanic constructing his own models, and had utilitarian objectives in mind. Nevertheless, he never moved beyond the point of constructing models, ingenious models but models nevertheless. He walked right up to the threshold of glorious discoveries and lingered there, but never crossed it.

The final triumph: Savery and Newcomen

In the very same year (1698) that marks the radical turn in Papin's designs, Thomas Savery was acquiring his patent for the first working steam engine invented using the power of the atmosphere. He was exhibiting his apparatus to the Royal Society the next year and publishing an account of it in 1702.[30] Savery's design (depicted in Figure 1.10) is too well known to warrant extensive discussion. It incorporated elements found in models as recent as that of Papin, but also others going back to della Porta's apparatus at the beginning of the seventeenth century; in some ways it showed signs of brilliant innovation, in some others it was a setback when compared with Papin's early conceptualizations. It was an engine that performed two distinct operations, the second of which consisted in using two separate vessels and the power of steam to force water to a higher level; in this regard it was virtually identical with della Porta's device. The first operation, using the same vessels to lift water from a depth below the vessels, through the creation of a vacuum and the use of atmospheric pressure, was bound to be lacking in della Porta's design since the notion of vacuum was still undiscovered; and it was certainly more innovative than Papin's 1690 design, since it used two vessels, but inferior to his in

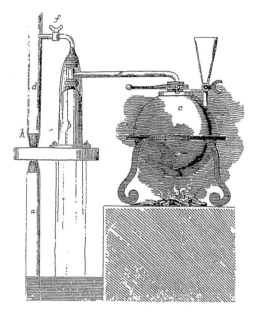

Figure 1.10 Savery's engine. The engine depicted here is based on an actual
engine constructed by Savery himself at Camden House, Kensington,
c. 1711; it is somewhat different in design from the model described
in *The Miner's Friend*. Steam is generated in the boiler *c*, passes
through a pipe to a receiver *b*, and is condensed by turning the cock *f*,
which sprays water at the outside of the receiver. The pressure of the
atmosphere forces the water through the pipe *a* and into the receiver.
The cock *f* is then closed and the communication between the boiler
and the receiver is re-opened, introducing steam into the boiler. The
pressure of the steam forces the water from the receiver into the pipe *d*;
the valve *h*, opening upward, prevents it from flowing into *a*.

Source: Stuart, *A Descriptive History*, pp. 42–44.

that it did not utilize a piston. It was an engine that incorporated considerable
conceptual flaws. In the second operation steam would come into direct contact
with cold water, diminishing its power to lift it to considerable heights; the alternative
was to increase the quantity of steam generated, but at the risk of deranging the
joints of the vessels and causing explosions.

There is no doubt that Savery's efforts preceded his patent by at least a couple
of years, and thus there was a parallel race between him and Papin; this speculation
seems reasonable since the engineering skills of the period required a good amount
of time to bring his model into the state of a workable engine and with extra time
required for experimentation before incurring the expenses involved in the acquisition of a patent. Savery might have even drawn some inspiration from the summary of
Papin's 1690 device in the *Philosophical Transactions* (1697). But there is no doubt
that he came up with the first workable steam engine followed by the savvy step

of exhibiting it in front of the king and the Royal Society at a time when Newton's position at its helm lent enormous prestige. But there is also no doubt that the adoption of the Savery engine could not have been, and was not, very widespread. Savery himself envisioned the use of his engine to raise water in fountains and cisterns, for fen drainage, and as a supporting device for waterwheels. But, as the title of his book indicates, he was mostly keen to see it adopted in mines, expanding their output and also having beneficial effects on related trades (e.g., carpentry, tool-making), leaving some to speculate that the title by which he was addressed ("Captain") was owed to him for being the proprietor or director of a mine.[31]

Such expectations, however, were not met, particularly when it came to mines. The condensation of steam during the first operation cycle of the engine could raise water from a depth of 20–30 feet. To raise it another 64 feet above the receiver would require the raising of steam whose pressure was four atmospheres, exerting a pressure of 30 pounds per square inch inside the vessels, something that would have been borderline unsafe; in fact, raising water with a single engine to a *total* height of 60–80 feet was considered the safest choice even with the use of copper vessels. But even at the maximum height of 90 feet or 15 fathoms, to drain a mine at the time would have required the use of up to four engines used in tandem and installed one on top of the other, because mines were reaching depths up to 50–60 fathoms. There were usually problems associated with such a solution. The purchase and installation cost would have been very considerable; adding to this cost, the consumption of fuel in these engines was excessive, an issue of particular concern in regions that lacked coal deposits (e.g., Cornwall); the engine required the presence of an attendant to turn the cocks, which added not only to the cost but also to the risk of accidents; in the case of explosions or technical mishaps the entire operation would come to a halt and some of the engines could be destroyed due to flooding.

The fate of an engine Savery himself installed at a coal mine in Wednesbury (Staffordshire) bears testimony to such defects. The quantity of water to be raised was so large that, when the quantity of steam was raised to excessive levels, the engine burst into pieces. Similarly unsuccessful were his efforts to introduce it to Cornwall. But the engine encountered difficulties in its adoption for other uses. Applying it to fen drainage was also not practicable because despite the low height to which water had to be raised, the quantity of water that had to be displaced was way too large and thus a great number of engines would have to be erected. A Savery engine was also installed at York Buildings in the Strand to raise water from the Thames. It was worked to the extent of generating steam exerting a pressure of 117–47 pounds per square inch, leading the joints of the engine to blow open, and it was deemed useless. In the end, the limited effectiveness of the engine was partly due to the poor quality of materials and workmanship, but also due to its design flaws. A small number of engines were erected under the authority of the patent but mostly to work fountains and, to a lesser extent, to provide a flow of water to overshot wheels. Savery succeeded in being the first individual to come up with a true steam engine, but it was an engine of very limited potential in terms of economic benefits.

It was Thomas Newcomen who succeeded in coming up with technical improvements to the steam engine that translated into economic benefits.[32] We are not in a position to know when Newcomen, a humble ironmonger from Devon, initiated his efforts. According to Triewald – a Swedish engineer who came to England in 1716 to study industrial methods, met Newcomen, and helped erect his engine both in England and Sweden – Newcomen knew nothing of Savery's efforts prior to the latter's patent (1698). The idea of working on a steam engine came to him while visiting the tin mines of Cornwall, where he would sell iron tools, due to the endemic flooding they faced. Similar views are expressed by Switzer, a contemporary writer. But if Savery and Newcomen worked parallel to each other, each ignorant of the other's efforts, the question is, how much earlier did Newcomen initiate his work? According to one account (by Dr John Robison), Newcomen knew Robert Hooke, a fellow Devonian, who passed to him some of his notes on Papin's projects; if true, that would indicate that Newcomen started his work well before Savery's patent. But there is no evidence to corroborate this claim, though it is possible that Newcomen became aware of Papin's work through the summary of his experiments published in the *Philosophical Transactions*, something that would place him somewhat behind Savery. We also do not know much about Newcomen's activities for the twelve years following Savery's patent, i.e., until he started being engaged in the erection of his engines. What we do know, however, is that he agreed to erect his engines under Savery's patent through an agreement signed in 1705.

The question of who crossed the line first is less important than what Newcomen actually achieved. Many of the engine's parts and conceptual designs were already in existence. The use of a piston within a cylinder goes back to von Guericke, Huygens, and Papin. The separation of the boiler from the receiver was Savery's idea. The boiler itself was already used in brewing, including the material it was made of (copper); in fact, it was similar to the one built by Savery. It is not clear whether other elements were products of Newcomen's ingenuity or of his copying skills, one of them being the use of the working beam and lift pump. It is highly unlikely that this combination of parts was employed in mining at the time, i.e., using the former to operate the latter. If Newcomen had access to Agricola's mining book he would have come across many reciprocating lift pumps, but he would have been left with the impression that the only way to operate them was through a crank and connecting rod. But there was a design that came very close to his, illustrated in a book published in London in 1696 by Venturus Mandey and James Moxon. It depicted a cam-operated pumping mechanism that used the sector-and-flat-chain arrangement and it was an exact reproduction of a drawing found in a book published in France by Philippe de la Hire, a mathematician and member of the French Academy who used this type of pump to supply water to a castle near Paris. If Newcomen came across the former book he simply modified the shape of the beam from curved to straight. There are a couple of elements, however, that were clearly unique to his model. The conception of the valve gear that allowed the engine to operate in a sequential fashion may have been inspired by some particular mechanism present in medieval clocks, but it was quite different and more complex. In addition, Papin's conception of spraying water outside the cylinder was transformed into spraying inside, speeding up condensation and producing 12–14 strokes/minute instead of 3–4. But most significantly, and although some elements were adopted or adapted, the overall assemblage of parts revealed a unique design. Moreover, borrowing disparate design elements from various sources and bringing them together in a manner that would allow the engine to operate smoothly are two different issues and, hence, Newcomen deserves credit not only for his conceptual synthesis but also his engineering skills. The engine exhibited a level of ingenuity well above the standards of craftsmanship at the time (see Figure 1.11).

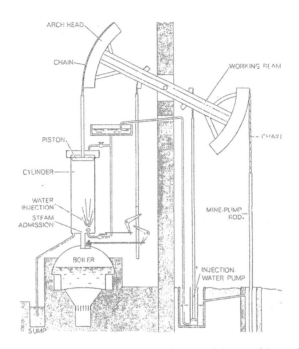

Figure 1.11 Newcomen engine. The essential parts of the engine are the boiler, the cylinder on top of which fits a piston made tight by the packing of leather or soft rope and with a water seal on top, the tank injecting water into the cylinder (depicted at the top right of the cylinder), the working beam, and the pump rod, which draws water out of the mine. Let us assume that the piston is at the top of the cylinder and steam is allowed to come into the cylinder from the boiler underneath by opening a cock. When the quantity of steam in the cylinder is sufficient, the cock is turned off and a quantity of water is injected into the cylinder from the water tank. Condensation ensues, a vacuum is produced, and the pressure of the atmosphere presses the piston down, lifting the outer end of the working beam and thus the pump rod, which brings water out of the mine. The steam cock is opened again, forcing the piston up, water is injected, causing condensation and a vacuum, and the cycle begins anew. The first Newcomen engines had cylinders of twenty-one inches in diameter and a working stroke of c. six feet and, at fourteen working strokes/minute, they developed about 6 hp. Later engines increased to a cylinder diameter of seven feet and a stroke of ten feet, developing well over 100 hp.

Source: Ferguson, "The Origins of the Steam Engine," pp. 102–3.

The Newcomen engine was clearly superior to Savery's. Instead of using, as the latter did, both the power of the atmosphere and that of steam to force water up a pipe, in the process reducing its efficiency by having steam coming in contact with water (thereby wasting energy that could have been transformed into useful work), Newcomen used steam as an auxiliary power to create a vacuum, leaving the atmosphere and the piston to do all the work in a safer fashion. Part of the gain in efficiency was lost through the transmission of power from the engine to the pump but, on balance, the gain was positive. Farey came up with some interesting contrasts between the two models, showing that to have a Savery engine raise the same quantity of water from the bottom of a pit as an 8 hp Newcomen engine would require one of two options: either to generate a quantity of steam that would exact a pressure of 59 pounds per square inch in the receiver's interior, double the level of the safety's threshold; or to have two Savery engines working in tandem one above the other, involving a greater expenditure of fuel and higher labor cost.[33] The Newcomen model did have, however, one major flaw relating to the condensation of steam: if too much water was sprayed inside the cylinder, the vacuum created would be perfect, but the cylinder would have been cooled to such a degree that it would require an excessive amount of steam to heat it up again; moderating the amount of sprayed water, on the other hand, would entail a less than perfect condensation, some vapor left in the cylinder, and thus some amount of resistance to the descending piston at the expense of mechanical power.

The story of the invention of the steam engine comes to completion in the next several decades with a number of minor improvements on existing models. The Savery model was neglected but not forgotten. In 1718 Desaguliers constructed an improved version of it, the main modification being that instead of achieving condensation by spraying the cylinder's exterior, it was done by spraying a smaller quantity inside it. Many years later, in 1766, Blakely obtained a patent aimed at addressing the main flaw of this model, i.e., the contact of the cold water with the hot steam. He used both oil floating on the surface of the water in the receiver in order to act as some sort of piston, and compressed air to separate the steam from the water. Both methods proved fruitless.[34]

But, as would be expected, it was the more promising Newcomen model that drew the most attention on the part of engineers going through a number of improvements.[35] The performance of these engines hinged to a large extent on the degree of attentiveness in shutting and opening cocks, something that had to be done 14 times/minute. Failure to act at the precise moment could lead to a diminishing mechanical efficiency or even shake the engine to pieces. This problem was solved by 1713 with the invention of a system of strings allowing the engine to operate automatically and increase the number of strokes per minute. No one knows who came up with this improvement, but the story of Humphrey Potter has been told many times, the young boy who was assigned to attend a Newcomen engine and, envious of his friends playing at a distance, invented the system of strings so he could join them. In 1718 these strings were replaced with rigid vertical rods fixed to the beam and connected to small pegs that turned the valves. These modifications were introduced by Henry Beighton, an engineer from Newcastle who directed construction of several Newcomen engines and also introduced an important safety valve.

Another major problem was the imperfect fit of the piston in the cylinder. At the beginning of the eighteenth century the art of boring cylinders and fitting pistons tightly in them was still in its infancy. It was only cannon and pump makers who were in need of boring cylinders, but the level of expertise at the time could not accommodate the construction of cylinders of more than 7 inches, while the poor fit of the piston was dealt with by placing a leather flap around it and a seal of water on the top to close the gaps between piston and cylinder. The company with the best reputation in boring cylinders was Coalbrookdale; the first record in this regard comes from 1723, and a new boring mill was put together in 1734. The Carron Ironworks were also known for boring, mainly cannons. By 1769 the premises proved too small, and thus Smeaton came in to design two boring mills for them, one for guns, the other one for cylinders.[36] The material of construction also drew considerable reflection. Brass proved to be the material of choice because it could be cast at less than 1 inch thick. Cast iron was an alternative, but it could not be cast at less than half an inch thick and thus heating and cooling were not as fast, at the expense of efficiency. Brass was more expensive, but saved money in the long run. Coalbrookdale was at the cutting edge of experimentation, making cylinders from spelter in the 1740s that proved to be as good as brass, and it even came up with cast iron ones of a superior quality by using pit-coal, but they were still imperfect in that the rust of iron created resistance for the piston.

An even more fundamental problem at the time was the failure of engineers to look at steam engines as interdependent elements of a whole and see that the right proportions mattered in putting together the various parts as, for example, in the case of boilers and cylinders; faulty proportions and working gear led to problems such as the piston's not descending all the way to the bottom on the downstroke. The result was that in many cases Newcomen engines performed half of the useful work defined by their potential. The responses of engineers to such problems were often misguided. In some cases they would attribute the problem exclusively to boilers; in fact, this period was characterized by a great deal of experimentation in this regard. In some other cases, when they felt that more power was needed, they would seek engines with a piston of larger diameter without asking how that affected its velocity or fuel consumption. The celebrated Smeaton addressed these problems by thinking of steam engines as systems with interdependent parts. His modifications allowed atmospheric engines to pump more water and decrease fuel consumption, and his designs reduced their cost of construction. As an illustration, the brass cylinder of an engine erected in Scotland in 1727 cost £250 and the entire engine £1,200. Smeaton estimated later on that an engine with the same details but based on his modified design, including a cylinder a third larger, should not exceed a total cost of £750, though it should be noted that part of the savings came from cost reductions in the production of metals, especially through the use of coal instead of charcoal.

Another challenge arose when later on flywheels were connected to Newcomen engines, with very slight modifications needed in the arrangement of their parts, in order to use them for mill work. The flywheel did have the capacity to impose some regularity on the gear connected to millwork despite the irregularity of the piston. The main problem, however, arose due to the time it took to condense the steam in the interior of a cylinder through water-spraying; at that point the piston was suspended for a while at the top of the cycle. The problem was resolved only when Boulton & Watt came on to the scene, by having the condenser and air pump of Watt's design added to these Newcomen engines, which allowed steam to be exhausted, instead of being sprayed with cold water. B & W sued and demanded payments for licenses, but in the end these modified Newcomen engines proved simpler and cheaper than B & W engines, and were especially preferred in regions of cheap coal. Finally, there was a series of other miscellaneous issues associated with the working of Newcomen engines, such as the practice of having engine attendants heap coals in the center of the fire grate, making a heat that was intense at the center of the boiler but insufficient at the circumference; or paying very little attention to cleaning accumulated crust from the interior of the boiler.

Some of the aforementioned defects were especially pronounced in Newcomen engines of low hp. In some instances they proved to be inferior to Savery engines. Engines erected in Cornwall were constructed with more attention to detail compared with engines in other regions (e.g., Newcastle). But the differences were not dramatic and the defects often translated to annual fuel bills rising to the excessive amount of £3,000. The reason so many defects persisted for such a long time is that few individuals had the time or material resources to engage in experiments. Smeaton, however, was an exception in that he combined keen intellectual acumen with advanced engineering skills as well as the ability to engage in experiments for four years with a small Newcomen engine he erected at his house. Some of his experiments involved sophisticated observations; others, however, identified problems easy to resolve, such as reducing fuel consumption by one-sixth just by keeping a fire evenly spread over the grate. It should be stressed that while engineers such as Smeaton were making progress on improving the first truly workable steam engine model during the decades preceding Watt's appearance, continental efforts in this field were clearly overshadowed. The only notable exception was Leupold's engine, designed in 1720, the first high-pressure engine utilizing the beam mechanism. This engine, combining elements of Papin's 1707 design with Newcomen's working beam, was celebrated for its simplicity (see Figure 1.12).

A long-drawn-out evolutionary process

In summarizing the evidence, it would be useful to provide a classification of the various steam engine devices and to outline particular phases of their evolution, summarized in Table 1.1. The first phase covers the years from 1543 to either 1629 or 1663; ambiguity arises because we do not know enough about Ramsay's and Somerset's inventions. During this phase steam devices fell into two types, both of them involving fairly simple designs. Type A involves the use of a steam

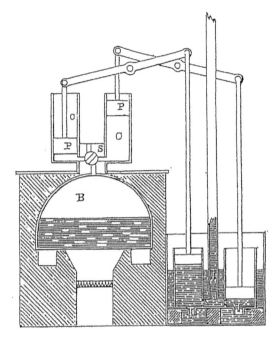

Figure 1.12 Leupold's engine. In this engine steam is passed from the boiler *B* into the two cylinders via a four-way cock *S*, raising the pistons, which are connected through beams to plungers. The steam causes the piston to ascend (and once this is done steam is allowed to escape into the air) and the plunger on the other side of the beam forces water up a pipe. The admission of steam into each cylinder is done in an alternate fashion.

Source: Hodge, *The Steam Engine*, pp. 31–32.

jet pressing against a wheel (De Garay and Branca) and it is the design that bears the closest affinity to Hero's apparatus. Type B involves the power of steam pressing against water and forcing it up a pipe (della Porta, de Caus, and perhaps Somerset). Then between the years 1641 and 1661 the crucial experiments of Berti, Torricelli, Pascal, and von Guericke take place, proving the potential of creating a vacuum. These purely scientific breakthroughs along with the utilization of the piston, a device borrowed from already existing technologies, define the designs of steam engines in a second phase that begins in 1678 and ends in 1707.[37]

Two types of designs appear during this phase. The first one (type C) is a hybrid in that it borrows the element of steam pressing against water (from type B) and incorporates the product of the aforementioned scientific discoveries (vacuum) or the piston but not both (Savery and Papin's 1707 device). The fourth type of design (type D) represents the pinnacle of achievement in this evolutionary scale because it completely discards elements predating the relevant scientific discoveries and incorporates both a piston and a vacuum in producing mechanical work

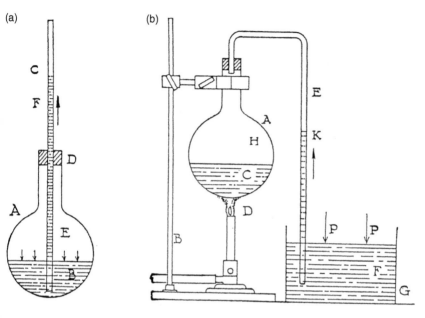

Figure 1.13 Two experiments depicting the effect of scientific breakthroughs on steam engine design. 1.13a depicts a flask containing some water and a glass tube that is inserted into it through the airtight mouth of the flask *D*. Once we heat the water every cubic inch of it produces steam, which expands to 1,700 cubic inches. Assuming the flask is strong enough, the steam fills the space *E* and starts pressing on the water, which is expelled up the tube. This experiment demonstrates the principle incorporated in the designs of della Porta, de Caus, and, possibly, Somerset (type B in the text). In 1.13b, we have a flask partially filled with water and connected with a bended tube to a tank of water. When the water in the flask is heated it produces steam, which expels the air from space *H* through the tube *E,* and this expulsion of air produces bubbles in the tank *G*. Once the bubbles cease, the fire is withdrawn, the steam in the flask condenses, and the atmospheric pressure pushes on the water of the tank, which is forced up the tube and, since it faces no resistance due to the presence of a vacuum, the water fills the flask. This experiment incorporates the conceptual gains regarding the vacuum made in the period 1641–61 and found applications in the devices by Hautefeuille, Papin's 1690 cylinder, Savery, and Newcomen (types C and D in the text). See Hart, *James Watt*, pp. 86–90, 110–11.

Hautefeuille, Papin's 1690 device, Newcomen). It is interesting that types C and D do not follow a neat chronological succession; it becomes apparent that type D could have succeeded B had Hautefeuille followed through with his brilliant ideas and had Papin not been delayed in transforming his primitive little 1690 cylinder into a working engine, possibly because Savery got there first. Finally, we have Leupold's high-pressure engine, which stands in a class of its own (type E) appearing nearly a century before such design became a practical prototype.

Table 1.1 Key technological and scientific (in italics) developments in the invention of steam engines

Inventor and date	Main working principles of the device	Intended purpose
Hero, 150BC	Steam is channeled into a globe, causing rotation [A]	Curiosity value/toy
De Garay, 1543	Steam is directed against a central wheel which provides motion to paddle-wheels	Used in ships
Della Porta, 1601	Steam is directed against water, forcing it up a pipe [B]	Toy
De Caus, 1615	Steam is directed against water, forcing it up a pipe [B]	Toy
Branca, 1629	Steam is directed against a wheel [A]	Moving stampers suspended over mortars
Ramsay, 1630	Unknown	Mine drainage

Experiments on the existence of vacuum by Berti (1641–2), Torricelli (1643), Pascal (1648), Guericke (1650). Guericke exhausts air from a cylinder, vacuum allows atmospheric pressure to push piston thereby lifting weights through pulleys (1654 and 1661)

Somerset, 1663	Unknown, but probably similar to della Porta's or de Caus's devices [B?]	Various uses, among them mine drainage devices
Hautefeuille, 1678	Sketch of a device using piston and steam condensation to produce mechanical effects [D]	
Morland, 1682/1685	Unknown	Mine drainage
Papin I, 1690	Vacuum through steam condensation, piston is pushed down by atmosphere [D]	Various uses, among them mine drainage
Papin II, 1707	Steam is used to press upon water through the mediation of a floating piston, no vacuum [C]	"
Savery, 1698	(a) Use of vacuum to lift water; (b) direct pressure of steam on water lifting it to a higher level [C]	Mine drainage
Newcomen, prior to 1705	Vacuum through condensation and complete reliance on the atmosphere to do mechanical work by pushing on a piston [D]	Mine drainage
Leupold, 1720	No condensation, steam acts upon pistons connected to beams and plungers forcing water up pipes (high-pressure principle) [E]	

The review of the evidence shows that the invention of the steam engine was the product of a long evolutionary process, sometimes marked by setbacks in the degree of sophistication of the designs of the various devices, but more often than not involving a process of cumulative improvement in which discoveries at one stage acted as inspiration for improvements in successive ones; in some cases inspiration was drawn from direct contact between inventors.[38] To cite a few examples, Ramsay was part of the royal court in London at the same time de Caus was there and involved with the design of his steam device; and while Ramsay was part of the court, Somerset's grandfather was Keeper of the Privy Seal about the same time (1616–21), implying that the future Marquis of Worcester grew up in an environment that may have acquainted him with Ramsay and his subsequent work; and there is a good chance that Morland was acquainted with Somerset's engine since he lived in Vauxhall where the marquis erected his engine.

These chains of inspiration continued through the very end of the inventive process. It is plausible, for instance, that Savery knew and was inspired by the work of della Porta, de Caus, and Somerset, since elements of their devices were incorporated in his engine.[39] The connections between Newcomen and his predecessors, particularly Papin, are more tentative. It is possible that Newcomen became acquainted with Papin's 1690 device through the latter's publications in Latin and French via the influx to Devon of Huguenot refugees following the Revocation of the Edict of Nantes. Baptist preachers, Newcomen being one of them, were known for their proclivity toward learning. The review of Papin's piston-and-cylinder device in the *Philosophical Transactions* was another possible channel of information, though one may point out that scientific work emanating from London rarely trickled down to remote Devonshire. And it has been claimed that Newcomen may have become acquainted with Papin's work through contacts with Hooke, though this claim has been discredited.[40] There is no doubt that there was a huge leap between Papin's experimental little device and the complexity of Newcomen's engine, the very first one to generate economic benefits; despite, however, the level of ingenuity involved in the latter, it is hard to fathom the possibility that Newcomen knew nothing of the conceptualizations of von Guericke and Papin.[41] Finally, there is no doubt that Papin inspired Leupold's work in terms of some of the components he borrowed, such as the four-way cock. The same connections can be claimed for the realm of experimental science, one example being the witnessing of Berti's experiments by Kircher and the transmission of this knowledge to Schott, von Guericke, and Boyle. The case of Pascal and Torricelli working on similar experiments almost instantaneously without knowing, up to a point, each other's work, is the only notable exception that proves the rule.

One is struck, however, by how slowly knowledge was transmitted in this era. The second half of the sixteenth century was marked by the rediscovery and dissemination of Hero's work, and when finally steam devices came into the fore at the dawn of the seventeenth century they ended up being simple designs. It is only in the last quarter of the century that the degree of sophistication scores notable improvements. The same principle applies to the work of scientists. Torricelli's experiments reached Pascal fairly quickly in the 1640s, but the transmission of knowledge from Berti's experiments in 1641–42 to Kircher, Schott, and von Guericke finally reached Boyle in 1657. Part of the reason lies in the time involved in travel, with a trip from London to Edinburgh, for instance, taking nearly three weeks to complete.[42] But perhaps the main reason is that knowledge transmission became institutionalized very slowly. Royal courts and progressive members of the aristocracy provided material support and sometimes offered an opportunity for savants to meet each other (e.g., de Caus, Ramsay, Somerset, Morland, Papin). Some degree of interaction among savants was also achieved through institutionalization following the formation of scientific academies (e.g., Huygens, Papin, Boyle). But by and large, the seventeenth century remained an era marked by the heroic efforts of independent inventors and scientists (e.g., della Porta, Branca, Galileo, Torricelli, Berti, Kircher, Schott, von Guericke, Savery, Newcomen).

The last point that needs to be emphasized is that the first phase of steam devices is dominated by Italians and Frenchmen – particularly when we also take into account translations of Hero's work and the crucial scientific breakthroughs – producing mostly models with no economic value. However, despite statements to the contrary by modern historians, there are a couple of instances in which the motives of inventors were utilitarian or had economic applications (de Garay, Branca). But it is also profoundly interesting to note that although British inventors enter the scene late (with Ramsay in 1630), they end up dominating developments in the second phase and, without exception, they are driven by utilitarian motives, mine drainage being preeminent among them.[43] This is not a mere coincidence. It is an observation that goes to the core of the question why England was the first country to invent the steam engine, as opposed to its continental rivals.

Notes

1   Clark, *An elementary treatise,* pp. 7–9, has a visual description of Hero's apparatus used in Egyptian temples.
2   Cited in Alderson, *An essay on the nature and application of steam,* p. 17.
3   Clark, *An elementary treatise,* pp. 14–15, 19; Hart, *James Watt,* pp. 92–3; Russell, *A treatise on the steam engine,* pp. 14, 16; Smiles, *Lives of Boulton and Watt,* p. 7; Thurston, *A history of the growth of the steam engine,* pp. 10–11, 18–19.
4   Arago, "History of the steam engine", pp. 6–8.
5   Ibid., p. 7; Clark, *An elementary treatise,* p. 13.
6   Russell, *A treatise on the steam engine,* pp. 14–16; Clark, *An elementary treatise,* pp. 15–16; Stuart, *Historical and descriptive anecdotes,* pp. 24–5.
7   Arago, "History of the steam engine", pp. 8–9; Clark, *An elementary treatise,* pp. 16–17; Dickinson, *A short history of the steam engine,* pp. 12–13; Rolt, *Thomas Newcomen,* pp. 21–2; Russell, *A treatise on the steam engine,* pp. 16–17; Jenkins, "The heat engine idea", pp. 1–2.
8   Clark, *An elementary treatise,* pp. 17–18; Arago, "History of the steam engine", p. 9; Partington, *A course of lectures,* p. 5; Stuart, *Historical and descriptive anecdotes,* pp. 32–3.
9   Stuart, *A descriptive history of the steam engine,* pp. 9–10; Dickinson, *A short history of the steam engine,* p. 13; Galloway, *Annals,* p. 196; Hart, *James Watt,* p. 100; Thurston, *A history of the growth of the steam engine,* pp. 17–18; Jenkins, "The heat engine idea", pp. 2–3.

10 The following paragraphs are based on these sources: Hall and Hall, *A brief history of science*, pp. 173–5; Hart, *James Watt*, pp. 69–77, 82–4; Pacey, *The maze of ingenuity*, pp. 83–5; Goldstone, *Why Europe?* p. 152; Bourne, *A treatise on the steam engine*, pp. 5–6; Clark, *An elementary treatise*, pp. 20–1; Stuart, *Historical and descriptive anecdotes*, pp. 36–7.

11 An illustration of the firm hold of Aristotelian ideas on the issue of vacuum as late as the 1630s is Bate, *The mysteryes of nature and art*, pp. 3–4. According to Bate, "Ayre, and Water doe insert themselves into all manner of concavities, as hollownesses."

12 Hall and Hall, *A brief history of science*, p. 174.

13 Arago, *The life of James Watt*, pp. 52–3; Arago, "History of the steam engine", pp. 9–11, 16; Hodge, *The steam engine*, pp. 19–20; Millington, *An epitome*, pp. 243–4; Stuart, *Historical and descriptive anecdotes*, pp. 54–6, 66–9, 160–2; Stuart, *A descriptive history*, pp. 14–20; Clark, *An elementary treatise*, pp. 19–20; Dickinson, *A short history*, pp. 13–16; Muirhead, *The life of James Watt*, pp. 114–17; Partington, *The century of inventions*, pp. 62–3, 99–103, 107–9; Smiles, *Lives of Boultan and Watt*, pp. 18–23.

14 Partington, *The century of inventions*, p. 62.

15 Ibid., p. 63.

16 Such as making a watch run for one's lifetime once it is wound up; or making a vessel go upstream in a river, the faster the current, the faster the speed of the vessel; and flying an "artificial bird" in every direction and as long as he pleased. See Stuart, *Historical and descriptive anecdotes*, pp. 54–5.

17 The bill came to the House of Lords on 16 March 1663 and was then referred to a committee that proceeded to make some alterations. Subsequently, the bill came to the House of Commons on 2 April and was also referred to a committee there. Several amendments were introduced, and it went back to the House of Lords for approval of the House of Commons amendments. Finally, the royal assent was given on 3 June 1663. See Muirhead, *The life of James Watt*, pp. 115–16.

18 Cited in Stuart, *Historical and descriptive anecdotes*, p. 56.

19 Thurston, *A history of the growth of the steam engine*, pp. 24–5; Clark, *An elementary treatise*, pp. 23–24; Hart, *James Watt*, p. 107.

20 Cited in Jenkins, "A contribution", p. 44.

21 Cited in Rolt, *Thomas Newcomen*, p. 26.

22 Cited in Jenkins, "A contribution", p. 45.

23 Cited in Arago, "History of the steam engine", p. 12.

24 Jenkins, "A contribution", pp. 43–7; see also Arago, "History of the steam engine", pp. 11–12; Stuart, *Historical and descriptive anecdotes*, pp. 73–77; Stuart, *A descriptive history of the steam engine*, pp. 21–4; Dickinson, *A short history of the steam engine*, p. 16; Hart, *James Watt*, p. 109; Rolt, *Thomas Newcomen*, pp. 26–9; Thurston, *A history of the growth of the steam engine*, pp. 28–9; Clark, *An elementary treatise*, pp. 22–3. Clark includes a presumed description of Morland's engine, but it should be borne in mind that if North's sketch does refer to Morland, then Clark's interpretation of the device is not correct, because it does not include the use of a piston.

25 Arago, *Life of James Watt*, pp. 61–2; idem, "History of the steam engine", pp. 12–15; Farey, *A Treatise on the steam engine*, pp. 97–9; Stuart, *A descriptive history*, pp. 27–8, 49–53; Bourne, *A treatise on the steam engine*, p. 6; Briggs, *The power of steam*, pp. 21–3; Clark, *An elementary treatise*, pp. 25–8; Daumas, *A history of technology and invention*, pp. 446–53, 456–9, 462–3; Dickinson, *A short history of the steam engine*, pp. 8–11; Armytage, *A social history of engineering*, pp. 78–9; Galloway, *The steam engine*, pp. 14–16, 26–51; Hart, *James Watt*, pp. 108–9; Thurston, *A history of the growth of the steam engine*, pp. 25–6; Klemm, *A history of western technology*, pp. 220–6; Jenkins, "The heat engine idea", pp. 4–5; Basalla, *The evolution of technology*, pp. 92–3.

26 Cited in Daumas, *A history of technological invention*, p. 450.

27 Cited in Arago, "History of the steam engine", p. 14.

28 Ibid., p. 14.
29 That Papin's mind was clearly focused on the problem of mine drainage is also reflected in his design of a fairly complex machine utilizing a waterwheel and air pumps to extract water from mines; he referred to this machine in a paper he read to the Royal Society in 1687, right before he left England. A description of it can be found in Galloway, *The steam engine,* pp. 35–9.
30 Savery, *The miner's friend,* pp. 8–10, 13–14, 17–21; Arago, "History of the steam engine", pp. 16–18; Stuart, *Historical and descriptive anecdotes,* pp. 108, 133–4, 141, 158–9; Alderson, *An essay on the nature and application of steam,* pp. 28–9; Stuart, *A descriptive history of the steam engine,* pp. 53–5; Farey, *A treatise on the steam engine,* pp. 110, 116–18; Mathias, *The first industrial nation,* pp. 134–5; Dickinson, *A short history of the steam engine,* pp. 26–7; Fletcher and Crowe, *An early steam engine,* p. 2; Pole, *A treatise on the Cornish pumping engine,* pp. 7–8; Smiles, *Lives of the engineers,* pp. 452–3. A note of caution is in order when it comes to Arago's evaluation of Savery's engine. Arago, in an effort to elevate the status of a fellow Frenchman, compares it to de Caus's device when, in fact, Savery incorporated elements more akin to della Porta's design.
31 There is a considerable void of information when it comes to his personal and professional background. Some authors deduced from his title of "captain" that he was a seafaring man, but Stuart dismisses this claim by citing Savery's declaring himself ignorant on nautical matters and despite his invention of a useful nautical device that he submitted to Newton, soliciting his opinion; see Stuart, *Historical and descriptive anecdotes,* pp. 102–3, 106.
32 Landes, *The unbound Prometheus,* p. 101; Stuart, *Historical and descriptive anecdotes,* pp. 154–5; van Riemsdijk and Brown, *The pictorial history of steam power,* p. 25; Arago, *Life of James Watt,* pp. 66–71; Farey, *A treatise on the steam engine,* pp. 127–31; Cohen, "Inside Newcomen's fire engine", p. 117; Ferguson, "The origins of the steam engine", pp. 103–5; Hodge, *The steam engine,* pp. 30, 49–50; Lardner, *Popular lectures,* pp. 53–4, 59–60; Dickinson, *A short history of the steam engine,* pp. 29–30, 32–3; Stowers, "Thomas Newcomen's first steam engine", p. 146; Stuart, *A descriptive history of the steam engine,* pp. 59–60; Jenkins, "Savery, Newcomen, and the early history of the steam engine", pp. 117–18; Galloway, *The steam engine,* pp. 54–5; Rolt, *Thomas Newcomen,* pp. 50–1.
33 Farey, *A treatise on the steam engine,* pp. 131–3.
34 Ibid., pp. 110–16, 121.
35 Mantoux, *The Industrial Revolution,* pp. 316–17; von Tunzelmann, *Steam power,* pp. 16–17; Arago, *Life of James Watt,* pp. 65–72; Ferguson, "The origins of the steam engine", p. 102; Hodge, *The steam engine,* pp. 30–1; Farey, *A treatise on the steam engine,* pp. 128, 231–2, 234–7, 272, 291, 410–13, 671; Stuart, *Historical and descriptive anecdotes,* pp. 155, 169–70, 179, 185–8, 226–7, 292–4, 303–5; Dickinson, *A short history of the steam engine,* p. 33; "Methods in early engine manufacture", pp. 22–3; Millington, *An epitome,* p. 265.
36 Boring cylinders was done in the same way as the boring of trees for wooden pipes used in water-works. The cylinder was placed on a sledge and fastened by chains; the sledge moved along a roadway toward the borer. The latter was a circular iron disk fitting into the cylinder the same way a piston would do and provided with 6–8 steel cutters in its circumference. The sledge would move toward the borer, allowing it to gradually grind its interior, the operation having to be repeated several times to achieve a smooth finish in the cylinder's interior. See Farey, *A treatise on the steam engine,* p. 291.
37 A rod with a piston appears in the context of suction pumps sometime in the early modern period, replacing pumps with chain and sockets. The new suction pump was tried in English collieries by 1618, when a certain Robert Crump was awarded a patent for it. Steam engine designs begin incorporating the piston from suction pumps

beginning in the last quarter of the eighteenth century, as shown by the use of a leather border to surround the piston in these pumps, a practice directly copied by steam engines. See Nef, *The rise of the British coal industry*, 2, pp. 450–1. To appreciate the conceptual significance of these scientific breakthroughs on steam engine design, see the experimental illustrations in Figure 1.13.

38 Pacey, *The maze of ingenuity*, pp. 90–2; Thurston, *A history of the growth of the steam engine*, pp. 29–30; Jenkins, "The heat engine idea", pp. 3–7; Basalla, *The evolution of technology*, p. 95; Hart, *James Watt*, p. 77; Stuart, *Historical and descriptive anecdotes*, p. 188.

39 The belief is based on references made by Savery in *The miner's friend* to old devices that proved "troublesome and expensive, yet of no manner of use" and "short of performing what they pretended to." Savery neither names specific predecessors of his nor makes it explicit that he refers to steam devices, but in the same paragraph refers to his engines as one of the "inventions of this nature" and several lines below discusses the issue of water drainage. See Savery, *The miner's friend*, p. 8.

40 The alleged connection between Newcomen and Hooke was made for the first time by Dr. John Robison, a close friend of James Watt, in his article "Steam engine" in the *Encyclopaedia Britannica* (1797) and was repeated by later writers such as Arago and Hodge. Robison's article abounds in conceptual and factual mistakes. Moreover, modern writers have examined the same records of the Royal Society but found no trace of correspondence between Hooke and Newcomen. Some of Robison's mistakes are pointed out in Jenkins, "The heat engine idea", pp. 6–7. See also Rolt, *Thomas Newcomen*, pp. 49–50; Arago, "History of the steam engine", p. 19; Hodge, *The steam engine*, p. 27; Stuart, *A descriptive history of the steam engine*, p. 59.

41 There is also a fairly good chance that Savery and Newcomen may have met each other. Savery visited Dartmouth several times once he became treasurer of the Sick and Wounded Commission in 1705 and met with the town's mayor, who was a local agent of the commission. The mayor knew Newcomen and thus may have acted as a catalyst for the meeting between the two inventors. This meeting, if it took place, would have been instrumental, given the time period, solely for the creation of the business partnership between Savery and Newcomen. See Rolt and Allen, *The steam engine of Thomas Newcomen*, p. 38.

42 Kronick, *A history of scientific and technical periodicals*, p. 48.

43 Let us not forget that even Papin, nominally a Frenchman, did a significant part of his work in England, also having in mind mine drainage. On this point, see Rolt, *Thomas Newcomen*, p. 23.

Bibliography

Alderson, M. A., *An essay on the nature and application of steam* (London: Sherwood, Gilbert, and Piper, 1834).

Arago, M., "History of the steam engine, with a reply to the criticisms to which the first publication of the article gave rise", *Annual of the Board of Longitude, 1836*.

Arago, M., *Life of James Watt*, 3rd ed. (Edinburgh: A. & C. Black, 1839).

Armytage, W. H. G., *A social history of engineering*, 4th ed. (London: Faber and Faber, 1976).

Basalla, G., *The evolution of technology* (Cambridge, England and New York: Cambridge University Press, 1988).

Bate, J., *The mysteryes of nature and art* (London: 1st edition printed by T. Harper for R. Mab, 1634; facsimile edition Norwood, NJ: Walter J. Johnson, 1977).

Bourne, J., *A treatise on the steam engine in its application to mines, mills, steam navigation, and railways* (London: Longman, Brown, Green & Longmans, 1846).

Briggs, A., *The power of steam: an illustrated history of the world's steam age* (Chicago: University of Chicago Press, 1982).

Clark, D. K., *An elementary treatise on steam and the steam-engine, stationary and portable* (London: Lockwood & Co., 1875).

Cohen, H. F., "Inside Newcomen's fire engine, or: the scientific revolution and the rise of the modern world", *History of Technology*, 25 (2004), pp. 111–32.

Daumas, M., ed., *A history of technology and invention, progress through the ages. Vol. 2, The first stages of mechanization* (New York: Crown Publishers Inc., 1969).

Dickinson, H. W., with a new introduction by A. E. Musson. *A short history of the steam engine* (New York: Augustus M. Kelley, 1965).

Farey, J., *A treatise on the steam engine, historical, practical and descriptive* (London: Longman, Rees, Orme, Brown and Green, 1827).

Ferguson, E. S., "The origins of the steam engine", *Scientific American*, 210, 1 (Jan. 1964), pp. 98–107.

Fletcher, J. M., and A. J. Crowe, *An early steam engine in Wednesbury: some papers relating to the coal mines of the Fidoe family, 1727–9* (Wednesbury: Central Library, 1966).

Galloway, R. L., *The steam engine and its inventors: a historical sketch* (London: Macmillan, 1881).

Galloway, R., *Annals of coal-mining and the coal trade: the invention of the steam engine and the origin of the railway*, 2 vols. (London: Colliery Guardian, 1898–1904).

Goldstone, J., *Why Europe? The rise of the West in world history, 1500–1850* (New York: McGraw-Hill Companies, 2009).

Hall, R. A., and M. Boas Hall, *A brief history of science* (Ames: Iowa State University Press, 1988).

Hart, I. B., *James Watt and the history of steam power* (New York: Henry Schuman, 1949).

Hodge, P. R., *The steam engine: its origin and gradual improvement, from the time of Hero to the present day* (New York: D. Appleton, 1840).

Jenkins, R., "A contribution to the history of the steam engine", Paper read before the Newcomen Society, 22 January 1936; reprinted in R. Jenkins, *Links in the history of engineering*, pp. 40–7.

Jenkins, R., "The heat engine idea in the seventeenth century: a contribution to the history of the steam engine", *Transactions of the Newcomen Society*, 17 (1936–7), pp. 1–11.

Jenkins, R., *Links in the history of engineering and technology from Tudor times: the collected papers of Rhys Jenkins* (Cambridge: Newcomen Society, 1936).

Jenkins, R., "Savery, Newcomen, and the early history of the steam engine", *Transactions of the Newcomen Society 4* (1923–4), pp. 113–31.

Klemm, F., *A history of western technology* (Ames: Iowa State University Press, 1991).

Kronick, D. A., *A history of scientific and technical periodicals: the origins and development of the scientific and technical press 1665–1790*, 2nd ed. (Metuchen, NJ: Scarecrow Press, 1976).

Landes, D., *The unbound Prometheus* (Cambridge: Cambridge University Press, 1969).

Lardner, D., *Popular lectures on the steam engine* (New York: Printed for E. Bliss, 1828).

Mantoux, P., *The Industrial Revolution in the 18th century* (Chicago: University of Chicago Press, 1983).

Mathias, P., *The first industrial nation: an economic history of Britain, 1700–1914* (New York: Scribner, 1969).

"Methods in early engine manufacture (1712–1800)", *The Hoyt Notched Ingot*, 50 (Jul 1953), pp. 18–26.

Millington, J., *An epitome of the elementary principles of natural and experimental philosophy* (London: Printed for and sold by the author, 1823).

Muirhead, J. P., *Life of James Watt with selections from his correspondence* (London: John Murray, 1858).

Nef, J., *The rise of the British coal industry, Vol. 2* (London: George Routledge & Sons, 1932).

Pacey, A., *The maze of ingenuity: ideas and idealism in the development of technology*, 2nd ed. (Cambridge, MA and London: MIT Press, 1992).

Partington, C. F., *The century of inventions of the Marquis of Worcester from the original manuscripts with historical and explanatory notes and a biographical memoir* (London: John Murray, 1825).

Partington, C. F., *A course of lectures on the steam engine* (London: G. Virtue, 1826).

Pole, W., *A treatise on the Cornish pumping engine* (London: John Weale, 1844).

Rolt, L. T. C., *Thomas Newcomen: The prehistory of the steam engine* (Dawlish, U.K.: David and Charles, 1963).

Rolt, L. T. C., and J. S. Allen, *The steam engine of Thomas Newcomen* (New York: Science History Publications, 1977).

Russell, J. S., *A treatise on the steam engine: from the seventh edition of the Encyclopaedia Britannica* (Edinburgh: A. & C. Black, 1846).

Savery, T., *The miner's friend, or an engine to raise water by fire described and of the manner of fixing it in mines* (London, 1702, reprinted 1827 for S. Crouch).

Sewell, J., *Elementary treatise on steam and locomotion, Vol. 1* (London: J. Weale, 1852).

Smiles, S., *Lives of Boulton and Watt* (Philadelphia: J. B. Lippincott and Company, and London: John Murray, 1865).

Smiles, S., *Lives of the engineers, Vol. 4* (London: John Murray, 1874).

Stowers, A., "Thomas Newcomen's first steam engine 250 years ago and the initial development of steam power", *Transactions of the Newcomen Society*, 34 (1961–2): 133–49.

Stuart (Meikleham), R., *A descriptive history of the steam engine* (London: John Knight and Henry Lacey, 1824).

Stuart (Meikleham), R., *Historical and descriptive anecdotes of steam engines* (London: Wightman and Cramp, 1829).

Thurston, A., *A history of the growth of the steam engine* (New York: D. Appleton and Company, 1897).

Van Riemsdjik, J. T., and Kenneth Brown, *The pictorial history of steam power* (London: Octopus Books, 1980).

Von Tunzelmann, G. N., *Steam power and British industrialization to 1860* (Oxford: Clarendon Press, 1978).

2 Why did England invent the steam engine?

The role of science, economic incentives, institutions, and technical skills

The invention of the steam engine represented a spectacular leap in technological sophistication and produced sizeable economic effects by contributing to a dramatic increase of coal output and eventually of other sectors by becoming a general-purpose technology through subsequent modifications introduced by Watt; one may argue that it also played a critical role in spreading the factory system, a key institutional element of capitalism. In light of these multi-faceted transformations it brought, it is puzzling that only recently economic historians have attempted to provide a theoretical framework referring to the critical factor(s) behind the genesis of this technology.

Three explanatory frameworks have been offered in addressing the question as to why England was the country which came up with this invention first, despite the fact it was a laggard compared to three other European countries (Germany, France, Italy) in mining technology and in generating the science that was directly relevant to this invention. The first of these theories, by Joel Mokyr, does not deal exclusively with steam engines but with the cultural foundations of the Industrial Revolution and the uniqueness of England in this respect. Mokyr stresses certain key transformations which took place in the early modern period such as the decline of superstition, the rise of the new science, and the growth of literacy and numeracy, all of them being of crucial importance in generating the set of innovations which defined the Industrial Revolution. The uniqueness of England lay in establishing the most dynamic dialogue through channels of communication between savants, fabricants, and entrepreneurs.[1]

Robert Allen concurs with Mokyr on the importance of these factors but breaks away from him by arguing that since factors such as literacy rates, and hence the potential supply of inventors, were fairly similar across northwestern Europe, cultural factors may explain why the invention of the steam engine and the emergence of the Industrial Revolution took place in that part of Europe, as opposed to Asia; but they do not explain why these events took place in Britain. The critical factor lay, instead, on the demand side taking the form of the existence of rich mineral deposits waiting to be exploited, particularly coal, in the midst of a high wage economy.[2]

Unlike the previous two accounts which follow the tradition of grand historical narratives, Graham Hollister-Short provided a well-argued and detailed comparison of mining technologies in England vs. key continental regions but devoid of the wider economic, scientific, and institutional context in which this contrast of techniques emerged.[3] This theory places a great emphasis on England's natural resource endowments and peculiar climatic conditions. The timber scarcity faced by the country in the early modern period was exacerbated by the lack of winter precipitation in the form of snow which elsewhere allowed the utilization of timber inaccessible to transportation through float/flume operations.[4] The country was forced to exploit an alternative energy source, coal, but this sector of the economy was trapped in a state of palaeotechnic development when it comes to addressing the serious problem of draining water from mines. Unlike other major mining regions in Europe, particularly in Germany and southern Belgium, which adopted a sophisticated technology of mine drainage capable of solving the problem (*Stangenkunst*), England stuck to more primitive methods and thus was forced to seek alternative technological options.

This chapter will argue that the monocausal explanations offered by these theories mask the complexity involved in the process of invention of the steam engine. An alternative explanation will be offered arguing that all of these factors were indispensable components of the story but they were tied together in a chain of causation which was triggered by certain institutional transformations, the latter being the critical socio-economic element in this regard. The first section of the chapter will focus on the dichotomy which marked early modern European history in terms of religious and epistemological strife and its impact on the diffusion of knowledge pertinent to this invention. The second section will address the economic context, particularly the size of the British mining industry contrasted to that of other continental regions. The final section will assess the state of English mining technology compared to continental practices.

Religious and epistemological disputes across Europe

Prior to the Scientific Revolution knowledge was tied to its ancient and medieval heritage infused with wildly imaginative elements borrowed from "magical" traditions; knowledge acquisition was based on a crude empiricism of sense perception, common sense and *a priori* aphorisms. By contrast, the critical element of the new scientific spirit was its methodology which stressed its reliance on experimentation for the validation of knowledge claims.[5] It succeeded in discarding, very slowly, mystical beliefs and imposing a sense of mental discipline. It taught its practitioners the importance of quantification and accurate measurements, the difference between correlation and causation, of breaking down a problem to its component parts and holding all variables constant but one in order to measure its effects; it was a method which was formulated by thinkers such as Newton but trickled down to engineers such as Smeaton.[6] By the time this intellectual transformation was over it had replaced a wild optimism over the control of nature – manifesting itself, for instance, in the obsession with perpetual motion machines – with a grounded and more realistic optimism defined by what was feasible. In light of this context, the invention of the steam engine was not the direct product of pre-existing theories; seventeenth-century theories of heat were quite irrelevant in this regard. Instead, a puzzle posed by the inability of water to rise above a certain height in the well of the Grand Duke of Tuscany, something Galileo was unable to explain, brought to the fore a contradiction between an empirical observation and received doctrines borrowed from antiquity. The contradiction was addressed through the experimental method which led to the establishment of a new scientific doctrine, i.e., the presence of vacuum. This new doctrine, coupled with the use of a cylinder and piston in Guericke's experiments (two elements borrowed from an existing technique, i.e., the pump), established the core elements which eventually led to the invention of economically useful steam engines.

Observers of the Scientific Revolution, going back to nineteenth-century thinkers (e.g., Thurston) all the way to Mokyr and Allen, have treated the phenomenon as having spread in a pan-European context.[7] This is clearly an erroneous assessment. In referring to the eighteenth century (although the comment is even more applicable to the seventeenth), Jacob points out that "the ability to think mechanically – that is, scientifically, in the modern meaning of that word – permeated Western societies only selectively."[8] This was clearly the case in the invention of the steam engine. The experiments which produced the relevant science took place in Italy, France, and Germany while England dominated in terms of developments marking the final stretch leading to its invention. No other European country played a direct role in this regard. This section will attempt to explain this dichotomy by outlining the demarcation lines drawn in the continent between the spread of Protestantism and the Baconian model of the new science contrasted to the attitudes of the Catholic church towards the new science and its eventual embrace of the Cartesian philosophy.

The new scientific spirit met the least amount of resistance in England because its main adversaries, Aristotelian philosophy and the old clergy of the Roman church, were defeated following the Reformation under Henry VIII. This led to the domination by the king of bishops and ministers and to a unified church whose function was subsumed under the national interest; in contrast continental Protestantism was plagued by sectarian divisions. By the middle of the next century (1641) Parliament dealt a final blow to the power of the Anglican Church to meddle with secular intellectual affairs by taking away its prerogative when it came to censorship; as a result more books and pamphlets were published in the period 1640–60 than in the rest of the century combined. But it is important to stress that the Anglican Church was not as keen on imposing barriers to the dissemination of the new scientific spirit to begin with as were churches on the continent. Quite the contrary, its leadership, like Protestants elsewhere, viewed the empiricism and experimental methodology of the new science as an ideological vehicle by which to oppose papal authority.[9]

The genesis of the English scientific tradition is identified with the writings of Francis Bacon and continued through a number of savants writing in the second half of the sixteenth century.[10] Collectively, this tradition challenged Aristotle's infallibility, instead promoting the power of reason, the usefulness of experiments, and the notion that Man is perfectible and has the potential to understand and dominate nature. In fact, one may argue that the experimental method, in a crude, empirical sense, has ancient roots and certainly precedes Bacon. The concoction of drugs in an effort to find special remedies for particular diseases, which by the late sixteenth century vied successfully with theories derived from Galen, is one illustration. The experimentation with the right sequence of crops and adoption of field systems in an effort to increase yields dating back to the Middle Ages is another. The effort to adopt crops and products of the New World (from corn and potatoes to chocolate and tobacco) is a third, and so on. But this was an empiricism that until Bacon's time was often infused with an obsessive interest in metaphysical properties and the occult, often inspiring tricks by charlatans to impress the ignorant public.

With Bacon, the break from the past becomes decisive by separating empiricism from the occult and discarding the latter and by condemning the Hermetic tradition.[11] The creation of knowledge, he argued, ought to start from a clean slate, a *tabula rasa*, with the first step in filling the void being a massive project of collation and classification of facts, an idea very much reminiscent of the *modus operandi* of the scholastic intellectual tradition. Half of the 36 fellows comprising the scientific elite described in the *New Atlantis*, a utopian fable, would be preoccupied with the collection and taxonomy of past knowledge in order to observe regularities of patterns and exceptions that would allow the formulation of general principles. But it was the work of the remaining fellows that was the most critical by indentifying more complex problems: by designing and executing experiments (often involving the use of instruments), applying inductive reasoning, and synthesizing and interpreting the results they intended to establish the basis of new knowledge. Mathematics and pure reasoning, unless promoting the inductive method, have nothing to offer in this regard. By this method, the crude empiricism of sense perception was to be challenged and tested, a notion that was counter-intuitive and thus radical and revolutionary. Bacon's conception of the universe was colored by a religious vision but his method for understanding the universe was supremely secular.

It was this aspect which captured the imagination of the English middle class whose voracious appetite for the new science lay behind the spectacular reception they gave to the *New Atlantis*. It went through sixteen editions and ranked fifth in the list of best sellers in fiction, and was the most important work of scientific interest during the seventeenth century. The middle class also played a critical role in the dissemination of scientific and technical periodicals as well as by sponsoring, through subscriptions, the lectures of traveling popularizers of science. The democratization of science, so to speak, was clearly a critical element in Bacon's vision through his perception of the experimental method as an instrument for the improvement of "useful arts", i.e., manufacturing production and crafts. The Royal Society in England was founded precisely on this premise, thus setting the tone for the dynamic "dialogue" between scientists, manufacturers, merchants and a middle class driven by curiosity over scientific matters which became the hallmark of social and economic life through the Industrial Revolution. Jacob, Mokyr, and Allen, all agree that the divide between savants and fabricants in England was the least pronounced, creating a feedback mechanism that proved useful to both sides.[12]

The vision encapsulated in the Baconian paradigm did meet with some resistance. The Baconian notion that artisans and craftsmen had a role to play, equally useful to that played by those engaged in speculative and abstract theory, was a friction point clashing with the aristocratic ideal which looked down on practical and often uneducated artisans. A true gentleman was supposed to hunt, to fight, and to know things but not necessarily of a useful sort. The nail in the coffin of such resistance, however, was put in place towards the end of the century when Newton came to embrace the Baconian methodology:

> Analysis consists in making Experiments and Observations, and in drawing general Conclusions from them by induction, and admitting of no Objections against the Conclusions, but such as are taken from Experiments, or other certain Truths . . . And although the arguing from Experiments and Observations by Induction be no Demonstration of general Conclusions; yet it is the best way of arguing which the nature of Things admits of . . .[13]

Newtonian laws may have been expressed through the principles of mathematical physics but the foundation of his claims was built on induction and the experimental method.

The latitudinarian wing of the Anglican Church viewed the Newtonian model as the best explanation for a universe driven by a mechanical regularity akin to perfection and under the impact of a single force, gravity. The latter was seen as the manifestation of God's wisdom and the perfect regularity of the universe as divine harmony. In the end, the role of the Church was one of the crucial institutional factors which allowed the dissemination of the new science, not only by not posing obstacles to it but, in fact, by promoting it. The presence of a relatively free press, the formation of scientific societies at the provincial level, and the itinerant lecturers were all manifestations of the progressive role played by the Church, as were other key institutional factors such as the protection of property rights for the commercial elite which viewed the engineering profession and the technological applications of the new science as means towards profit maximization.

> The route out of the *Principia* (1687) to the coal mines of Derbyshire or the canals of the Midlands was mapped by Newtonian explicators who made the application of mechanics as natural as the very harmony and order of Newton's grand mathematical system.[14]

The genesis of the new science neither remained an affair insular to England nor, however, gained universal acceptance throughout Europe; instead, its adoption was particularly noticeable in two other countries.[15] The Dutch Republic known for its free press which allowed the publication of scientific treatises, was particularly receptive to Baconian and Newtonian ideas. It made no contribution, however, to the development of the steam engine partly because, as Jacob suggested, mechanical aptitude was not fostered in the context of a republic with a weak state and powerful urban elites whose prosperity was built mainly on foreign trade. Germany was the other territory where the stars were aligned even more favorably, in the sense that it had established a tradition of openness to new scientific ideas and whose artisans were well-known for their skills. The first modern translation of Hero's *Pneumatica* was accomplished by a German (Regiomontanus) in the fifteenth century, a time when its printing industry was taking off, establishing presses in sixty towns by the end of the century and going through even more phenomenal growth during the next century. It developed a literature which covered a wide range of scientific subjects, among them industrial technology and engineering and, most importantly, it was heavily focused on empirical problems and practical needs. Large parts of the country were also on the "right" side of the cultural wars between Catholics and Protestants and welcoming to refugees from the latter group. It was a German (Guericke) who first combined in one apparatus the two elements essential for the construction of a workable steam engine (creation of a vacuum and a piston); and despite the fact that Germans did not cross the finish line first, it was Leupold who designed the most advanced steam engine prior to Watt.

The Baconian and Newtonian theories failed to become popular in other parts of Europe, with the Catholic church playing an instrumental part in resisting them.[16] To the Catholic intelligentsia the force of gravity sounded a lot like magic and, most importantly, the experimental method had the potential of being too unpredictable to minds defined by rigid religious dogma. This approach came to forge an uneasy alliance with the Cartesian philosophy which presented itself as the main rival to the English philosophers in terms of what the proper method of the new science ought to be. Like Bacon, Descartes rejected every type of past knowledge, including ancient and religious doctrines, as well as his own sensory experiences. The universe, created by God, must be perfect, and the way to unlock its secrets is to apply deductive, mathematical reasoning. We logically perceive space in the universe because there is something there (hence empty space, a vacuum, is inconceivable) and that "something", according to Descartes, consisted of invisible particles whose motions and interactions create our sensory perceptions. Descartes's reliance on pure deductive reasoning and mathematical logic led him to reject the value of experiments and to make a number of erroneous inferences.[17] When his publications started appearing in the 1630s they aroused a universal hostility among both Catholics and Protestants; a universe whose mechanics were driven by moving particles without active divine intervention was unthinkable to them. But attitudes changed in the following decades as Jesuits in France, Italy, Spain, and southern Germany, as well as some members of the secular intelligentsia (e.g., members of the French Academy) came to tolerate and eventually embrace his mathematical and logical approach. His physics were more difficult to swallow but they ended up reasoning that God's will was not part of the material world and that He could intervene in the latter at will.

These reactions to the English version of the new science played out in somewhat different ways across Catholic Europe. This anti-Enlightenment mentality claimed Spain and Italy as its first and most obvious victims.[18] Italy, the country which played a crucial role in generating the science that eventually led to the invention of modern steam engines, came under the strongest grip of papal authority to the point of putting on trial proponents of the new science in Naples in the 1690s. The intellectual climate was such as to present substantial obstacles to the dissemination of the new science; it certainly rendered it virtually impossible for a culture of applied mechanics to be formed, what Jacob calls the "cultural packaging" of science, i.e., "the informal learning, the mechanical illustrations, the hands-on use of devices, the relatively egalitarian philosophical society".[19] The result was that "despite the interests of select Italian intellectuals or the Piedmontese state, applied science for industrial purposes never took root before 1800. There was simply too much opposition and too much censorship affecting its fortunes."[20] An interesting illustration of how far Italy fell behind is that when a Watt engine was installed in Padua in the 1790s local engineers did not understand its working mechanism. In contrast, by that time English engineers had installed and managed many hundreds of such engines.

In the case of France there were forces at play which rendered more ambivalent its placement in the context of these cultural wars.[21] Here papal authority was weaker than in Spain and Italy because a portion of the French clergy resented pontifical interference in its internal ecclesiastical affairs; but there was an even stronger resentment against Protestant ideas, culminating in the Edict of Nantes, and their alliance with the new science. However, the French monarchy clearly sought to foster science and its useful applications through the instrumental role of Colbert who played a decisive role in the creation of the French Academy (1666), founded on the same utilitarian premise as the Royal Society. It is true that the former retained more the character of an elite institution; the Cartesian paradigm became increasingly popular among its members and came to dominate the curriculum of French colleges and universities from the 1690s through the 1740s, the time when theoretical and applied Newtonian mechanics started making inroads. These developments did prevent the full-blown institutionalization of science, as is evident from the fact that scientific and technical periodicals catered more for the intelligentsia in contrast to England where their readership was more widespread. But Descartes's writings in the 1630s did not prevent Pascal in the following decade from using instruments in the context of experiments to prove the existence of a vacuum; and the Cartesian model did come to dominate intellectual circles by the 1690s, but this was a gradual process allowing in the meantime scientists such as Huygens, Papin and Hautefeuille to work on devices incorporating the notion of vacuum. If Spain/Italy and England represented two opposite poles, France was placed in between; developments there were such as to prevent it from crossing the finish line first but not obstructive enough to prevent some very important contributions from its scientific community.[22] One thing is certain, however: while in the countries surveyed so far debates on the proper scientific paradigm did take place, regardless of where the chips may have fallen in the end, such debates barely touched intellectual and political elites in other parts of Europe.[23]

In the end, what was the outcome of this friction that engulfed Europe over what was the proper scientific method which was needed in order to fill the void left by the condemnation of religious dogma and magic, and how had the role of the church shaped the resolution of this friction? I have noted that, by the 1640s, Italy was the undisputed leader in generating the science pertinent to the eventual invention of modern steam engines along with some devices in the form of toys. France was right next to it with England and Germany not far behind. The review of developments in this section helps us explain why Italy was cut out of the race and why the contradictory inertia that developed among the political, intellectual and religious elite of France slowed down the contributions of this country. But disputes over science and religion do not help us understand why, among the remaining contenders, it was England that crossed the line before Germany and why the Dutch Republic, despite its quick assimilation of English science, failed to preoccupy itself with the invention of the steam engine. Let us turn now to the economics of the story.

Economic incentives and property rights in the coal mining industry

The discovery of the vacuum and, even more so, the debates between Newtonians and Cartesians on ontological matters and what constitutes the proper methodology of science would have been rendered irrelevant had not the focus of scientists and artisans been directed towards the solution of practical problems. As noted in the previous section, few territories in Europe rivaled England in this regard. The official objective of the Royal Society was stated thus: "to improve the knowledge of natural things, and all useful arts, manufactures, Mechanic practices, Engynes and Inventions by experiment."[24] A couple of years later one of its most prominent members, Robert Hooke, stated that its members do not reject experiments of theoretical usefulness "but they principally aim at such, whose Applications will improve and facilitate the present way of Manual Arts".[25] These were not empty words. Experiments and reports aimed at useful applications in industry and agriculture received at least equal weight to other subjects in the pages of the *Philosophical Transactions*.

One of the most pressing problems was that of mine drainage, plaguing this critical sector of the economy throughout the seventeenth century. The Newcastle coalfield was the epicenter of the problem. Sir George Selby, testifying before Parliament in 1610, sounded the alarm by stating that "the coal mines at Newcastle would not hold out the term of their lease of twenty-one years."[26] Financial losses and even loss of life due to flooding were commonplace. There is an excellent survey referring to the parish of Wickham, located a few miles southwest of Newcastle, which is indicative of the problem.[27] In the late sixteenth century, Thomas Liddell attempted to exploit the coalfield in the rector's glebe land at Allerdeans but for ten years he failed to recover his investment because "for ditches, dikes, water and other like accidents no worke out of the same [could] be had."[28] His successors were more fortunate in working this particular mine by 1617 but at the great cost of employing twenty men. Similar problems existed in the nearby Baldwinflat where William Sherwood, one of the local owners, observed in 1619 that "the cause of mane dealers in Collieries to be at great chardges in sinking and working of pitts and to loose all their chardges by the drowning of [them]."[29] Success was recorded during the first quarter of the century but only at the considerable expense of employing horses, pumps, and men. The growing level of expenses was, in most cases, unavoidable given the scale of investment already undertaken by leaseholders.

High expenses could be afforded because coal prices tripled between the middle of the sixteenth and the beginning of the seventeenth century prompting a nearly proportional increase in output; figures from Newcastle's port books suggest that output doubled during the period from 1608–9 to 1633–4. But the more output increased, along with profits (often in the range of £5,000–8,000 above rent), the deeper mines had to go (some of them reaching 180 ft or 30 fathoms) demanding even greater expenses and adherence to higher standards of safety; pits had to be "well and sufficiently timbered with wood and tymber to keepe and hinder the ground from thrusting together".[30] But the high prices and profits could not be sustained for long. During the second quarter of the seventeenth century the bubble burst as a result of cut-throat competition between collieries in the midst of glutted markets. An assessment made in 1636 revealed that many previously highly productive seams ceased to exist, while others slowed down production, with only one new colliery appearing that year. Things became worse by the early 1640s because of the Scottish raids and the Civil War. Production resumed after these events but a survey of 1652 revealed that output was at very low levels. The report is peppered with instances of particular coalfields that were worked to the limits allowed by existing technologies and then abandoned and overtaken by drowning. Similar stories continued through the end of the century. The attempt to exploit a colliery in Elswick, located on the north side of the Tyne, ended in failure due to encountering overwhelming quantities of water in sinking the pit.[31]

The problem was not limited to the northeastern coalfield.[32] Colliery owners in Staffordshire went through the same process of exploiting the fields in which coal lay nearest the surface and used existing techniques to try to get deeper but without much in the way of gains. The problem was such that local iron manufacturers feared a possible scarcity of coal affecting their capacity to sustain output. Similar evidence comes from Cornish tin mines where shaft mining began c. 1500, initially with some impressive levels of output. By the time of Queen Elizabeth, however, the first complaints about mine drainage appeared. As early as 1568 a German engineer, Burchard Kranich, experimented with different devices trying to resolve the problem. By 1602 Carew describes a feverish battle with underground water, despite his praise of the technical skills of local miners:

In Cornwall they pray in aide of sundry devices, as addits, pumps and wheeles driven by a streame, and interchangeably filling and emptying two Buckets with many such like; all which notwithstanding, the springs do so incroche upon there inventions as in sundry places they are driven to keep men, and some where horses also at worke both day and night without ceasing; and in some all this will not serve the time. For supplying such hand service they have always fresh men at hand.[33]

The problem surely persisted through the time Newcomen appeared in the local scene. Triewald wrote that:

he was induced to undertake this by considering the heavy cost of lifting water by means of horses, which Mr. Newcomen found existing in the English tin mines. These mines Mr. Newcomen often visited in the capacity of a dealer in iron tools with which he used to furnish many of the tin mines.[34]

Newcomen must have known through his conversations with the local miners that the problem was not limited to mines in the southwest but persisted throughout the country.

There were two types of methods dealing with the problem, often used in tandem, both being very expensive.[35] The first one was to construct soughs which sometimes extended to a mile or longer in some instances, serving several adjacent collieries. Maintenance costs were low but construction costs could run to a few thousand pounds; £4,000 was spent in the 1620s at Bedworth colliery, mainly for the construction of a sough. Drainage machines provided a cheaper alternative in terms of initial cost – few of them would cost more than £100 during the seventeenth century – but they were unreliable when operated by wind or water power or expensive in terms of running cost when operated by horses which often proved to have short lives.[36] There is evidence for the early part of the century referring to the tin mines of Cornwall showing that in some cases drainage costs could account for 75 percent of mining costs. By the early part of the eighteenth century, when Newcomen engines offered a lower cost alternative, draining with horses was still very expensive. From a very detailed report prepared by the mining agent of James Lowther, the owner of a colliery at Whitehaven, Cumberland, it was estimated that to extract the quantity of water from a drowned pit would amount to £222 taking 125 days to accomplish the task, while the subsequent maintenance cost would reach £360 per year. The annual cost of draining at Griff colliery, Warwickshire, using over fifty horses, amounted to £900.

Problems associated with mine drainage could result in anything from severe difficulties to bankruptcy.[37] During severe flooding coal extraction would cease but not the operating expenses of a mine having to deal with the logistics of inventories and the feed of horses and cattle. Expenses associated with mine drainage contributed to the ballooning of the entry cost in the mining industry. During the reign of Queen Elizabeth £100–200 was the norm in terms of starting a colliery but by the turn of the century the figure went up from a few hundred pounds to £2,000–3,000. By the reign of James I £6,000–8,000 was the norm and by 1700 it reached around £15,000–20,000; these figures do not include expenses sometimes associated with coastal collieries for harbor infrastructure which could add as much as £10,000. Such expenditures did not always guarantee success. The literature is peppered with instances of collieries, both in England and Scotland, whose losses reached sometimes up to £20,000, with flooding being the leading cause. It is important to get a perspective on what these figures mean in the context of the early modern economy. During Elizabethan times it was questionable whether there were fifty men capable of financing single-handedly the entry cost of the largest colliery of the day. By 1695 out of a list of 140 joint-stock enterprises only five (among them the East India and Royal Africa Companies along with the Bank of England) had capitalization rates exceeding that of the largest colliery in the Tyne. In the end, expenses associated with mine drainage contributed to the huge increase in the entry and operating costs of mining enterprises, thus rendering them susceptible to the potential of financial ruin.

Both the magnitude of the problem and the potential profit to be had from resolving it were such that a growing number of aspiring innovators focused on it.[38] Of the 317 patents issued by England in the period 1561–1688, 43 (14 percent) involved devices designed to address mine drainage. What is more interesting is that during the years 1561–90 only six such patents were issued but by 1611–40 the figure had risen to 14 and by 1660–88 to 23. Beginning in 1630 a number of English inventors (as well as Papin, working on English soil) were preoccupied with the resolution of the problem by utilizing the power of steam. By the last quarter of the century the subject of mine drainage was at the top of the list when it comes to types of invention, its importance being reflected on the fact that Savery's patent was extended in 1699 from 14 to 35 years.

The eagerness by which the problem was addressed in England can be understood by looking at the weight of mining output, especially coal mining, in the context of the national economy.[39] The coal industry faced severe limitations during the Middle Ages due to constraints imposed by the existing technology, with exploitation limited to outcrops; the limited quantities that were extracted were used for lime-burning, blacksmithing, and salt production. The catalyst that led to the take-off of English coal mining was the confiscation of monastic lands by Henry VIII, particularly in the output-rich areas of Durham, Shropshire, and South Wales. Monastic administrators undertook little capital investment when exploiting mines themselves; and they granted short leases and placed ceilings on annual output when leasing lands hence making it difficult for lessees to risk their own capital. Once the lands were passed on to lay owners, leases were usually extended to 21 years making investment projects more viable. Indicative of the zeal with which the gentry undertook the exploitation of coal was the example of the Willoughby family of Wollaton Hall, Nottingham which started exploiting coal pits near Nottingham in 1542. By the 1590s they were investing nearly £20,000 a year on mining and ironworks and by the turn of the century were considering shipping coal to London through river and coastal navigation.

This institutional transformation was clearly more relevant to the initial growth of coal output, and the need it created for new technological solutions regarding drainage, compared to purely economic configurations. There has been a lively debate on whether England's "timber crisis" was general or localized. Regardless of where the truth lies on this issue, it is more relevant to look at the timing of this crisis. In a well-argued account on the issue of energy consumption, Warde pointed out that "fears of a general 'timber famine' by the early 17th century may have been well-founded."[40] A long series of charcoal prices in the southeast of England analyzed by Malanima pinpoints more accurately a steady rise of such prices, and hence presumably the beginning of a timber famine, starting in the second quarter of the seventeenth century.[41] Nevertheless, "coal became a more important provider of thermal energy than wood around about, or a little earlier than 1620."[42] In other words, the rise in English coal production starts at the time following the dissolution of the monasteries when charcoal prices were exhibiting a fairly stable pattern and precedes by several decades the timber famine.[43] It follows that the critical factor was the institutional transformation brought about by the alteration of property rights, though the timber famine was important in providing further impetus to the growth of the coal industry and the need to find alternative technological solutions to the drainage problem.

National statistics on coal output begin in 1854 and thus the further we go back the less reliable records become.[44] But the existing estimates suggest that the sharp rise started in the middle of the sixteenth century, increasing from an annual output of 50,000 tons to 210,000 tons during the period 1530–60; the northeastern coalfield was by far the most important coal-producing region accounting for about 40 percent of national output by the latter year and shipping a good portion of it to London and elsewhere. A century later (1660) Britain produced 2.1–2.25 million tons, 3–4 times the output of Europe, production levels in the continent scarcely rising above medieval levels by that time. By 1700, British output was of the order of 2.5–3.0 million tons annually, and, if we adopt the latter figure, coal consumption per capita stood at 9 cwt, a fairly impressive level; the significance of the northeastern coalfield actually rose somewhat, accounting for 43–47 percent of the total depending which aggregate figure we adopt. By that time Britain was the undisputed leader of the industry, the only other region worth noting being what is today southern Belgium (along the Liège–Mons axis).

A contributory factor to this impressive growth was household consumption, absorbing 47.6 percent of aggregate output in 1700, fed in particular by London's urban explosion, from 55,000 in 1520 to over 500,000 by 1700. Such demand was not present throughout the country but forthcoming from districts near coalfields and from urban centers which could draw supplies at a fairly low transportation cost (e.g., London drawing supplies from the northeastern coalfield). Despite the fact, however, that household consumption was of paramount importance there was a wide array of manufacturing industries, absorbing a total of 39.2 percent of output, which came to depend for fuel on the coal industry. The salt industry was probably at the top of the list but potters, brewers, distillers, dyers, and blacksmiths also used it; it was also the main fuel for chafery forges, working bar-iron, but the use of coal for the smelting of iron defied efforts despite Dudley's persistence in this regard. It becomes apparent that the ability of the coal industry to expand its supplies over time was tied to the growth rates of a number of manufacturing sectors which were important in the context of regional settings if not the national economy as a whole. With the exception of the Liège district, this statement would not be applicable to any part of continental Europe.[45]

In trying to gain a broader perspective on the distinctions between Britain and continental Europe, one may argue that if we ignore coal momentarily there would not be much difference between the two. Surely the availability of metals would be different but the weight of mining within each respective economy would not be particularly significant, despite the gains scored by Britain when it comes to particular metals. Copper production, for instance, was only 100 tons in Britain in 1570, 200 tons in Sweden but 1,500 in Germany. By 1712, British production increased tenfold, Swedish by sixfold, whereas in Germany there was a decline down to 700 tons/year.[46] But when we introduce coal into the picture the gap between Britain and the continent seems like a chasm. According to Allen, in 1700 England produced 80 percent by tonnage and 59 percent by value of all mining output in Europe. Germany, the leader in the field in the later Middle Ages, accounted for only 4 and 9 percent respectively.[47]

In concluding this section, one is justified in arguing that when national and regional disparities in the economic contexts of the period are introduced and viewed in conjunction with the religious and epistemological disputes, the picture becomes sharper in trying to pinpoint the most likely candidates in the invention of the steam engines. Italy, and to a large extent France, despite the leading role they played in generating the science that led to the invention of the steam engine, got themselves on the "wrong" side of the scientific disputes of the period; the lack of economic incentives due to the absence of extensive mining sectors compounded the problem. The Netherlands found itself with the "right" religion, allowing it to become receptive to the new science of Bacon and Newton but it lacked a mining industry that would have created the incentive to resolve the water flooding problem. It is true that the struggle with land reclamation projects offered another potential source of incentives to work towards the invention of the steam engine. But this problem was pretty much resolved successfully by the middle of the seventeenth century by utilizing sluices and windmills. The discussion of economic configurations across Europe, however, introduces a new potential candidate when it comes to the invention of the steam engine, that is, the region of today's southern Belgium with its rich coal supplies. The region did not rival the magnitude of British coal output but coal mining was of paramount importance in the context of this narrow geographical area, similar to the importance of the northeastern coalfield in England, and thus provided strong incentives for the invention of effective water draining devices. The obvious question is: why did it not play a role in this regard?

The case of southern Belgium is particularly relevant in assessing Allen's thesis. Mons was part of the Spanish Netherlands during the seventeenth century while Liège was the seat of the principality bearing the same name, an independent state within the Holy Roman Empire controlled by the local bishop. The struggle against the Reformation was particularly noticeable in Liège but radical ideas were successfully suppressed during the reign of Gerard of Groesbeeck (1564–80). The control of the educational system, including the local university, by the Catholic Church became so complete and dominated by scholastic and Cartesian texts that when the French took control of the Belgian educational system after 1795 they discovered that there was a lot to be done in order to gear it away from "pure science" and towards applications; Newtonian science and illustrations of mechanical devices were entirely absent. That is not to say that voices of enlightened secularism were absent nor that the region failed to develop ties and partnerships between mining entrepreneurs and engineers. But in addition to the educational system which did not promote innovation, there were other institutional obstacles. Most of the bishops of Liège in the seventeenth century were foreigners, holding several bishoprics at once and thus often absent; in contrast to the situation across the channel where the monarchy often played a pivotal role in supporting the new science, the bishops of Liège were more interested in the collection of taxes. Furthermore, the local mines in the region were controlled by owners, both clerical and aristocratic, who sought to maximize short-run profits which in turn translated into favoring short-term leases; the latter were obviously neither conducive to undertaking investment projects that would address mine drainage in the long run nor fostering innovation in that field. In the end, while southern Belgium possessed an economic profile similar to the one of regional British coalfields, there were certain institutional rigidities reminiscent of those present in France in the seventeenth century that made it difficult for the interaction between entrepreneurs and engineers to become as dynamic and systematic as it became across the Channel.[48]

By the end of the century it was only England and Germany that were left standing as the territories most likely to invent the steam engine but, given the differences in the size of their mining industries, the former had a sizeable advantage over the latter. Differences in mining technology and the relevant skills associated with it, the subject of the next section, accentuated even more the demarcation in the structure of incentives existing between the two countries.

English vs. continental technological trajectories in mining

There is an overall impression that England lagged behind continental Europe, particularly Germany, when it comes to mining technology during the Middle Ages. If there was a lag it was not very large either in terms of the size of mines or of the technology employed. England possessed some large royal silver and lead mines in Devon (Bere Alston, Bere Ferris, Combe Martin, Birland) which were leased or mortgaged to major European mining companies against loans taken by the Crown as early as the thirteenth century. This facilitated the adoption of some continental methods and techniques, the use of adits and soughs being one of them.[49] This was the preferred method of drainage, assuming the terrain allowed it, when the operators of the mine had long-term objectives in mind. Digging of soughs could be a cheap affair in hilly terrains, and British collieries were mainly hilly. But even in such terrains the cost could easily go up because the deeper the mine was, the longer the distance that had to be dug to discharge the water. Another factor that could add to the cost was that as the exploitation of coal seams expanded, additional channels had to be dug to connect them with the sough. The limited scale of mining rendered such cost considerations largely irrelevant during the Middle Ages. But adits were certainly time-consuming projects, as an agreement between a Yorkshire colliery owner and two workmen shows; the distance the latter were able to dig in a five-year period was only 540 yards.

The first use of adits is recorded in Germany in 1213 and by the end of the century there is evidence of them in England. The use of adits is documented at Bere Ferris once the mine was leased to the Frescobaldi company of Florence in 1295. The method spread subsequently throughout Devon and Cornwall and it was used in the small mines of Lancashire by 1303/5. When a mine at Cossall (Nottinghamshire) was leased in 1316 it was specified that the lessees would be responsible for repairing the gutter. The accounts kept for a mine at Kilvey (Glamorgan) reveal an elaborate underground network of conduits, gutters, and sluices. The fifteenth-century leases of the Bishop of Durham make frequent references to underground tunnels and in one case the bishop promises to reduce the rent if the lessee agrees to undertake a large expense in such underground work. Adit drainage was not a universal method; for instance, it was not used in the large mines of the Mendips. But that may have been because this method was not suitable given the physical configuration of certain mines, not because of the lack of knowledge. The timeline when it comes to the appearance of adits is suggestive of the pace of technological diffusion in the Middle Ages but, as Burt suggests, the notion of diffusion may not be relevant in this case since this is a simple method that could have been discovered independently in multiple locations.[50]

If the construction of adits proved not to be feasible for geological or financial reasons, there were other alternatives, some being primitive methods, others more sophisticated, especially as time went on.[51] One of them was to cease operations until the water level fell in late spring or summer. Another was to try to displace the water to nearby swallets or bring it to the surface by using large leather buckets; there is a record from a Flintshire mine, for instance, dating from the reign of Henry VIII, stating that four workers were employed for forty days carrying buckets of water from the mine to the surface.

In terms of machinery, the most common equipment in the Middle Ages was the endless chain with buckets attached and moved by a man-powered windlass at the pit head. The windlass was used to raise water but also ore and debris to the surface. It was a crude and inefficient method due to the time-consuming nature of the task in removing the buckets at the pit in order to fill them with water or ore and doing the same thing at the surface to empty them; not to mention that the vibration of the buckets (having a 60-gallon capacity), when going up and down, caused spilling of water in the form of a constant cascade down the shaft. But one improvement was scored by replacing the thin bar over the pit with a drum or barrel of a large diameter, making it easier to move the bucket up and down, and by substituting iron axles for wooden ones. Treadmills operated by men or gins operated by horses were often used in the place of the windlass. The cog-and-rung gin was comprised of a horizontal wheel turned by horses transmitting power to the teeth of cogs which turned the rungs or bars of a drum spread across the mouth of the shaft in order to operate the rope. Such devices were not terribly sophisticated but they had the merit of being simple to build and operate, assemble and dismantle; they were suitable for shallow pits with short lives since they could only draw a small quantity of water with the two buckets attached; and they were cheap up to the point when the rope was replaced by an iron chain – there is a reference to it in a Durham colliery from the late fifteenth century – because if a single bolt gave way the entire apparatus would come crushing down at the pit with disastrous results.

There were also chain pumps which were of two types, the bucket-and-chain, and the rag-and-chain. The former was a more sophisticated version of the previous devices, consisting of a chain to which wooden or leather buckets were also attached; as they lifted water they became inverted when they reached the top of the shaft, emptying the water into a trough which carried it at a considerable distance to make sure it did not find its way into the mine. The rag-and-chain pump consisted of a chain passing through a hollow pipe to which were attached, at intervals, the so-called suckers made of metal or leather. As the chain descended down to the sump, water was trapped between the suckers and it was lifted up as the chain ascended; the water was discarded into a trough which carried it away. Such pumps, operated by horses or water-wheels, appeared between the late fifteenth and the middle of the sixteenth century in a wide range of locations, e.g., Bere Ferris in Devon, Wollaton colliery near Nottingham and Finchale Priory in Durham, where a horse-driven pump cost over £9. In light of the fact that similar machinery appears among Agricola's sketches, it proves that up to that point England was not a backwater in terms of mining technology compared to the continent. Finally, the vacuum pump, patented by Robert Crump in 1618, consisted of a piston attached to a rod working inside a pipe and designed in such a way as to allow the water to pass over the piston in the downstroke forcing it to the top of the pipe. None of these devices was capable of raising water far more than twenty fathoms though in some cases, as in Ravensworth colliery on the Tyne (1672), water was drawn from level to level before it reached the surface.

But while England seems to have kept up with continental methods of mine drainage up to the second half of the sixteenth century, a picture of a growing gap emerges thereafter with parts of the continent forging ahead and English technology stalling.[52] Continental methods up to the middle of the sixteenth century would be familiar to Englishmen: from the use of pumps with pistons bringing the water up in two or three stages to the chain of buckets worked by water-wheels or men. But a major innovation appeared at that time in German-speaking territories with the emergence of the *Stangenkunst*, roughly translated as "rod work with crank". It was introduced in Erzgebirge (Ore mountains, on the border of Saxony/ Bohemia) and the Harz mountains (Saxony/Thuringia) in the period 1550–65, with its full development progressing in subsequent decades. *Stangenkunst* used a water-wheel to transmit power through wooden flatrods (*Feldstangen*) over extensive distances above ground (up to a mile), the rods ending over the mine shaft where they connected to pump rods drawing the water from the mine. The flatrods were fitted with iron joints designed in a way that allowed them to be fitted one into another and secured with bolts and screws. At the point where the flatrods met the lifting rods over the mine shaft a cross-shaped lever (*Kunstkreuz*) and crank were fitted to transform the horizontal movement of the former into the vertical of the latter. *Stangenkunst* had the advantage of being able to transmit power over long distances. Its obvious disadvantage was that it was feasible only if water power was available nearby, as well as losing efficiency owing to the transmission of power through multiple rods.

The diffusion of the technique was fairly quick but only in selective territories. The Freiberg mine director Martin Planer stated that he had installed several of these machines by 1570 and there are numerous descriptions and drawings of it referring to Central European mines in which Germans played a leading role. Outside of the German world, the coal mines of the Liège area were the most notable in terms of adopting it. The Liège coal mines witnessed the exhaustion of shallow pits by 1570, prompting the Prince Bishop Ernst von Bayern to declare by public proclamation in 1582 that whoever succeeded in resolving the problem of drainage would be allowed to reap the benefits by working the mines. That seems to have been the main reason why *Stangenkunst* technology reached Liège by the late 1580s. The results were spectacular. A German chronicler of the Harz mines, Hardanus Hake, wrote in 1583 that the previous generation of miners achieved depths of c. 70 ft. At Liège depths of 600 ft were achieved by 1674 partially thanks to the hilly morphology of the area which allowed the extensive use of adits but mainly through the adoption of *Stangenkunst* later on. However such benefits did not spread throughout Europe. The Dutch did not have much use for it given the limited number of mines they possessed and also since they succeeded in draining sea water by using other methods, nor did Spaniards and Turks have any reason to adopt it since coalfields are virtually non-existent in the Mediterranean region. *Stangenkunst* did appear in France, where it was part of the mechanism of the famous Marly waterworks (1681–8), but with a very significant time lag.

The evidence, being stronger for the second half of the seventeenth century than earlier, suggests that *Stangenkunst* technology had not reached England for most of this period.[53] One of the most valuable sources of information on the state of mining technology in the middle of the century is R. D'Acres' treatise *The art of water drawing*.[54] D'Acres' purpose was not to list all existing techniques but to focus on new machines and to suggest potential improvements. Not a single reference is made by him to *Stangenkunst* or anything resembling it. Subsequent written accounts coming from every mining region of England, with the unfortunate exception of Cornwall, project the same impression. A account published in 1667 by Stephen Primatt makes references to pumps driven by horse-, tread- and water-wheels as being the norm in the Tyne and Wear while in the hilly Derbyshire lead mines a wider use of soughs was made along with rag-and-chain pumps. It is unlikely the author was uninformed in light of the fact that the second edition of his book (1680) was not revised when it comes to references on drainage and because other authors corroborate Primatt's account. Another account published in the 1680s by Francis North states that in one of the several mines he visited, the great Lumley Park mine, chain pumps were the most common method of drainage. North's statement is corroborated by Fordyce, a well-known nineteenth-century author, who argues that in 1676 mines in Lumley Park, Hetton, and Jesmond were using chain pumps worked by water-wheels. He adds that horses were widely used through the time of the Newcomen engine and that windmills were erected in 1708 in Scotland but proved ineffective in calm weather. The following year an innovative Scottish mine owner, John Earl of Mar, sent his manager to inspect technical standards in the Newcastle district. His report verified the wide use of water-wheels and horse engines with chain pumps; the expense of sinking was cited at £55 and the cost of a horse gin at £28. Similar statements are made in a booklet whose author is cited by his initials (J.C.), published in 1708, painting a picture little changed from previous decades. J.C. argues that the most common method was to draw both water and coal to the surface by using horses or water-wheels. Traditional methods of drainage persisted well after the introduction of steam engines. In a letter written in 1757 referring to a Cornish mine, William Lemon noted: "I have heard of £50 a month for a water course for driving a wheel engine."[55]

Another set of evidence pointing to the fact that England was not familiar with *Stangenkunst* technology comes from the reports of Englishmen who had visited continental mines. One of them was Edward Browne who had no name for the technology he witnessed in Liège and elsewhere which suggests that either he never visited any English mines or that such technology was unknown to England, with the latter explanation being more likely when the entire range of the evidence is taken into account. When another Englishman, Sir Joseph Williamson, started planning a trip to the continent in 1673 the Royal Society drafted a list of questions to which he was asked to find some answers. The trip was to involve stays in Aachen and Liège, and Williamson was asked to inquire about the depth of the pits and the engines used to drain them. Upon his return he did report that depths in Liège reached down to 100 fathoms but he did not have much to say about the technology used. Again, this episode indicates the failure of Englishmen to transfer continental technology and expertise.[56]

The reliance on traditional drainage techniques is indirectly corroborated by the depths sunk in English mines.[57] While in Germany depths well over 50–60 fathoms were achieved by the middle of the seventeenth century, the norm in England was up to 20–30 fathoms, a figure which was virtually identical through 1744 when Desaguliers was writing, and only in a few selected mines were depths of over 50–60 fathoms achieved (e.g., Derbyshire lead mines, Forest of Dean). Iron mines were particularly shallow, up to five fathoms c. 1600 rising to 10–15 subsequently, the main reason being the prevailing belief that iron ore did not exist at deeper levels. Pumps could not raise water for more than 15–20 fathoms. When water had to be drawn from 30 fathoms two pits were sunk near each other, one of them 30 fathoms long, the other half that distance. Water would be drawn half way up the longer pit, channeled to the shorter one and from there drawn up to the surface. In deeper mines the same method would be applied by sinking three pits. In either case various engines would be used to draw water at different levels. At the Tyne mine of Ravensworth three water-wheels were employed to lift the water in three stages from a total depth of 40 fathoms.

One is left with the overall impression that England relied throughout the seventeenth century on traditional techniques which may have witnessed minor cumulative improvements, arising, for example, from the growing experience with the construction of soughs which in some instances became extensive to a degree that permitted drainage from several square miles. This conclusion relies mainly on evidence by Hollister-Short but other authors have drawn similar conclusions. Burt, for instance, also depicts a largely stagnant picture.[58] There were certainly a few large mines (e.g., Mines Royal) but the majority of them were small enterprises and pretty much all utilized techniques little changed since the Middle Ages. Techniques were not only outdated but the cost of pumping (and other operations) was unnecessarily high due to shafts not being straight: "meandering shafts and the irregular layout of levels and stopes required the multiple articulation of drive systems, which was both complex to design and manufacture and grossly wasteful of power through friction."[59] The reason for the persistence of these patterns was the fact that many mining operations were the result of opportunistic associations of individuals who had little incentive to engage in expensive fixed capital investment, including a more rational redesign of the shaft pattern. According to Burt, "the system . . . was highly labour intensive, low in productivity and, above all, that the opportunity for heavy capital investment to break this long-jam was very restricted."[60] Hatcher comes to similar conclusions:

> Drainage technology had made substantial progress in the late Middle Ages and the early modern centuries, and most collieries were adequately served by a combination of sough and simple engine. Yet the great collieries usually required more, and although relatively inexpensive engines capable of lifting larger quantities of water existed, they were unreliable and, unless they were able to be powered by water, extremely costly to operate. Here if anywhere we have a significant technological restraint upon our industry.[61]

Despite the diversity and weight of this evidence, Hollister-Short has argued that *Stangenkunst* technology did reach England c. 1700 but in an incomplete and partially assimilated form, in the sense that machinery incorporating some of its essential elements (e.g., relying on a tier of pumps), but also lacking some major and minor features of it (e.g., master rods), did make its appearance in

English mines in an improvised form.[62] The evidence comes from Cornwall where Joachim Becher, a German engineer, introduced a version of the technology in the 1680s and from Griff colliery in the 1710s where it may have appeared as a result of imprecise and vague reports regarding its working mechanism leading to less sophisticated versions of it. But the critical question is why this technology was not introduced earlier. Hollister-Short makes a very compelling case that in fact it was, specifically in the copper mines of Cumberland which drew the interest of the finance house of Haug & Co. and witnessed an influx of German engineers in 1568. A report regarding Newlands mine drafted in 1602 makes reference to a leat 1,200 yards long bringing the water used to operate "the double wheel" and "many pumps" with such an efficiency that the authors of the report who descended to the bottom were impressed by the lack of water. Meager evidence suggests that *Stangenkunst* technology may have been introduced in the same mine c. 1570 by the well-known German engineer Daniel Hochstetter. If that was the case it would suggest a remarkable speed of diffusion since the technique reached Cumberland less than twenty years after it originated in Saxony and twenty years prior to reaching Liège. But then why did it fail to diffuse throughout the country? Hollister-Short speculates that the early demise of the copper mines (Haug & Co. lost £19,000 before abandoning this venture) meant that the technology failed to become the expertise of English engineers. Imagining a strict division of labor along ethnic lines, with German engineers operating this technology and English workers performing unskilled labor, satisfies common sense. But if copper mining had proven to be a long-lasting enterprise and given the assimilation and intermarriage of Germans with the local population, it would be a matter of a single generation before the knowledge of this technology had spread to English engineers who would have carried its diffusion to other mining regions.

There are two outstanding issues involved. First, while Hollister-Short's evidence does seem to support his claim that *Stangenkunst* technology may have appeared in England in the second half of the sixteenth century, but then got lost only to reappear in an improvised and imperfect form a century later, his explanation leaves a lot to be desired. If language was the main barrier, why this technology was adopted fairly quickly in the French-speaking Liège region but much later in France? If the presence of a strong mining industry was the necessary inducement mechanism, why was it adopted in Liège but not in England through most of the seventeenth century with its much larger mining sector?[63]

Language and having access to German expertise could not have been an issue since, at about the same time German engineers were brought to Cumberland, Burchard Cranage offered his services in Derbyshire and subsequently in Cornwall and Devon. Moreover, he received an exclusive license for twenty years for the use of a mine-drainage technique which, most likely, he brought from Germany. Not to mention that Sir Francis Godolphin also introduced in Cornwall miners from the continent around 1580. Why did Englishmen succeed in introducing techniques from the continent up to that point, such as the rag-and-chain pump, but failed to do so subsequently? At least some English mine owners such as

Sir Francis Willoughby, owner of Wollaton colliery, were relentless in pursuing solutions to the drainage problem by perusing the pages of *De Re Metallica* and trying virtually all known means for draining their mines, from soughs to various kinds of pumps, and utilizing all kinds of motive powers, from men and horses to wind and water. And there were Englishmen who kept traveling abroad looking for solutions such as the engineer who approached Willoughby in 1610 claiming he could solve the problem by exhibiting models of all the worthy technologies used in Italy, Germany, and the Low Countries; or the millwright of Montrose who was sent to Holland in 1708 at the expense of the town to study windmills. Nor could it be a problem to finance such research and development efforts given the high profitability of some mines such as those of Culross collieries in Fife (formerly part of Perthshire) which contributed to the building of the abbey of Culross or some of the greatest collieries in the Newcastle area which could produce 25,000 chalders of coal and generate a net profit of £5,000/annum by about 1700. In the end, one possibility is that *Stangenkunst* technology, even in an improvised form, was more prevalent in the seventeenth century but the evidence has not been discovered yet, a hypothesis that would be consistent with the otherwise multiple signs of good entrepreneurial reflexes of the English mining community. Alternatively, the time gap referring to its absence pointed out by Hollister-Short is real which is consistent with the fact that every single English inventor (as well as Papin) who became involved with the effort to come up with a steam device, beginning with Ramsay in 1630, had mine drainage in mind. The author is agnostic in this regard, though the latter hypothesis is more consistent with the argument of this paper.

The second issue to address is the extent to which *Stangenkunst* technology resolved the problem in the mining districts where it was adopted. Hollister-Short believes that was indeed the case and one key piece of evidence he cites, and others do too, is the impressions recorded by Edward Browne following his 1673 trip to the Erzgebirge, Hungary, and Liège.[64] Browne did not describe particular machines but he clearly suggested that flooding was not a problem. Referring to an 84-fathom mine called *Auff der Halsbrucker*, near Freiberg, he clearly states that its owners were not troubled by water, that they had good engines to draw it out. And speaking of installations he saw in Liège, he notes: "Their pumps and engines to draw out the water are very considerable at these mines; in some places moved by wheels at above a furlong's distance to which they are continued by strong woodwork, which moves backwards and forwards continuously."[65] It appears that *Stangenkunst* was quite effective but that does not imply that it could be adopted in every mine throughout Central Europe. Browne witnessed severe flooding problem at Schemnitz where there was a complete absence of water above ground, and thus no option of using water-wheels, combined with strong currents below ground. Klemm mentions another mine in the Harz mountains lacking water power, a problem which Leibniz attempted to resolve by means of a wind-powered apparatus, a plan which proved entirely unsuccessful.[66] Even Papin received an offer (which he ultimately rejected) to work on the same problem in the mines of a Bohemian prince in the 1690s.[67] German miners may have had access to technology superior to that of their English counterparts but the problem persisted in particular areas.

A 'perfect storm' in England

The invention of the steam engine in England was not the outcome of a single factor but of several, all acting as necessary conditions towards this outcome. But it is also important to stress that these factors were not all of equal significance in terms of putting the puzzle together; instead, the role of the institutional framework was critical in that it initiated a chain of causation or a domino effect which eventually led to the inventor being Newcomen, an Englishman rather than a foreigner.

Henry VIII's divorce was, indirectly, the first domino which initiated two crucial transformations. The first of these was the passing of the ownership of mines from monastic hands to the members of the gentry who came to exploit mineral deposits with a more aggressive entrepreneurial zeal; or if they leased out their mines, they extended the length of leases and lifted restrictions on the quantity of annual output that was allowed to be extracted. Other regions in Europe possessed rich mineral deposits such as coal but it was in England where changes to property rights led to the spectacular exploitation of such potential that was reflected in the quadrupling of coal output in the twenty years following the dissolution of the monasteries. Beginning in the second quarter of the seventeenth century the timber famine accentuated the growth of the coal industry and the concomitant need for more effective technological solutions to the drainage problem.

The second major outcome of the institutional changes was the domination of religious institutions by secular authority. This led eventually to the Anglican Church losing its censorship prerogative and coming to embrace the new science, viewing it as a symbol of resistance to papal authority. The triumph of the new science in England was critical not simply because it allowed its scientists to be the first to discover the principle of the existence of vacuum. England, along with Germany, lagged behind in this area, but that was not a decisive issue since this knowledge could be disseminated via curious savants across borders even where hostile attitudes towards the new science prevailed. But "knowledge in itself is no guarantee of success," as Jacob pointed out.[68] Instead, it was crucial to establish a culture in which the validation of knowledge claims was disassociated from religious dogma and the magical tradition, and it was crucial for that culture to be tied to the experimental method. Among countries that shared similar literacy rates, the decisive element that made the difference was the existence of unobtrusive institutions that fostered a more intense dialogue among savants and between them and fabricants.

In the end, there were two decisive factors behind England's success: the country's availability of rich natural resources – a matter of sheer luck – and its institutional framework; the former defined the necessary economic incentives, the latter created the dynamic interaction between landowners, mining entrepreneurs, savants and fabricants that responded to such incentives. Germany came really close to duplicating this 'perfect storm' of factors but the technological ingenuity of its engineers, already crystallized in the *Stangenkunst* technique, dampened the incentive to seek alternative solutions to the drainage problem.

Beyond these two countries the rest of Europe was, to one degree or another, less competitive in this race. The Dutch Republic had the right institutions and embraced the new science very quickly but was not endowed with plentiful mineral resources, the region around Maastricht being an exception. France and southern Belgium were blessed in this regard, particularly the latter, but entrepreneurial responsiveness was blunted by the inertia created by Catholic dogma. This inertia was not, however, impregnable. The French Academy was founded upon utilitarian principles albeit the majority of its members opted eventually for the Cartesian model. The bishops of Liège played a decisive role in suppressing the new science, though one of them was instrumental in establishing the institutional incentives for resolving the drainage problem which was addressed by adopting the *Stangenkunst* and thus eliminating the incentive to seek alternative techniques. Italy, whose scientists discovered the principle of vacuum, became irrelevant in this race due to the absence of a large mining industry and to Catholic opposition to the new science. Spain found itself in the same boat. Institutional rigidities imposed by Ottoman sultans and feudal lords across the eastern frontier of Europe since the late fifteenth century rendered those areas even less relevant. Institutions were geared towards the redistribution, as opposed to the creation, of wealth and thus the aggressive and optimistic attitudes of the new science in seeking to master nature did not find a receptive audience here.

Notes

1 Mokyr, *The gifts of Athena*.
2 Allen, *The British Industrial Revolution*, esp. pp. 267–9.
3 Hollister-Short, "Leads and lags", esp. p. 164.
4 Float/flume operations were intricate networks of floatways which allowed timber to be transported from inaccessible areas when these floatways were formed in the spring following the melting of snow; timber was collected at the other end by erecting a rake made of timber and placed across the torrent. See ibid.
5 Cohen, "Inside Newcomen's fire engine", pp. 118–19; Cardwell, *From Watt to Clausius*, pp. 1–7, 17–21; Mendelssohn, *Science and western domination*, pp. 32–3; Hall, "Cultural, intellectual, social foundations", p. 114; Mathias, *The first industrial nation*, p. 12; idem, *The transformation of England*, pp. 84–5; idem, *Science and society*, pp. 61–2.
6 The degree to which experimentation was valued over theoretical propositions was still evident throughout the time Smeaton became prominent. According to one of his biographers "the rule of his practice and one which he adhered to with the most undeviating firmness was never to trust to deductions drawn from a theory, in any case where he could have an opportunity of trial"; cited in Stuart, *Historical and descriptive anecdotes*, p. 379.
7 Allen, *The British Industrial Revolution*, p. 268; Thurston, *A history of the growth of the steam engine*, p. 24.
8 Jacob, *Scientific culture*, p. 132.
9 Ibid., pp. 27, 29, 54.
10 But Stearns has argued that the growth of this tradition dates back to Robert Grosseteste and, especially, Roger Bacon. He places these intellectual trends in the

wider socio-economic context of the time by stressing the importance of the discoveries, the commercial expansion of the period, and the rise of the middle class as important stimuli fostering the utilitarian approach of the new science. The connection between the latter and the rising bourgeoisie is evidenced by the fact that nearly all the scientific treatises of the period were written in English. See Stearns, "The scientific spirit in England"; also Hall and Hall, *A brief history of science*, p. 171.

11 Mathias, *Science and society*, p. 13; Hall and Hall, *A brief history of science*, pp. 170–2.

12 Mokyr, *The gifts of Athena*, p. 65; Allen, *The British Industrial Revolution*, p. 267; see also Goldstone, *Why Europe?*, pp. 158–61; Kronick, *A history of scientific & technical periodicals*, pp. 38, 40–4.

13 Cited in Hall and Hall, *A brief history of science*, p. 170; see also Goldstone, *Why Europe?*, p. 154; Jacob, *Scientific culture*, pp. 29–30.

14 Jacob, *Scientific culture*, p. 107; see also, Goldstone, *Why Europe?*, pp. 155–61.

15 Eamon, *Science and the secrets of nature*, p. 95; Jacob, *Scientific culture*, pp. 32–3, 141–54.

16 On the role of the Catholic Church and its alliance with the Cartesian philosophy, see Goldstone, *Why Europe?*, pp. 151–61.

17 While the majority of the Cartesian thinkers, especially French, did reject the experimental method, a few did not; his followers, for instance, promoted the value of experiments towards the end of the seventeenth century. See Jacob, *Scientific culture*, p. 46.

18 Ibid., pp. 27–8, 141.

19 Ibid., p. 107.

20 Ibid., p. 164.

21 Kronick, *A history of scientific & technical periodicals*, p. 38; Goldstone, *Why Europe?*, pp. 158–61; Jacob, *Scientific culture*, pp. 27, 32–3, 134–41; Mathias, *Science and society*, p. 61.

22 This is an important point to make because some older and more recent historians (e.g., Thurston, Goldstone) tend to draw a sharper demarcation line in this regard between England and continental Europe, particularly its Catholic segment; the French case cannot be classified as being in either camp. See Thurston, *A history of the growth of the steam engine*, p. 26; Goldstone, *Why Europe?*, pp. 151–5.

23 Russia, for instance, was very backward in this regard. As late as 1780 British engineers exhibited steam engines in the presence of senior Russian military officers, presumably trained in engineering principles; nevertheless, some of them could not comprehend the operating principles of such engines. See Jacob, *Scientific culture*, p. 132.

24 Cited in Mathias, *Science and society*, p. 61; see also p. 62.

25 Cited in Hall, "Cultural, intellectual, social foundations", p. 114.

26 Cited in Galloway, *Annals of coal mining*, p. 128.

27 Levine and Wrightson, *The making of an industrial society*, pp. 38–43.

28 Ibid., p. 38.

29 Ibid., p. 38.

30 Ibid., p. 39.

31 Galloway, *Annals of coal mining*, p. 129.

32 Smiles, *Lives of the engineers*, p. 52; Rolt and Allen, *The steam engine of Thomas Newcomen*, p. 36; Briggs, *The power of steam*, p. 23; Rolt, *Thomas Newcomen*, pp. 23–4.

33 Cited in Harris, "Engineering in Cornwall", pp. 111–12.

34 Cited in Rolt, *Thomas Newcomen*, p. 51.

35 Stuart, *Historical and descriptive anecdotes*, p. 619; Allen, "The 1715 and other Newcomen engines", pp. 242, 261–3; Hatcher, *The history of the British coal industry*, pp. 213–5, 226–8; Armytage, *A social history of engineering*, p. 71.

36 Being cheaper did not mean that the total cost involved in using engines was low. Sir Ralph Delaval spent £2,300, largely "spent upon engines", to drain his colliery

at Seaton Delaval. When horses were involved, 50–60 of them would often be necessary, each one costing £6–7 c. 1700, not to mention their voracious appetites. See Hatcher, *The history of the British coal industry*, p. 227.

37 Nef, *The rise of the British coal industry*, pp. 377–80; Hatcher, *The history of the British coal industry*, p. 212; Scott, *The constitution and finance of English, Scottish and Irish joint stock companies*, p. 186.

38 Dickinson, *A short history of the steam engine*, p. 16; Mott, "The Newcomen engine", p. 70; Forbes, *Man the maker*, p. 197; Merton, *Science, technology & society*, pp. 143–4. The following sources provide references to specific inventors and their devices: Rees, *Industry before the Industrial Revolution*, pp. 149, 152–6; Scott, *The constitution and finance of English, Scottish and Irish joint-stock companies, Vol. II*, pp. 479–80, 482–3; ibid, *Vol. III*, pp. 186–7; Harris, "Engineering in Cornwall", pp. 112–13.

39 Chaloner and Musson, *Industry and technology*, pp. 24–5; Allen, *The British Industrial Revolution*, p. 81.

40 Warde, *Energy consumption*, p. 39.

41 Malanima, "The path towards the modern economy", p. 19, graph 9.

42 Warde, *Energy consumption*, p. 67.

43 Warde also concurs with the notion that the beginning of the timber famine in the seventeenth century "does not indicate that wood shortage was the *cause* of the transition to fossil fuel use"; ibid., p. 39, emphasis in the original.

44 Ashton and Sykes, *The coal industry*, p. 13; Hatcher, *The history of the British coal industry*, p. 68; Chaloner and Musson, *Industry and technology*, pp. 24–5; Armytage, *A social history of engineering*, p. 70; Flinn, *The history of the British coal industry*, pp. 26, 28; Mundella, "What are the conditions on which the commercial and manufacturing supremacy of Great Britain depend", p. 109; Allen, *The British Industrial Revolution*, p. 81.

45 Farey, *A treatise on the steam engine*, p. 272; Flinn, *The history of the British coal industry*, pp. 252–3; Forbes, *Man the maker*, p. 196; Hollister-Short, "Leads and lags", p. 162; Allen, "Was there a timber crisis in early modern Europe?", p. 472.

46 Tylecote, *A history of metallurgy*, p. 131.

47 Allen, *The British Industrial Revolution*, pp. 161–2; see also Hollister-Short, "Leads and lags", p. 161.

48 Jacob, *Scientific culture*, pp. 154–8.

49 On the use of adits, see Hatcher, *The history of the British coal industry*, pp. 212–17.

50 Burt, "The international diffusion of technology", p. 255.

51 The evidence cited in this and the following two paragraphs relies on the following sources: Burt, "The international diffusion of technology", pp. 255–6; Hatcher, *The history of the British coal industry*, pp. 213, 217–24; Nef, *The rise of the British coal industry, Vol. II*, pp. 449–50; Chaloner and Musson, *Industry and technology*, p. 25; Ashton and Sykes, *The coal industry*, pp. 34–5; Bald, *A general view*, p. 6; Rees, *Industry, Vol. I*, p. 148.

52 Rees, *Industry, Vol. I*, p. 148; Hollister-Short, "Leads and lags", pp. 162–4, 172–3; Multhauf, *Mine pumping* (with useful illustrations); Malanima, "The path towards the modern economy", p. 19.

53 Hollister-Short, "Leads and lags", pp. 165, 170–4; Fordyce, *A history of coal, coke, coal fields*, p. 16; Bald, *A general view*, pp. 7–8.

54 Hollister-Short remarks that if Jenkins' speculation that the author's name was a pseudonym for Robert Thornton living near Daventry then his knowledge of mining techniques would be solid since his residence was near the Warwickshire coalfield. See his "Leads and lags", p.165.

55 Cited in Harris, "Engineering in Cornwall", p. 113.

56 Another possible explanation, however, is that the Royal Society failed to systematically collect knowledge on the subject in light of the fact that it did not approach and

consult people like Walter Pope and Edward Browne who had visited continental mines and published relevant papers in the *Philosophical Transactions*. See Hollister-Short, "Leads and lags", pp. 162, 170.

57 Hollister-Short, "Leads and lags", pp. 163, 171; Ashton and Sykes, *The coal industry*, p. 33; Bald, *A general view*, p. 9; Hatcher, *The history of the British coal industry*, pp. 226–7; Nef, *The rise of the British coal industry, Vol. II*, p. 451; Schumbert, *History of the British iron and steel industry*, p. 211; Burt, "The international diffusion of technology", p. 263.

58 Burt, "The international diffusion of technology", pp. 262–3; see also Ashton and Sykes, *The coal industry*, pp. 33–4.

59 Burt, "The international diffusion of technology", p. 262.

60 Ibid., p. 263.

61 Hatcher, *The history of the British coal industry*, pp. 230–1.

62 Hollister-Short, "Leads and lags", pp. 165–9, 174–8.

63 For evidence regarding the questions raised in this paragraph, see Bald, *A general view*, pp. 5, 7, 9–10; Hatcher, *The history of the British coal industry*, pp. 221, 224–6; Rees, *Industry, Vol. I*, p. 149; Schumbert, *History of the British iron and steel industry*, pp. 211–12; Harris, "Engineering in Cornwall", pp. 111–12.

64 Hollister-Short, "Leads and lags", pp. 169–70; see also Multhauf, *Mine pumping*.

65 Cited in Hollister-Short, "Leads and lags", p. 170.

66 Klemm, *A history of western technology*, pp. 208–11.

67 Ibid., pp. 220–1.

68 Jacob, *Scientific culture*, p. 185.

Bibliography

Allen, J. S., "The 1715 and other Newcomen engines at Whitehaven, Cumberland", *Transactions of the Newcomen Society*, 45 (1972–3) pp. 237–68.

Allen, R., "Was there a timber crisis in early modern Europe?", in S. Cavaciocchi, ed., *Economia e energia*, pp. 469–82.

Allen, R., *The British Industrial Revolution in global perspective* (Cambridge: Cambridge University Press, 2009).

Armytage, W. H. G., *A social history of engineering*, 4th ed. (London: Faber and Faber, 1976).

Ashton, T. S., and J. Sykes, *The coal industry of the eighteenth century* (New York: Augustus M. Kelley, 1967).

Bald, R., *A general view of the coal trade of Scotland* (Edinburgh: Oliphant & Brown, 1808).

Briggs, A., *The power of steam: an illustrated history of the world's steam age* (Chicago: University of Chicago Press, 1982).

Burt, R., "The international diffusion of technology in the early modern period: the case of the British non-ferrous mining industry", *Economic History Review*, 44 (1991), pp. 249–71.

Cardwell, D. S. L., *From Watt to Clausius: the rise of thermodynamics in the early industrial age* (Ames: Iowa State University Press, 1989).

Cavaciocchi S., ed., *Economia e energia secc. XIII–XVIII*, Istituto Internazionale di Storia economica "F. Datini" (Florence: Le Monnier, 2003).

Chaloner, W. H., and A. E. Musson, *Industry and technology* (London: Vista Books, 1963).

Cohen, H. F., "Inside Newcomen's fire engine, or: the scientific revolution and the rise of the modern world", *History of Technology*, 25 (2004), pp. 111–32.

Dickinson, H. W., with a new intro by A. E. Musson, *A short history of the steam engine* (New York: Kelley, 1965).

Eamon, W., *Science and the secrets of nature: books of secrets in medieval and early modern culture* (Princeton, NJ: Princeton University Press, 1994).

Farey, J., *A treatise on the steam engine, historical, practical and descriptive* (London: Longman, Rees, Orme, Brown, and Green, 1827).

Flinn, M. W., *The history of the British coal industry, Vol. 2, 1700–1830: The industrial revolution* (Oxford: Clarendon Press, 1984).

Forbes, R. J., *Man the maker: a history of technology and engineering* (London and New York: Abelard-Schuman, 1958).

Fordyce, W., *A history of coal, coke, coal fields . . .* (London: S. Low, Son, and Co.; New York, Scribner & Co, 1860).

Galloway, R., *Annals of coal-mining and the coal trade: the invention of the steam engine and the origin of the railway*, 2 vols. (London: Colliery Guardian, 1898–1904).

Goldstone, J., *Why Europe? The rise of the West in world history, 1500–1850* (New York: McGraw Hill Higher Education, 2009).

Hall, R. A., "Cultural, intellectual, social foundations, 1600–1750", in Kranzberg and Purcell, eds., *Technology in western civilization,* pp. 107–17.

Hall, R. A., and M. Boas Hall, *A brief history of science* (Ames: Iowa State University Press, 1988).

Harris, T. R., "Engineering in Cornwall before 1775", *Transactions of the Newcomen Society*, 25 (1945), pp. 111–22.

Hatcher, J., *The history of the British coal industry, Vol. 1, Before 1700: towards the age of coal* (Oxford: Clarendon Press, 1993).

Hollister-Short, C. J., "Leads and lags in late seventeenth century English technology", *History of Technology*, 1 (1976), pp. 159–83.

Jacob, M. C., *Scientific culture and the making of the industrial west* (New York and Oxford: Oxford University Press, 1997).

Klemm, F., *A history of western technology* (Ames: Iowa State University Press, 1991).

Kranzberg, M., and C. W. Purcell, Jr., eds., *Technology in western civilization, Vol. 1, The emergence of modern industrial society, earliest times to 1900* (New York: Oxford University Press, 1967).

Kronick, D. A., *A history of scientific and technical periodicals: the origins and development of the scientific and technical press 1665–1790*, 2nd ed. (Metuchen, NJ: Scarecrow Press, 1976).

Levine, D., and K. Wrightson, *The making of an industrial society: Whickham, 1560–1765* (Oxford: Clarendon Press; New York: Oxford University Press, 1991).

Malanima, P., "The path towards the modern economy: the role of energy", *Rivista di Politica Economica*, Aprile/Giugno (2010–11), pp. 1–29.

Mathias, P., *The first industrial nation: an economic history of Britain, 1700–1914* (New York: Scribner, 1969).

Mathias, P., ed., *Science and society, 1600–1900* (Cambridge: Cambridge University Press, 1972).

Mathias, P., *The transformation of England: essays in the economic and social history of England in the eighteenth century* (New York: Columbia University Press, 1979).

Mendelssohn, K., *Science and western domination* (London: Thames and Hudson, 1976).

Merton, R. K., *Science, technology and society in seventeenth century England* (New York, Evanston, and London: Harper Torchbooks, 1970).

Mokyr, J., *The gifts of Athena: historical origins of the knowledge economy* (Princeton, NJ and Oxford: Princeton University Press, 2002).

Mott, R. A., "The Newcomen engine in the eighteenth century", *Transactions of the Newcomen Society*, 35 (1962–3), pp. 69–86.

Multhauf, R., "Mine pumping in Agricola's time & later", Paper 7, *Contributions from the Museum of History and Technology* (Washington: Smithsonian Institution, 1959).

Mundella, A. J., "What are the conditions on which the commercial and manufacturing supremacy of Great Britain depend, and is there any reason to think they may have been or may be endangered?" *Journal of the Royal Statistical Society*, XLI (1878), pp. 87–134.

Nef, J., *The rise of the British coal industry*, 2 vols. (London: George Routledge & Sons, 1932).

Rees, W., *Industry before the industrial revolution, vols. I and II* (Cardiff: University of Wales Press, 1968).

Rolt, L. T. C., *Thomas Newcomen: the prehistory of the steam engine* (Dawlish, England: David and Charles, 1963).

Rolt, L. T. C., and J. S. Allen, *The steam engine of Thomas Newcomen* (New York: Science History Publications, 1977).

Schumbert, H. R., *History of the British iron and steel industry from c. 450 B.C. to A.D. 1775* (London: Routledge and Kegan Paul, 1957).

Scott, W. R., The *constitution and finance of English, Scottish and Irish joint stock companies to 1720, vols. 2 and 3* (Cambridge: Cambridge University Press, 1910–11).

Smiles, S., *Lives of the engineers, Vol. 4* (London: John Murray, 1874).

Stearns, R. P., "The scientific spirit in England in early modern times (c. 1600)", *Isis*, 96 (1943), pp. 293–300.

Stuart (Meikleham), R., *Historical and descriptive anecdotes of steam engines* (London: Wightman and Cramp, 1829).

Thurston, A., *A history of the growth of the steam engine* (New York: D. Appleton and Co., 1897).

Tylecote R. F., *A history of metallurgy* (London: The Metals Society, 1976).

Warde, P., *Energy consumption in England & Wales, 1560–2000* (Consiglio Nazionale delle Ricerche, 2007).

Part II

The diffusion of Newcomen engines, 1706–73

Introduction

The British economy, or any other for that matter, was one that at the dawn of the eighteenth century relied largely on animate sources of energy, though the contribution of water and wind was not trivial. But it was about to enter a new era, one that we are still going through, in which technologies relying on fossil fuels used for production purposes came to dominate the generation of energy. The Newcomen engine initiated this new era and, before the genius of James Watt made its appearance, it became a familiar sight in the island's landscape. The diffusion process of this technology is of paramount importance. In terms of economic outcomes, there is little value in a nation being the first one to come up with a major invention since its contribution to economic growth hinges exclusively on the speed of adoption of this technology.

Part II of this book delves into the diffusion of Newcomen engines from the time of their first commercial appearance (1706) to the year prior to the first commercial application of the Watt model (1773). Chapter 3 offers a methodology for measuring the diffusion of steam power during this period which is quite different, in several respects, in comparison with previous accounts. It is followed by three chapters which attempt to provide an interpretative framework in order to explain the various facets of the diffusion process which was characterized by regional and sectoral asymmetries.

It may be useful to offer some preliminary remarks, drawing from the standard literature of technological diffusion, in order to frame and organize the discussion on the determinants of this process. The amount of hp adopted at any given point in time was a function of several variables which can be classified in the following explanatory clusters:

Factors relating to *the evolution of cost of steam power* and its effect on profitability, paying special attention to the role of the patent premium (in effect through 1733) and the evolution of engineering skills.[1] The former was important in determining the fixed cost of the engine. The latter even more so in determining all the other components of fixed and operating cost per unit of thermodynamic output (hp), particularly the cost of fuel consumption; along with the elasticity of key capital inputs, it was also critical for the speed of installations of these engines. The development of such skills was endogenously determined by the diffusion process, i.e., the more diffusion unfolded, the more it carried forward the improvement of such skills, through learning-by-doing, resulting in cost reductions. In the absence of a formal education system, the transfer of engineering skills could come only from related labor markets and personal interaction and hence was bound to resemble a contagion effect with strong regional asymmetries that were ameliorated as time went by.

Next, *the cost and technical capabilities of alternative techniques* have to be taken into account. If an existing technique is complementary to the new one it is bound to induce diffusion of the latter. On the other hand, if the new technology causes the displacement of the old one then the question of the relative costs per unit of energy output comes to the forefront. The general principle which conditions the decision-making process is that the total (fixed plus operating) cost of the new technique has to be lower than the operating cost of the old one.[2]

The cost of a newly introduced technology often stands higher compared to the cost of an existing one. Learning-by-doing will eventually lead to improvements and reduction of cost though the gap may persist for some time especially if the existing technique goes through improvements itself. The diffusion rate will stall during this period but the potential of acceleration presents itself once the gap closes and the threshold point of the cost curves is pierced. There may be, however, further delay depending on the age distribution of the old fixed capital and its rate of replacement; if it has a low depreciation rate and/or if the adopting sectors go through a phase of slow growth then the adoption of the new technology will be delayed; when the time is ripe for its adoption, it is a comparison of total costs of both techniques that matters. Another delay may be caused if there are expectations for upcoming improvements of the new technology creating a widening gap between best and average practice. It will be shown, however, that this was not an important factor in the case of the Newcomen engine.[3]

A note of caution is in order. *Ex ante* investment decisions are by definition tentative due to the uncertainty surrounding the future behavior of variables in product and factor markets. Compounding the difficulties involved, the level of sophistication of such modeling exercises was beyond business concepts prevailing in the eighteenth century. Hence it is important not to confuse *ex post* outcomes with *ex ante* ultra rational decision making; hindsight, in this case, becomes the enemy of accurate historical analysis. Managerial attitudes towards risk, fed by uncertainty over the technical characteristics and capabilities of the new technique and how they impact profitability, become of paramount importance. Uncertainty is diminished the further down the road we are in terms of the knowledge transmission mechanism even in the face of imperfect business concepts.[4]

Finally, *the nature of markets and the size of firms*, a factor largely neglected by the literature on the diffusion of steam power, played a decisive role. It will be shown that the existing transportation network led to a fragmentation of markets for final products placing limits on the size of firms and hence their ability to afford the purchase of engines.

Some studies referring to modern innovations have found no clear link between firm size and propensity to adopt an innovation. However, in an age lacking a well-developed financial network, the size distribution of firms would seem to play some role in their ability to finance the purchase of a technique through their own profits. That would have been particularly the case for Newcomen engines given their fairly high purchasing cost. One would expect diffusion to be faster in sectors with firms sufficiently large to self-finance the fixed and operating costs of the new technique, particularly if firm sizes were characterized by limited variations in a particular market cluster, the latter characteristic inducing a competitive drive towards adoption. Such competitive forces would be especially keen once adoption reaches a certain momentum, in the dynamic segment of the diffusion curve, since non-adopters would face an increased risk of becoming less efficient and profitable compared to pioneering firms. On the contrary, in markets with low entry barriers and a large number of small firms, the latter would be less conducive to adopt a new expensive technology.[5]

An important question that has to be addressed in this context is whether a firm size or certain level of output, either acting as a threshold for the adoption of innovations, can be defined, as Soete has suggested.[6] It will be argued that such specification is feasible, as well as useful, as long as we bear in mind that it is only necessary for a potential adopter to approach the threshold size of output since the adoption of the technology will achieve the goal of reaching it.

The above list is not exhaustive. Does the presence of certain individuals in the right place and the right time play a role, as Mansfield pointed out?[7] And, in the context of the Schumpeterian model of long-term structural change and long waves, is diffusion retarded in the depressive phase of the cycle and does it pick up pace during the upswing? Or, as some studies have suggested, does the business cycle play no role in the process?[8] These are, however, questions which are easier posed than answered, for different reasons.

Notes

1 Metcalfe, "Impulse and diffusion", pp. 350, 356–7; Soete, "Long cycles", p. 221; Georghiou et al., *Post-innovation performance*, pp. 74–6; Radnor, et al., eds., *The diffusion of innovations*, p. 29; Dosi, "The research on innovation diffusion", p. 187; Brown, *Innovation diffusion*, pp. 183–4.
2 Von Tunzelmann, "Technical progress", p. 152.
3 Rosenberg, *Inside the black box*, pp. 26–7; idem, *Perspectives on technology*, p. 193; Brown, *Innovation diffusion*, pp. 154–5; Soete, "Long cycles", p. 222; Frankel, "Obsolescence and technological change", p. 299; Stoneman, *The economic analysis of technological change*, p. 147; Radnor, et al., *The diffusion of innovations*, p. 37.
4 Stoneman, *The economic analysis of technological change*, p. 147; Mansfield, "Determinants of the speed of application of new technology", p. 211.
5 Utterback, "Innovation in industry", p. 625; Davies, *The diffusion of process innovations*, p. 160; Romeo, "The rate of imitation", p. 67; Nabseth and Ray, eds., *The diffusion of new industrial processes*, pp. 13, 307; Georghiou et al., *Post-innovation performance*, p. 77. Mansfield came up with a simple model suggesting that, along with the profitability of the innovation, the size of investment in it as a percentage of the value of the total assets of the firm were the two most important factors. See Mansfield, "The speed of response of firms to new techniques", p. 309–10; idem, *Industrial research*, pp. 155–8; idem, "Determinants of the speed of application of new technology", pp. 207–8.

6 Soete, "Long cycles", p. 220.
7 "The speed of response of firms to new techniques", p. 311.
8 Soete, "Long cycles", p. 221; Utterback, "Innovation in industry", p. 624.

Bibliography

Brown, L., *Innovation diffusion: a new perspective* (London and New York: Methuen, 1981).

Davies, S., *The diffusion of process innovations* (Cambridge: Cambridge University Press, 1979).

Dosi, G., "The research on innovation diffusion: an assessment", in Nakinenovic and Grubler, eds., *Diffusion of technologies*, pp. 179–208.

Floud, R., and D. McCloskey, eds., *The economic history of Britain since 1700, Vol. I* (Cambridge: Cambridge University Press, 1981).

Frankel, M., "Obsolescence and technological change", *American Economic Review*, 45 (1955), pp. 296–319.

Freeman, C., ed., *Design, innovation and long cycles in economic development* (London: Frances Pinter, 1986).

Georghiou, L., et al., *Post-innovation performance: technological development and competition* (Basingstoke and London: Macmillan, 1986).

Mansfield, E., "The speed of response of firms to new techniques", *Quarterly Journal of Economics*, 77, 2 (1963), pp. 290–311.

Mansfield, E., *Industrial research and technological innovation: an econometric analysis* (New York: Norton, 1968).

Mansfield, E. "Determinants of the speed of application of new technology", in B. R. Williams, *Science and technology*, pp. 199–216.

Metcalfe, J. S., "Impulse and diffusion in the study of technical change", *Futures*, 13 (1981), pp. 347–59.

Nabseth, L., and G. Ray, eds., *The diffusion of new industrial processes: an international study* (Cambridge: Cambridge University Press, 1974).

Nakinenovic, N., and A. Grubler, eds., *Diffusion of technologies and social behavior* (Berlin: Springer-Verlag, 1991).

Radnor, M., I. Feller and E. M. Rogers, eds., *The diffusion of innovations: an assessment* (Evanston, Ill.: Center for the Interdisciplinary Study of Science and Technology, Northwestern University, 1978).

Romeo, A, "The rate of imitation of a capital embodied process innovation", *Economica*, 44 (1977), pp. 63–9.

Rosenberg, N., *Perspectives on technology* (Cambridge: Cambridge University Press, 1976).

Rosenberg, N., *Inside the black box* (Cambridge: Cambridge University Press, 1982).

Soete, L., "Long cycles," in Freeman, ed., *Design, innovation and long cycles*, pp. 214–30.

Stoneman, P., *The economic analysis of technological change* (Oxford: Oxford University Press, 1983).

Utterback, J. M., "Innovation in industry and the diffusion of technology", *Science*, 183 (February 1974), pp. 620–6.

Von Tunzelmann, G. N., "Technical progress", in Floud and McCloskey, eds., *The economic history of Britain*, pp. 143–63.

Williams, B. R., ed., *Science and technology in economic growth* (New York and Toronto: John Wiley & Sons, 1973).

3 Reassessing the diffusion of Newcomen engines, 1706–73

The prevailing view among economic historians is that steam power, as a general purpose technology, played a pivotal role in shaping the *long-run* trajectory of the British Industrial Revolution although its role was fairly limited in boosting productivity and aggregate economic growth prior to the nineteenth century. To appreciate the temporal impact of steam power, one needs to focus on its diffusion process by calibrating the analysis to take into account regional and sectoral patterns of diffusion, since the dynamic sectors of the British Industrial Revolution tended to exhibit a strong regional concentration.[1]

The first comprehensive effort (by Harris) to quantify the number of steam engines erected during the eighteenth century concluded that their diffusion exhibited a "remarkably dispersed geographical distribution" in light of the fact they were very expensive at the time of their appearance. This assessment carried weight among other experts such as Allen who also characterized their rate of adoption as "nothing short of remarkable" when contrasted with other technological innovations of the period. This impression became even stronger when Kanefsky and Robey revised the figure of the total number of engines adopted during the eighteenth century, nearly doubling Harris's figure, and allowing experts like Flinn to point out the "remarkably rapid" spread of steam power. The choice of superlatives is virtually identical in the latest assessment by Nuvolari, Verspagen and von Tunzelmann (2011) (henceforward NVT): "the spread of steam power technology appears to have been, from the very outset, remarkably wide."[2]

The author does not wish to argue with the previous assessments when the *absolute* number of adopted steam engines is taken into account; that was indeed remarkable by any standards. But it does wish to argue that the latest and most sophisticated attempt by NVT adopts a methodology which obscures the *relative* success rate of the diffusion process.

The NVT study counts the number of years it took to get to the midpoint of the diffusion process and the number of years needed to get from 10 to 90 percent of the "saturation level", the latter being defined as "the number of steam engines that will be installed at the end of the diffusion process" the authors examine, i.e., 1,800.[3] In other words, the saturation point of the diffusion process is identified with the actual adoption rate and the analysis revolves around the speed at which diffusion approaches the saturation point. I wish to address a different question: what was the extent of the gap by the end of the period between the actual adoption rate and the ideal one assuming the Newcomen engine was utilized by every potential user? The *ideal* rate of adoption is determined by the extent to which the engine could prove suitable to production needs across different sectors given its technical features. On the other hand, the *actual* rate of adoption is conditioned by economic considerations both on the demand and supply sides. Framing the analysis along these lines is in sync with a methodology prevalent in the literature of technological diffusion and it is more illuminating in appreciating the delay of steam power in having a radical impact on the rates of productivity and aggregate economic growth.

The methodology which will be used to assess the actual diffusion rate will utilize figures from an updated version of the Kanefsky database and it will be different to the one adopted by the NVT study in a couple of important respects: it will measure diffusion by relying on horsepower figures, as opposed to number of engines, to take into consideration the increased power of engines over time; and it will adjust these figures to account for their reduction due to engines falling out of use. In addition, it will suggest the utilization of some formulas referring to the technical features of engines which offer the potential of enriching the empirical evidence on which the econometric analysis of the chapter relies.

The chapter is divided into three main sections. The first one will point out several differences that were discovered between the original Kanefsky database and the secondary literature in terms of the precise number of steam engines installed, the year of their erection, and their technical characteristics; these differences necessitated a fair number of revisions.[4] It will describe the method utilized in deriving the data used to draw the diffusion trajectory and it will provide estimates regarding the horsepower installed over time. The section concludes by summarizing the statistics, particularly from an aggregate, sectoral, and regional perspective. The second and third sections weigh the rate of diffusion relative to the potential range of adoption by focusing on two sectors for which this assessment is easiest to undertake, mining and the use of steam engines in the operation of blast furnaces.

The actual diffusion rate

The first task at hand was to examine the degree of completeness of the original Kanefsky database by contrasting its entries with information found by means of a meticulous search in the secondary literature.[5] Three areas of concern were identified:

First, there were differences regarding the erection year of particular engines but no changes were made in this regard if they fell within four years from each other since they had a minimal impact on the diffusion trajectory. Second, there is a failure in some of the secondary sources to record engines cited in the database. But the reverse also holds true. For instance, the Kanefsky database cites only three engines as being erected in Derbyshire by 1730 but according to Barton this figure was "nine or more" by that year. In the case of Cornwall, Barton relies on a statement by Pryce who claimed that "above three score [above 60] have been erected" by 1739–75, whereas by 1777–8 there were "probably about 75 Newcomen engines". In contrast, the database's figures for Cornwall are 56 and 66 respectively.[6] In the end, the author was able to identify another dozen engines or so missing from the original database while a few others have been added by Dr. Kanefsky in recent years.[7] The third and final revision of the database involved supplementing it in terms of the technical characteristics of individual steam engines which, in some cases, allowed the calculation of their hp.[8]

The database incorporating the aforementioned revisions was then used to calculate the diffusion path by focusing on cumulative hp figures; this methodology comprises a radical departure from previous ones tracing diffusion based on the number of engines installed. The author finds the latter methodology problematic in light of the nearly fivefold increase scored in the hp of a typical engine from the beginning to the end of the period (see Appendix 3A). The hp figures used to draw the aggregate diffusion curve are reproduced in Figure 3.1.[9] A cursory look at the trend clearly indicates a fairly narrow range in the hp of engines during the 1730s and a growing one thereafter. Ignoring the substantial increase in energy output and counting engines as if each unit had the same economic impact amounts to a flawed methodology.

Following this reasoning, a list of 45 engines with known hp was compiled. The figures for 30 of them were provided by Kanefsky (but ignoring experimental engines of his original list since they had no economic impact); the figures for the remaining 15 engines were either found in the secondary literature but mostly

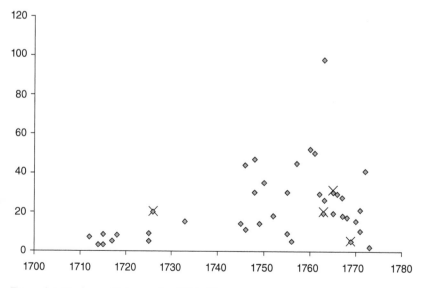

Figure 3.1 Engines with known hp, 1710–75

derived from the technical characteristics of engines, and in some cases led to revising the hp figures cited by Kanefsky.[10] Subsequently, four methods of imputing the unobserved hp data were tested, including three Monte Carlo simulations using static and rolling bins (see Appendix 3C). One of the latter proved to produce the most statistically robust results and was adopted in constructing the aggregate hp curve both in terms of the mean value along with the band defined by the standard deviations at a 95 percent confidence interval (Figure 3.2). This estimate shows a mean value of 13,239.7 hp installed by 1773.[11]

Horsepower diffusion figures derived by using this method are substantially higher than the useful power generated by these engines because part of it was wasted due to friction. No effort was made to account for this factor for two reasons: sources which state the hp of engines are often not explicit on this point and that precludes knowing whether they refer to indicated or effective hp, though most likely they refer to the former; and also because of the wildly different estimates on how to account for friction.[12] Burn, for instance, argues that the right method is to deduct 1.5 lbs from the load when applying a formula to calculate hp. Other experts opted to deduct a certain percentage from the indicated hp. Roper suggested that friction deducted 15 percent, Hawkins's figure was 30 percent, while others went as far as deducting half of the generated power. It should be noted that the proportion of lost power actually depended on the size of the engine, being higher in engines of smaller size.[13]

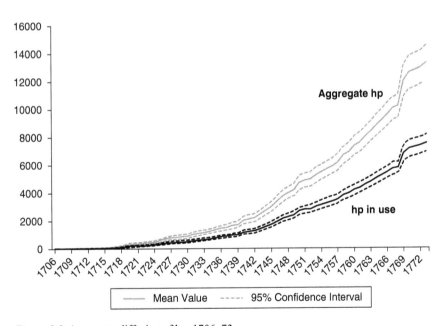

Figure 3.2 Aggregate diffusion of hp, 1706–73

Source: see Database K

However, adjustment of the diffusion figures was made in order to account for the fact that, at any given time, some engines were out of use.[14] The evidence in this regard is not ideal. Kanefsky ventured the estimate that by 1760, out of a possible total of 350 engines, at least 200 (57 percent), perhaps as many as 250 (71 percent), were at work.[15] There is a fair amount of evidence referring to the very end of the period, in line with Kanefsky's date, which supports the lower-bound figure of his range. Specifically, the database cites 34 engines erected at the Shropshire ironworks and coal and iron mines up to the end of 1775 but, according to an account cited by Trinder, there were "about" 20 of them working at the time (c. 59 percent).[16] Most importantly, out of the 99 engines compiled in the Brown list, only 57 of them were still working in 1769 (58 percent).[17] The evidence is compelling since it encompasses a substantial number of engines and refers to the two most important sectors in terms of their adoption (see the next two sections of this chapter). Unfortunately, the evidence is very weak regarding the years before 1760. The author is aware of only one estimate by Rogers referring to Cornwall, according to which there were only three engines still at work by 1741 out of seven installed by that time based on figures of the database revised by the author (42 percent).[18] In light of this evidence, it has been decided to adopt Kanefsky's lower-bound figure and reduce the cumulative diffusion figures for each year down to 57 percent despite the prospect the proportion of engines at work may have been lower for the pre-1760 decades.[19] The adjustment of the figures commences with the year 1714 when the first known engine went out of commission, that is, the Wheal Vor engine in Cornwall which is the third commercial engine in the database (erected in 1710).[20] The aggregate hp in use is also depicted in Figure 3.2. By the end of 1773 it reached a figure of 7,503.2 hp.

The data were further analyzed from several other perspectives. First, the data were broken down based on the type of engine involved. The diffusion of the Savery engine, either in its original or modified forms, was virtually non-existent during this period, not taking into account experimental engines. There were only four Savery engines adopted (1706, 1714, 1739, 1766), two of which were used to drain mines.[21] The remaining 563 non-experimental engines installed were of the Newcomen type.[22]

Second, the aggregate diffusion data (Figure 3.2) seem to reveal two structural break points of different levels of confidence.[23] The first break, the one with the highest confidence level, takes place in 1746 followed by another one in 1768. It should be noted that this trend is different from the one pointed out by previous authors who discern a two-phase pattern with the break point being the expiry of the patent in 1733. My tests, on the contrary, reveal that the patent's expiration did not have a discernible effect on the trend.[24] This finding is of paramount importance in assessing the contribution of several variables in conditioning the trajectory of diffusion, discussed in subsequent chapters. Lastly, the data were subjected to testing in order to discern whether a logistic growth or Gompertz curve fits them better; the latter was deemed a better model for both the aggregate hp curve and the aggregate hp in use (see Appendix 3C).

Third, there is a distinct bias from a sectoral point of view. Of the engines with known sectors of adoption, comprising the vast majority in the database, 87 percent of the total hp was installed in the mining industry.[25] The contribution of other sectors was minimal: ironworks trail mining far behind with 6 percent of total hp; the first one was adopted in 1731 but the bulk of them in the 1750s onwards. Waterworks come next (3 percent), the first engine being installed in 1714 and the rest of them spread fairly evenly through the entire period. Brassworks, canals, chemical works, oil/mustard, chocolate, paper, edge, and sugar mills complete the list each accounting for c. 1 percent or less.[26]

Fourth, an analysis of the data from a regional perspective reveals a striking concentration of hp in a very limited number of counties.[27] Table 3.1 illustrates this impression but by deviating from the structural breaks chronology. It has been deemed that a better perspective is gained if we trace diffusion through the first dozen years or so (1718) to identify the pioneering counties; followed by the year preceding the first structural break (1745); and bypassing the second structural break point, extending the analysis through to the end of the period a few years later. The top four counties accounted for over 60 percent of aggregate hp by 1718, followed by a drastic decline of the rate in the second phase and a partial recovery of it during the last three decades or so.

During the first phase the northeastern coalfield (Durham and Northumberland) clearly played the leading role (29 percent), followed by Staffordshire and Cornwall;[28] even when Warwickshire's hp is added to that of Staffordshire the combined share is distant second. Cornwall drops from the top-four list in the second phase but the northeast still retains its leading spot with over a fifth of the total hp followed by Staffordshire and Warwickshire with a combined 17 percent. But the gap between the northeast and other regions widens again in the third phase with the former accounting for 29 percent of the total, followed by Cornwall and Shropshire; even when bringing in Gloucestershire and Derbyshire to consider the top six counties (see Figure 3.3), the top three Midland counties are still far distant from the leading region.[29] Another interesting characteristic of the diffusion data is the very limited inroads the Newcomen engine made in Wales and Scotland

Table 3.1 Regional concentration ratios in the diffusion of Newcomen engines, top four counties at the end of three periods, aggregate hp and as a percentage of the total

1718		1745		1773	
Durham	20%	Northumberland	12%	Northumberland	17%
Staffordshire	19%	Warwickshire	10%	Durham	12%
Cornwall	14%	Durham	9%	Cornwall	11%
Northumberland	9%	Staffordshire	7%	Shropshire	7%
Total	62%	Total	38%	Total	47%

Note: Counties are classified on the basis of Method 4 outlined in Appendix 3C, since the more sophisticated econometric methods could not be applied at the county level. The data used were derived from the Kanefsky database once it had been revised by the author. The numbers are rounded to the nearest figure.

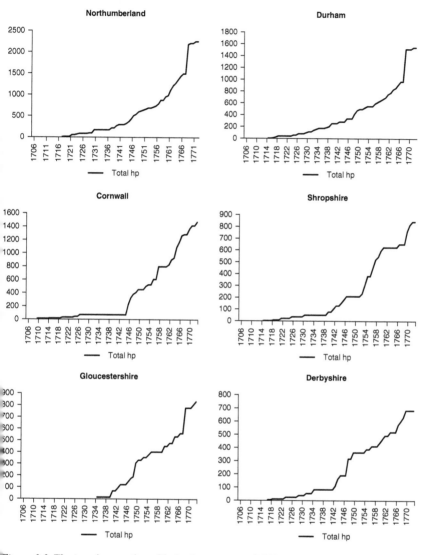

Figure 3.3 The top six counties with the fastest rates of diffusion, 1706–70/1

Source: see Database K

hroughout this period, with the former accounting for c. 5 percent and the later for c. 7 percent of the total by 1773. In some cases the engine was adopted
by a particular colliery but failed to find other imitators in nearby regions as, for
nstance, in the case of Stevenson colliery which adopted all five of the pre-1750
engines erected at the Ayrshire coalfield. In some other cases an entire county
ailed to adopt it until very late during this period, as was the case in Lanarkshire
which erected its first engine in 1760.[30]

Actual vs. 'ideal' diffusion in the mining sector

A substantial portion of the literature on technological diffusion has long established that the proper method of assessing the adoption rate of a technique is to measure the gap that exists between the level of adoption at any given point in time with the potential range of adoption at that moment.[31] Two methods often suggested are, first, to contrast the number of firms that have adopted the technology with the total potential pool of users at the firm level; or second, to measure the portion of total output produced by the technology. Neither of these methods, however, is straightforward. When counting firms, defining the denominator may be problematic because economic factors such as firm size may prevent adoption by all firms; and the productive capacity of a potential user has to be taken into account since a single firm may be capable of adopting multiple units of the technology in question. Most importantly, simply counting firms that may have adopted a single unit may provide a skewed picture of the rate of diffusion: if a couple of large firms have adopted it but the sector is comprised of several other smaller firms, the rate of adoption may appear falsely limited. When it comes to counting output, this method becomes problematic too if the technology can be used in only some aspects of an integrated production process but not in others or when the new technology is complementary to an old one in the context of the same production process.[32] Another important element to be taken into account is that the upper ceiling of adopters may be shifting due to technological improvements which expand the respective range; the latter is neither fixed nor homogeneous. In this case, the range of potential adoption is depicted as a step-like line superimposed above the diffusion curve.[33] However, in the case of Newcomen engines, this was not a major issue, given that technological improvements were not substantial enough to change dramatically the range of potential diffusion.

While we have some reasonably good estimates on the actual extent of the adoption of steam power, we tread on a riskier territory when it comes to the potential range of adopters for the top sector utilizing energy sources of any sort, namely mining (especially collieries). Let us start with some useful generalizations.[34] There were two tasks energy sources were necessary for: draining water from mines and winding coal or ore, with the devices used for either purpose being often the same in the pre-steam era. During the early modern period, when most mines were small and the quantities of water to be drained were limited, man-operated windlasses or horse gins would be adequate. Whenever possible, water-powered pumps were less expensive than devices powered by humans or horses and were capable of draining larger quantities, hence they were especially sought after in larger collieries. Water streams, however, were not always readily available and the specter of drought was always present. Wind-powered mechanisms were the least common method of drainage. Based on contemporary accounts from experts like J. C. and the assessments of modern historians, there seems to be no doubt that horses provided the bulk of power, water-draining methods playing a secondary role whereas human and wind power a very minor one.

When it comes to the drainage of collieries in particular, Galloway noted that "so long as the demand for coal was small, and supplies were attainable from shallow mines above the level of free drainage, the mining of coal had been comparatively easy. But about the beginning of the seventeenth century, this happy state of matters was coming to an end." By the beginning of the eighteenth century "in the great majority of cases water continued to harass or even altogether baffle the mines."[35]

The winding process kept relying on non-steam power sources following the introduction of the Newcomen engine due to technical impediments. Even the most prominent engineer of his era, Smeaton, was very resistant to the idea of turning the Newcomen engine into a rotative one by the simple addition of a connecting rod and crank, insisting that the only feasible arrangement was to act as a power auxiliary to water wheels. Smeaton's reservations were shared by many engineers at the time who thought that the variable stroke could cause the destruction of the engine, failing to appreciate that the crank would be able to control its variability. There were some isolated efforts to find a solution such as the ratchet device by Joseph Oxley and a similar one by John Stewart in 1766 but they both proved failures.[36]

By default, winding continued to rely on traditional methods all of which, however, failed to offer satisfactory solutions. To begin with, the use of horse gins created the potential of a bottleneck in the mining industry. A single horse gin could not raise more than 100 tons/day, hence restricting output to 30,000 tons annually. This figure was fairly high given the size of mines during the first half of the eighteenth century but the scale of operations gradually increased as the century progressed. In some isolated regions, such as the Scottish coalfield of Fife, wind power was utilized but obviously wind could not function as a universal solution. Water power could also be used but given its spatial and seasonal limitations, considerable efforts were made to use the Newcomen engine as an auxiliary force to it. In a very poorly documented case, Long Benton colliery seems to have attempted to use two engines pumping water over a water-wheel for winding purposes in 1749.[37] According to Galloway, the first documented case refers to Chesterhaugh colliery where, in 1753, a basket of coals was raised while a basket of water descended and the water was pumped up to the surface by a steam engine. Another engine was presumably used to operate a winding gin at Walker colliery in 1758. And in 1762 Joseph Oxley attempted to use steam power at Hartley colliery to pump water over a water-wheel but the effort proved unsuccessful. The full extent of these efforts is not clear but there is a consensus that the technical problems were finally resolved in the 1770s, Smeaton playing a critical role in this regard, and the method of using steam power to pump water to a cistern above a wheel became generalized. The important point to stress is that until then steam power failed to replace or even to aid to a substantial extent alternative sources of power when it came to winding.[38]

It follows that the process of drainage was the exclusive beneficiary of the adoption of steam power in the mining sector. The main question then to be addressed is how the c. 6,500 hp adopted in the draining of mines contrasts to the hp offered by other energy sources, something that will indicate the gap between actual and potential diffusion.[39] There were two types of mines, collieries and metal mines. It seems that in collieries the bulk of power in drainage was provided by steam engines supplemented to an undetermined degree by the use of adits; the latter were used in parts of the northeast, especially south and southwest of the High Main seam of Newcastle, all of the collieries in north Staffordshire, the lower half of Wales, Cumberland, Derbyshire, and Somerset. According to Kanefsky, the lack of water resources was so acute that they failed to play a significant role in both drainage and winding.[40]

The situation was substantially different in metal mines, with regional particularities stemming from the availability of water, the morphology of the terrain, and the size (and thus power needs) of mines producing a more diversified picture. Water power was both readily available and sufficient in the Pennines (500–1,000 hp), the Lake counties, and upland Wales (up to 500 hp in the country as a whole). On the other hand, the use of steam power was widespread in Cornwall, Denbighshire and Flintshire, as well as Shropshire, either because water resources were scarce or they were inadequate given the size of mines.

All in all, water power contributed to the mining sector 5,000 hp in 1760, a figure that remained unchanged through the end of the period this study covers.[41] If Kanefsky's judgment is valid, virtually all of it was utilized in metal mines.

But, presumably, part of this figure was utilized in the winding process as well as for other purposes (e.g., crushing) to an extent that can only be guessed through circumstantial evidence. Deriving his evidence from Cornwall, Kanefsky pointed out that the power capacity of water wheels used for drainage was clearly larger than that of those used for winding.[42] In light of the absence of other evidence I would venture the estimate that, of the 5,000 hp provided by water in metal mines, 4,000 hp was utilized in drainage and thus was part of the potential range of diffusion of steam power, with the remaining 1,000 hp being used in winding and other applications and thus not part of this range.

The contribution of other options is not clear. Horse gins were virtually eliminated from the effort to drain mines while wind power made a minimal contribution.[43] The role of soughs and adits, however, was not negligible. According to Flinn, their contribution was

> extremely limited since they required the existence, within a reasonable distance, of naturally drained land the surface of which was lower than that of the pit sump. Only mining in hilly districts could possibly meet these requirements, and it is clear that even in hilly areas not many hundreds of feet of depth would put a pit sump below the point at which it could be run out by driving a sough horizontally to an adjacent valley.

However, he admits that "at lesser depths this method was possible . . . and some coalfields . . . were in sufficiently hilly country."[44] I would venture the guess that the role of these drainage methods, particularly adits, amounted to c. 2,500 hp, accounting for nearly 20 percent of the total power required for drainage purposes (13,000 hp), behind steam (6,500 hp, 50 percent) and water (4,000 hp, c. 30 percent).[45]

These figures are based partly on solid evidence (for steam) and on reasonably good estimates (for water) but also on some risky extrapolations when it comes to the other sources of energy, notwithstanding that the consensus seems to be that they played a minor, albeit not trivial, role. As such, the figures are obviously not meant to be interpreted as being precise but simply conveying a reasonably good sense of the degree of deviation between the actual and ideal diffusion of steam power in the mining sector. It is also useful to keep in mind that while steam power scored significant inroads in collieries, it still had a long way to go in metal mines.

Actual vs. 'ideal' diffusion in the iron industry

Another sector in which the supply of a constant flow of power was of vital importance was ironworks, which traditionally utilized water power to blow the blast furnaces. Given the insufficient supply of water during summer months, steam engines were first used to return water to wheels. There was some confusion as to when the first returning engine was installed in blast furnaces. Farey placed the timing in the early 1760s, citing Coalbrookdale or Carron as the pioneering adopters. But, according to Hyde, the first such use was in the former firm in 1742. The subsequent use of such engines reveals a strong clustering pattern towards the iron industry of Shropshire.[46] Finally, during the late 1760s, blowing cylinders attached directly to an engine came to replace the leather bellows and supersede the use of water power.[47] It follows that for virtually the entire period examined here steam and water were complementary sources of power, unlike the mining industry where it was a matter of "either-or" in the use of these two energy sources.

There is also a lack of unanimity among economic historians when it comes to the degree to which water power was adequate in itself for powering blast furnaces. Hyde takes an optimistic stance by stating that "water power was often sufficient to operate a single coke blast furnace (coming into being for the first time in the early 1750s) and that steam engines were purchased only when a second or third furnace was added."[48] The crucial question amounts to how long a blast furnace could go with no or inadequate power before putting at risk its economic viability. The minimum amount of time furnaces had to close down for repairs was for 4–5 weeks, spread intermittently throughout the year. But Hyde also adds that water could provide power for eight months of the year (c. 34 weeks) which he considered the minimum amount of time for the operation of the bellows as long as it was consistent during the working period.[49] Richard Pegg, a "master workman" in Bradford (Yorkshire), stated in 1593 that, in order to generate a profit with a furnace, there had to be sufficient water to operate it for 20–30 weeks/year. By the eighteenth century, an operating period of thirty weeks was considered satisfactory.

It seems, however, that the norm, when utilizing water power, was falling below these figures.[50] Data from South Yorkshire indicate that the average operating span of furnaces during the period 1698–1756 was 26–30 weeks. Even more so, in regions such as the Black Country (south Staffordshire), rich in coal and iron deposits, exploitation of the latter could not have been feasible without steam power in light of its limited water resources. Raistrick has provided a detailed illustration of this claim in the case of Coalbrookdale.[51] Two blast furnaces utilized at the beginning of the century, named New and Old, worked with water-wheels relying on a natural stream of water, having an average combined annual output of 404 tons for the period 1719–27. Production was characterized by intense seasonal volatility with peaks in the winter and troughs in the summer. During the years 1733–4 the company faced a decline of power to the furnaces due to severe drought. At the same time, there was an expansion of demand for pig iron in Bristol and the building up of the trade for engine and pipe castings. In the face of this increased demand and power shortages, the company was forced to engage in efficiency improvements that came about in the form of learning-by-doing, better organization, and an improved device for pumping water powered by horses. The effect of these improvements was to raise the combined output of the Old and New furnaces to c. 600 tons per year during the period 1735–8. It is worth noting, however, that in July 1735 the firm's records report that despite the new pumping device there was an insufficiency of water for three-quarters of the 46 weeks the furnaces were blown. Once the installation of steam engines was initiated in 1743, the volatility of production figures disappeared and combined output figures for the two furnaces in selected years with surviving records were in the range of 1,200–1,600 tons.

In these instances water either failed to provide power for the minimum amount of time required or, if it did so, it was inadequate for most of the operating time of the furnaces. Its inherent inadequacy is also indicated by the fact that at any given point in time there were a number of furnaces in stock but not operating; weak demand may have been a contributory factor but mostly it was because of the unreliability of water power in providing the blast. In light of these facts, Kanefsky's assessment that the lack of adequate water power created a "serious bottleneck" seems well-founded: "in many works the need was sufficiently great to justify this expensive innovation [a steam engine]."[52]

The gap between actual and potential diffusion in the mining industry was quantified in terms of hp but this is not feasible in the iron industry. In order to determine the power of steam engines required in these locations we would need to know the water flows in every location of blast furnaces and the extent to which the quantity provided was sufficient, something that is well beyond the documentary evidence. And to define actual diffusion we need to know the hp of every single one of the 23 engines installed to aid blast furnaces, the amount of evidence again being inadequate. But this is not an intractable problem. There is strong circumstantial evidence which points to the fact that the engines installed were of sufficient power. We have figures for only two engines (both installed in the 1750s) which were of 30 and 45 hp, well above the decadal mean (c. 24 hp) and in comparison to some steam engines designed for this purpose by Smeaton shortly after the end of my period; the latter figures are also well above the typical hp of water wheels at the time used to power blast furnaces (10–12 hp).[53]

Moreover, it is not unreasonable to presume that since steam engines were introduced in this sector after a few decades of experience, engineers must have had enough sense to erect engines of adequate power in each blast furnace location. If that was the case, it is perfectly fine to contrast the number of engines installed with the number of blast furnaces, as Figure 3.4 does, since the gap would be the same compared to the method of using hp.

There are considerable discrepancies in the literature regarding the number of furnaces, particularly for the first half of the century, though this is not a serious problem since the bulk of engine installations took place afterwards. The author consulted the figures cited by Riden as well as those by Davies and Pollard, both sets of figures considered to be amongst the most authoritative. It should be noted that the former cites figures for furnaces in use whereas Davies and Pollard for the total number in stock (i.e., including those being idle). Interestingly enough, the expectation that the latter figures ought to have being higher than the former is not always met. But the differences between the two sets of figures are not overly wide with the exception of the early 1770s when Davies and Pollard's figures rise consistently above those of Riden and thus result in depicting a slower rate of diffusion.[54] In the end, the Davies-Pollard figures were utilized for the construction of the graph with the exception of the first two years since they begin in the 1750s; this choice was made because counting furnaces in stock is preferable since they include idle furnaces which, most likely, were such because of the absence of adequate water power. The rate of adoption comes to 29 percent of the ideal. But it should be stressed that the data overstate the rate of diffusion

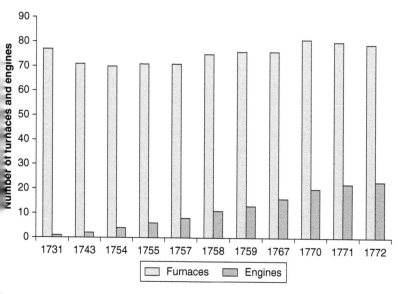

Figure 3.4 Number of furnaces and cumulative number of engines installed, 1731–72
Source: see text

because, presumably, an undetermined number of engines may have been out of use by the end of the period. If the previously adopted assumption of 57 percent engines in use applies in this case, then the proportion of blast furnaces having a steam engine is reduced from 29 down to 16.5 percent by 1772. On the other hand, there is also a reverse bias in that in some undetermined number of blast furnaces the use of steam engines may not have been imperative. In the end, the two biases may roughly cancel each other out.

Space limitations preclude extending the discussion to other sectors of the economy.[55] It is safe to argue that the diffusion process was certainly inadequate in waterworks which adopted 17 engines starting from early on (1714), replacing the use of horses. All but two of them were found in London, the other installations being in the very small town of York, while skipping the towns that trailed London, though by far, in the urban hierarchy of the period (e.g., Bristol, Birmingham, Liverpool, Manchester, Leeds, Sheffield). In other sectors, such as paper mills (350–400 by the end of the period) and brassworks, where steam could be used as an auxiliary power pumping water over wheels the diffusion process seems to have been weak with only one and six engines respectively being installed during the entire period.[56]

Assessing the evidence: a 'remarkable' diffusion?

The objective of this chapter was twofold. The first one was to take a fresh look at the Kanefsky database which has proven an invaluable tool in tracing the utilization of steam power in the British economy of the eighteenth century. It is clear that the database in its original form is not the definitive record of this process something its own author openly acknowledged. The discrepancies that were identified in relation to the erection year of engines, when not very much apart are not a serious flaw. But Kanefsky seems to have missed a number of engines which, if included in an updated version of the database, would bring the total to the figure he speculated was the true extent of diffusion. One wonders whether the erection of more engines awaits discovery. Another potential goldmine of information is the enrichment of the database with crucial technical characteristics of the engines installed, particularly the pressure on the piston and the velocity which could allow us to derive their horsepower by utilizing the formulas mentioned in Appendix 3B.

But the main objective of this exercise stems from the author's perception of what is the appropriate methodology in counting and assessing the diffusion path of Newcomen engines. To take the number of engines installed at a point in time and consider this the "saturation level" implies the impossibility of extending the diffusion process beyond this point; in other words, it implies a state of perfection. Furthermore, all this method allows us to do is to fit a curve between points A and B and test the nature of this curve. Instead, in my view, the right approach is to place the diffusion of any technology in a sectoral context and count the gap between actual and potential diffusion; such methodology would allow those economic historians interested in the pace of the Industrial Revolution to better assess the extent to which this technology contributed to productivity and aggregate growth.[57] And, in the context of this methodology, it makes little sense to pursue calculations on the basis of engines installed just because the latter offers a greater level of convenience but ignoring the fact that the power of the typical engine increased fivefold by the end of the period; nor does it make sense to ignore the amount of steam power falling out of use. Counting steam engines in a comparative context encompassing other power sources would be the equivalent of comparing passenger traffic handled by automobiles and railroad cars by counting them as units without taking into account their carrying capacity. There are admittedly gaps in the evidence referring to aggregate and in-use hp but they are not grave enough to preclude plausible generalizations with the use of sophisticated econometric techniques.

In the end, this new methodology does not overturn the long-held belief that the absolute number of Newcomen engines installed by the time Watt came on to the scene was indeed remarkable, particularly in light of the fact that the engine relied on an entirely novel working principle and was fairly complex. But it does create a more subdued assessment when we focus on the relative pace of diffusion. Steam power came to dominate the process of draining in collieries but had a long way to go in metal mines; it is worth repeating that in Cornwall, the county with the third highest figure of installed steam hp by 1773, the latter was barely on an equal footing with water power. In the mining sector as a whole, steam accounted by 1773 for about half of total power and even less in the iron industry.

Appendix 3A: The increasing power of Newcomen engines

Notes and comments: Decadal means of hp per engine were compiled beginning with the 1710s, the mean figure of which was projected back to the only commercial engine prior to that decade, specifically to an engine erected in 1706. At the other end of the chronology the mean hp per engine for the 1760s was calculated by incorporating data up to 1773. The figure adopted for the 1730s is more of an estimate rather than based on solid evidence.

It is important to compare my figures with others in the literature. First, the decadal means derived through this method are consistently somewhat above figures cited in Kanefsky and Robey ("Steam engines," p. 185, table 9; see also Kanefsky, *Diffusion of power technology*, pp. 261–2, 442). However, the author's sample relies on figures from 45 (non-experimental) engines, as opposed to 35 taken into account by Kanefsky and Robey.[58]

Period	1706–19	1720s	1730s	1740s	1750s	1760–73
Mean	5.66	13.5	15	26.66	23.66	27.36

Figure 3A.1 Mean hp per engine

Source: Based on data derived from the revision of the original Kanefsky database.

Another discrepancy emerges based on a statement made by Stuart according to whom the 57 engines in the Brown list still working in 1769 had an average hp of 20.84. A sample of 15 engines drawn from the Brown list by Farey presents an average of 25.1 hp; see Stuart, *Historical and descriptive anecdotes*, p. 292, and Farey, *Treatise on the steam engine*, p. 234. Both figures are below mine referring to the period 1760–73 (27.36). Most of the engines in the Brown list, and presumably in Farey's sample, were erected in the 1760s but few come from earlier decades when the typical steam engine was of lesser hp, presumably lowering unjustifiably their figures and thus accounting for the discrepancy with my estimates.

Finally, Stuart (*Historical and descriptive anecdotes*, p. 628) refers to a sample of 18 *large* Cornish engines working in 1770; according to Lord's speculation (*Capital and steam-power* p. 149), they had cylinder diameters in the range of 60–70 inches. The average hp of these 18 engines was 27.22, i.e., virtually identical with the average of my method regarding the period 1760–73. But the fact that these were large engines and the nine installed Cornish engines included in my sample for the period 1760–73 had somewhat lower hp compared to the overall mean of the sample seems to suggest the possibility of upward bias on my part. But it is a discrepancy that refers to only one county and thus it does not warrant placing excessive weight on it. That is not denying, however, that further research may very well revise the decadal hp figures adopted here.

Appendix 3B: Alternative methods of calculating hp

A really rough but very easy method to calculate nominal hp is to adopt a rule suggested by Farey according to which 90 square inches of cylinder diameter = 1 hp.[59] Mott reflects a similar view by arguing that "the potential power of an engine was proportional to the square of the diameter these engines were capable of developing."[60] If this rule was accurate we could use a fairly large amount of data on cylinder diameters provided by Kanefsky and supplement it by the approximately four dozen engines that can be positively identified in the Brown/Smeaton list whose diameters are also stated.[61] However, when this method was tested on engines for which both the hp and the cylinder diameter are known the results were very unsatisfactory. Simply put, an increase of cylinder diameters does not increase proportionally the amount of hp and that is evident even by a cursory examination of the two respective columns in the database.[62] In fact, it is puzzling that Farey even suggested such a method in light of his statement that Smeaton's observations on 15 engines erected in the Newcastle region (1769) proved that "the powers of the engines bore no settled proportion to the dimensions of the cylinder."[63]

The formal method of calculating nominal hp is to multiply the square of the diameter of the cylinder in inches by the cube root of the stroke in feet and divide by 47. This formula is based on assumptions regarding the load on the piston and its velocity, such assumptions differing from author to author. Once again, it does not provide a reliable method because, contrary to the belief that nominal and indicated hp were very similar in the eighteenth century, that is not borne out when we apply this formula to engines whose indicated hp is known.[64]

"The elements really entering into the number of horses-power which any engine will develop are, the average effective steam pressure, and the velocity of the piston."[65] There are a number of formulas which allow for the incorporation of either or both of these, most crucial, variables permitting us to calculate the indicated hp of an engine:

> **F1**: $P \times L \times A \times N/42,017$, where P = the pressure on the piston in lbs per square inch, A = the square of the diameter of the cylinder in circular inches, L = the length of the stroke in ft, N = the number of strokes per minute. The numerator of the fraction gives the duty whereas the figure in the denominator is used when A is expressed in circular inches as is the case in Kanefsky's database. If the diameter of the cylinder is expressed in square inches then the figure used in the denominator ought to be 33,000. To convert circular to square inches we multiply the square of the diameter by 0.7854.[66]

> **F2**: $A \times L \times N/6,000$.[67]

> **F3**: $(d-1)^2 \times L \times N/5,640$, where d is the diameter of the cylinder.[68]

The problem we have here, however, is that while we have *average* figures for a large number of engines regarding the pressure and the number of strokes, the author was able to find very few figures on these two variables referring to particular engines that would allow us to calculate their hp. An alternative method contemplated was to use mean figures and impute them to engines for which this information was missing in order to supplement data on cylinder diameters and length of stroke.

Regarding pressure, that of the atmosphere is 15 lbs/square inch but the vacuum in atmospheric engines was so imperfect that the effective pressure was bound to be lower. Watt believed that the typical figure before he came on the scene was 6.8 lbs/square inch for small engines and 6.94 for large ones (e.g., 100 hp); subsequent writers rounded up the figure to 7 lbs. On the other hand, Kanefsky has argued that the true figure was more like 9–10 lbs. Watt, however, seems to have been right on. The average pressure of 15 engines from the Brown list was 6.72 lbs and when supplemented by data on six other individual engines the range is 5-c. 11 lbs whereas the mean is 7 lbs.[69]

Regarding the number of strokes, we have data only from a handful of engines, the range being 6–15. Watt believed that the typical velocity of engines prior to his arrival on the scene was 128 feet; Kanefsky challenges this figure too, raising it to 200–250 feet and Rigg's estimate backs him up. However, to the author's surprise, these figures are way off the mark. Taking into account the average of 15 engines from the Brown list supplemented by figures on ten additional engines, provides a range of 50–105 feet and a mean of either 61.54 or 91.66 feet, well below any of the aforementioned estimates, including Watt's very conservative one.[70]

Attempts were made to compute the hp of individual engines by using the aforementioned means of pressure and velocity and applying F1, F2, and F3 but the results were not encouraging when testing these formulas on engines whose hp is already known. Given the wide range of deviations from both means, knowing the latter was not a good substitute for the lack of precise information on the pressure and velocity of specific engines.

However, the three or four technical features essential to deducing hp were known for about a dozen individual engines, allowing the calculation of hp figures, in a few cases leading to a revision of Kanefsky's data. The extracted figures were supplemented by a couple from the secondary literature and added to Kanefsky's unrevised figures, creating the sample of 45 engines. The author believes that other researchers who have done more meticulous research on the technical characteristics of steam engines can come forward and enrich this sample and lead to an enhancement of the robustness of results on diffusion derived by means of the paper's methodology.

Appendix 3C: Data augmentation techniques and logistic/ Gompertz testing
By Lawrence Costa and Michel D. Dilmanian

This appendix covers the chapter's testing methodology and presents statistical results. We cover (1) data augmentation techniques for imputing unobserved horsepower figures and (2) a Vuong test goodness-of-fit comparison between Gompertz and logistic models for tracking Newcomen engine diffusion. The data investigated are for aggregate horsepower installed, aggregate horsepower in use, and horsepower installed in the top six counties for steam power adoption by 1773.

Models

Following Verhulst's model as exemplified by Pearl and Reed, the logistic curves are estimated using the form $y = \dfrac{L}{1 + ae^{-bt}}$ where y represents the predicted horsepower figures, b and a are positive parameters, t represents the period/observation, and L is a scaling parameter.[71] We then define $Y = \ln\left(\dfrac{L}{y} - 1\right)$, $\alpha = \ln(a)$, and $\beta = -b$. Thus the logistic function is transformed to the linear form $Y = \alpha + \beta t$, which is estimated by least squares. The model is fit by choosing an L that minimizes the squared difference between the predicted y and the observed value. In our case, this optimization is performed using Microsoft Excel's Solver add-in.

The Gompertz model is approximated according to the method outlined by Franses.[72] We begin with the standard Gompertz form: $y_t = \alpha e^{-\beta e^{-\gamma t}}$ where y is the predicted horsepower figure; α, β, and γ are positive parameters; and t denotes the period. Taking the natural logarithm, we arrive at the equation $\ln(y_t) = \ln(\alpha) - \beta e^{-\gamma t}$.

Finally, we take first differences: $\ln\left(\Delta\ln(y_t)\right) = -\gamma t + \ln\left(\beta e^\gamma - \beta\right)$ where Δ represents the first difference operator, and estimate the equation using nonlinear least squares. Again, we make use of Excel's Solver for this estimation.

Motivation for and explanation of the Vuong test

We apply two tests to determine which model best fits the data. The first of these, derived by Franses, appears biased toward the logistic model and, unsurprisingly, indicates that it is a better fit across the board. Essentially, the Frances test rewrites both the Gompertz and logistic models in a similar fashion then tests whether some auxiliary terms in the logistic form are statistically different from zero. The problem lies in an asymmetry; the terms must be statistically zero for a Gompertz result whereas anything else indicates a logistic fit. For this reason, we discard the results of the Francis test.

A more satisfying approach follows from Lien and Vuong, who specify a likelihood test based on the theory developed by Vuong.[73] In this case, we compare the error terms from the predicted y values of each model and then use them to derive the Vuong statistic, denoted:

$$LR = \frac{\ln\left(\sum_{t=1}^{T} e_{G,t}^2 \big/ \sum_{t=1}^{T} e_{L,t}^2\right)}{\sqrt{\sum_{t=1}^{T}\left(\dfrac{e_{G,t}^2}{\sum_{s=1}^{T} e_{G,s}^2} - \dfrac{e_{L,t}^2}{\sum_{s=1}^{T} e_{L,s}^2}\right)^2}}$$

where e_G and e_L denote the Gompertz and logistic error terms respectively.

This Vuong statistic is reported on a t-scale and tests whether the two models' errors are significantly different. A significant negative result indicates that a Gompertz curve is a better relative fit – note that it is the first term in the numerator – and a significant positive result points toward the logistic model.

Data augmentation and testing methodology

Of the 567 engines considered in Database K, only 45 include an indicated horsepower figure. This necessitates some sort of data augmentation. Given such license, we employ four different procedures to help assure statistical rigor. Of the following tests, methods one and two are the most sophisticated (and method one is our preferred procedure). All Monte Carlo simulations are repeated 1,000 times via a VBA script in Excel. The Excel Analysis add-in is used for random sampling and, as mentioned above, Solver is used for Gompertz/logistic optimization.

Method 1 – Dynamic bins: We use a Monte Carlo simulation of an Approximate Bayesian Bootstrap (ABB) technique to impute unobserved horsepower values. In each iteration of the test, engines lacking a horsepower value receive one from the set of observed values within a 20 year band of the missing one. The ABB technique follows a two-stage process. In the first step, we take a random sample with replacement of the available horsepower values in the 20 year band; in the second, we choose an imputed value (again, with replacement) from the first stage sample. The bands ensure that an engine without an existing horsepower receives an imputed value from a contemporary engine, rather than one separated in time by as much as half a century.

Let us restate the preceding method mathematically. For each engine receiving an imputed value, we consider a sample $y_1, \ldots, y_n$, where the first i values are observed and the following n − i values are missing, and where i < n. In the first stage, we sample and replace i values from $Y_{observed} = (y_1, \ldots, y_i)$ to create the set $Y^*_{observed}$. In the second stage, we choose the imputed values from $Y^*_{observed}$. This creates the imputed set $Y^*_{missing} = (y_{i+1}, \ldots, y_n)$.

Finally, to illustrate the procedure in something closer to lay terminology, each iteration of the Monte Carlo simulation proceeds according to the following steps:

1   Impute horsepower figures to the 522 engines missing them.

    a   For each engine draw a first stage sample.
    b   From the first stage sample, draw a value to impute

2   Create a combined dataset of 45 observed horsepower figures and 522 with imputed values.
3   Calculate an aggregate horsepower figure for each year. These values are saved to calculate table 3C.3 below.
4   Fit a logistic model using the data from step (3).
5   Fit a Gompertz model using the data from step (3).
6   Compute a Vuong statistic for this iteration. This value is saved to calculate the Vuong statistics reported in tables 3C.1 and 3C.2 below.

Method 2 – Dynamic bins with imputation from a normal distribution: This procedure is nearly the same as *Method 1*, save for a slight change in the data imputation technique. Rather than draw an imputed value from the first stage sample (see step 1b above), we take the first stage sample and compute its mean and standard deviation. We then take this mean and standard deviation to characterize a normal distribution and randomly draw an imputed value from said distribution.

There is one caveat to this technique: it is possible for the imputed values to be negative, which obviously does not make sense for a horsepower figure. On average this problem affects 23 of the 522 imputed engines. We correct for it simply by using the absolute value when a calculation is negative. This correction does not seem to *materially* affect the distribution but it is for this reason that we prefer *Method 1* (simply by virtue of the fact that no fix is necessary). That having been noted, *Methods 1* and *2* return very similar results, which may be verified below

Method 3 – Static bins: Here we differ from *Method 1* in that a static bin of horsepower values is used for each decade, rather than a band around a given engine. Otherwise, the procedure is the same.

Method 4 – Decade-wise mean values: In this case, the ABB process is discarded in favor of simply filling in missing horsepower figures with the mean values for each decade (e.g., an engine from 1725 would receive the average horsepower value for 1720–29).

Results – Aggregate horsepower diffusion

In tables 3C.1, 3C.2, and 3C.3, we report results of the testing procedures described above.

Results – horsepower diffusion by county

Last, we find Vuong statistics by county (see Table 3C.4). ABB data imputation in this case is untenable given the sparseness of observations. Instead, we use decadal means to fill in unobserved horsepower values. To avoid large breaks resulting from gaps in the data, we also use linear interpolation to account for years when no engines are recorded as installed. Given that our Gompertz estimation makes use of the natural logarithm of first differences, it is unfeasible to simply repeat values. However, when approximating repeated values by making slight adjustments to the figures (e.g., by adding 0.1 hp per year over the span of the gap in the data), the results are not significantly different from those using linear interpolation.

Table 3C.1 Vuong statistics for aggregate horsepower installed

	Dynamic Bins – Method 1	Dynamic Bins – Method 2	Static Bins – Method 3	Decade-wise – Method 4
Vuong Statistic	−7.207	−7.182	−6.117	−6.303
Std. Deviation	0.865	1.12	1.047	N/A
Model Indicated	Gompertz	Gompertz	Gompertz	Gompertz
hp Observations	45	45	45	45
Years	68	68	68	68
Imputed Values	522	522	522	522
Simulations	1000	1000	986	1

Table 3C.2 Vuong statistics for aggregate horsepower in use

	Dynamic Bins – Method 1	Dynamic Bins – Method 2	Static Bins – Method 3	Decade-wise – Method 4
Vuong Statistic	−6.675	−6.566	−5.605	−5.743
Std. Deviation	0.901	0.984	1.008	N/A
Model Indicated	Gompertz	Gompertz	Gompertz	Gompertz
hp Observations	45	45	45	45
Years	68	68	68	68
Imputed Values	522	522	522	522
Simulations	1000	999	1000	1

Note: For in-use figures, we assume that all installed capacity is in use until 1714, when the first engine is taken out of service. From then on, we assume that 57 percent of installed capacity is in use.

Table 3C.3 Monte Carlo simulation aggregate horsepower values by year

Year	Mean Aggregate hp Method 1	Std. Deviation Aggregate hp Method 1	Mean Aggregate hp Method 2	Std. Deviation Aggregate hp Method 2	Mean in-use hp Method 1	Std. Deviation in-use hp Method 1	Mean in-use hp Method 2	Std. Deviation in-use hp Method 2
1706	5.30	2.26	5.27	2.47	5.346	2.274964	5.305764	2.461167
1707	5.30	2.26	5.27	2.47	5.346	2.274964	5.305764	2.461167
1708	5.30	2.26	5.27	2.47	5.346	2.274964	5.305764	2.461167
1709	5.30	2.26	5.27	2.47	5.346	2.274964	5.305764	2.461167
1710	16.60	4.25	16.50	4.13	16.416	4.192197	16.43501	4.213117
1711	16.60	4.25	16.50	4.13	16.416	4.192197	16.43501	4.213117
1712	23.60	4.25	23.50	4.13	23.416	4.192197	23.43501	4.213117
1713	23.60	4.25	23.50	4.13	23.416	4.192197	23.43501	4.213117
1714	32.41	4.67	32.15	4.67	18.27192	2.678815	18.34474	2.839424
1715	62.33	6.86	61.72	6.72	35.00769	3.753114	35.138	4.036799
1716	62.33	6.86	61.72	6.72	35.00769	3.753114	35.138	4.036799
1717	101.77	15.46	102.84	15.78	57.5586	8.194655	58.52601	8.366378
1718	143.95	21.14	146.35	21.33	81.94662	11.16928	83.78668	11.63948
1719	257.60	42.49	262.02	41.91	146.824	21.76925	152.1942	21.65169
1720	319.43	48.15	325.58	46.82	181.9816	25.48302	188.1547	24.37282
1721	328.35	48.50	334.62	46.94	187.0803	25.87023	193.2097	24.64301
1722	380.24	52.60	388.90	50.65	217.5399	27.68996	224.2418	26.64359
1723	409.17	53.62	418.05	52.08	233.9725	28.34456	240.8053	27.34579
1724	456.94	56.48	467.31	54.10	261.4088	29.79216	268.832	28.77179
1725	574.49	63.38	585.42	60.87	328.2106	33.90537	336.6223	32.7956
1726	673.01	65.98	684.11	62.59	384.0928	35.2357	393.2553	34.1082
1727	777.98	71.11	791.23	68.19	444.3133	38.50246	453.8241	37.38615
1728	791.14	71.17	804.11	68.27	451.6714	38.76612	460.8606	37.53636
1729	846.72	73.06	859.88	69.53	483.209	40.02258	492.3833	38.91599

1730	873.94	73.76	887.86	69.94	498.8919	40.4118	508.1229	39.20713
1731	1010.62	80.98	1028.16	77.50	578.2302	43.18468	587.4399	42.68948
1732	1065.76	81.95	1084.65	78.35	609.9177	44.01141	619.2537	43.36144
1733	1150.38	83.39	1169.29	79.73	657.9151	45.19398	667.2572	43.92838
1734	1219.37	85.05	1237.91	82.02	697.1054	46.70506	707.0644	44.92602
1735	1344.58	89.17	1364.69	85.16	768.0174	49.81928	779.4099	46.44141
1736	1446.86	97.14	1468.34	91.74	827.4206	52.74864	839.4495	51.13676
1737	1508.06	102.37	1534.78	96.83	864.2312	55.17831	876.2535	54.05877
1738	1642.29	112.20	1673.01	106.04	941.0575	62.025	954.7613	61.97371
1739	1692.90	114.05	1723.42	108.58	969.1818	62.91927	984.1859	62.7011
1740	2011.31	135.21	2042.11	135.96	1150.657	75.46238	1166.989	78.74145
1741	2114.28	140.07	2148.72	140.35	1211.054	78.1894	1228.771	81.89679
1742	2190.39	141.51	2226.90	142.65	1254.941	79.7228	1273.091	83.20494
1743	2443.71	150.46	2485.68	154.55	1398.785	84.37073	1419.694	90.69378
1744	2710.46	163.66	2756.34	165.17	1551.798	90.14417	1573.393	96.89095
1745	2975.79	172.52	3027.19	173.06	1705.146	97.24003	1726.666	102.0073
1746	3363.32	188.94	3418.31	188.60	1923.923	107	1949.536	110.3172
1747	3717.83	208.84	3778.58	200.64	2124.632	117.2083	2154.19	119.5919
1748	3969.58	216.56	4036.92	206.12	2269.641	120.5643	2300.069	122.125
1749	4159.71	224.14	4231.38	212.57	2376.741	125.0923	2411.361	125.3413
1750	4686.17	249.45	4766.80	239.78	2674.259	139.1522	2716.798	137.6096
1751	4857.24	254.35	4941.87	242.95	2774.848	140.9194	2816.471	139.4714
1752	4933.47	254.70	5018.68	243.60	2818.267	142.0543	2860.078	140.1283
1753	5246.55	264.72	5342.26	259.39	2998.359	148.1066	3044.273	147.5827
1754	5463.83	273.02	5565.82	267.34	3122.776	150.804	3174.644	152.4131
1755	5688.68	277.51	5794.43	268.30	3249.722	153.7143	3305.463	153.0473
1756	5883.18	286.54	5992.29	274.34	3358.733	156.194	3419.452	155.2873

(continued)

Table 3C.3 (continued)

Year	Mean Aggregate hp Method 1	Std. Deviation Aggregate hp Method 1	Mean Aggregate hp Method 2	Std. Deviation Aggregate hp Method 2	Mean in-use hp Method 1	Std. Deviation in-use hp Method 1	Mean in-use hp Method 2	Std. Deviation in-use hp Method 2
1757	6145.06	292.01	6261.79	282.68	3511.088	160.4764	3573.945	160.1401
1758	6670.84	310.95	6795.01	304.81	3807.65	168.8197	3881.756	168.3968
1759	6899.91	319.01	7025.08	313.83	3934.435	170.7907	4016.612	171.3288
1760	7348.81	341.75	7486.79	326.18	4186.73	178.0602	4282.929	179.995
1761	7559.11	344.35	7706.39	329.93	4304.195	180.7725	4406.15	182.7792
1762	7995.04	363.81	8161.88	346.47	4546.176	187.7256	4664.046	191.6487
1763	8342.47	367.39	8521.73	353.86	4742.02	190.0602	4867.399	194.3642
1764	8788.88	385.36	9011.58	370.14	4995.658	200.2839	5133.368	203.8065
1765	9160.01	393.03	9400.68	377.98	5205.028	205.7481	5353.933	208.0135
1766	9540.96	402.10	9805.70	391.02	5417.563	210.8437	5583.405	215.1593
1767	10008.24	415.48	10294.81	402.91	5679.941	218.5791	5860.704	221.9247
1768	10161.30	420.83	10453.46	408.09	5765.633	219.8327	5952.543	222.4619
1769	11990.81	572.83	12399.49	616.06	6802.271	292.347	7046.311	295.9487
1770	12574.71	597.38	13020.68	637.39	7132.601	300.5187	7395.059	311.1228
1771	12734.04	599.92	13187.62	635.43	7222.463	301.6676	7488.922	313.1137
1772	12922.41	602.30	13387.99	636.92	7328.112	302.8303	7602.805	315.0974
1773	13239.72	614.21	13725.34	643.77	7503.25	307.6172	7800.982	319.3359

Table 3C.4 Results for the Vuong statistic for horsepower by county (top 6)

	Cornwall	Derbyshire	Durham	Gloucestershire	Northumberland	Shropshire
Vuong Statistic	2.25	−1.18	1.80	3.28	4.06	3.75
Model	logistic	N/A	N/A	logistic	logistic	logistic
Years	64	57	60	39	56	59

Concluding remarks

Our results indicate that while most of the county-specific diffusion rates may be better approximated by a logistic model, the figures for aggregate installed horsepower and in use horsepower more closely fit the Gompertz equation.

We postulate that, given more horsepower observations, the county results may be different. The sparse data typically leads county diffusion tests to start with years after 1706. Since the early stages of a Gompertz diffusion are characterized by a slow initial period followed by a pronounced uptick, this truncation of the observed date range favors a logistic result. What would normally be the Gompertz upturn ends up occurring at the start of the observation range. Thus, it looks more akin to the very early stages of a logistic diffusion. Either way, we note that the county level results should be interpreted with care. While the aggregate diffusion tests are based on a significant number of observations, the county level data sets are smaller; furthermore, some years in those cases are interpolated rather than observed.

Appendix 3D: Structural change evaluation
By Lawrence Costa and Michel D. Dilmanian

Here, the data reported above in Table 3C.3 are evaluated for evidence of structural changes. A basic Chow test tends to indicate a structural change for any given year selected, which is not a particularly useful result. As such, we rely on a Bai-Perron test allowing us to test for an unknown number of structural breaks at unknown positions (i.e., years).[74] The results, reported below, indicate that there are potential breaks (in decreasing order of confidence) at 1746 and 1768. The evaluation is conducted using the econometric software Eviews 8.

In Table 3D.1 the trimming percentage column refers to a specification of the Bai-Perron test. A test trimmed at 10 percent requires at least 10 percent of observed values to be present during each structural period. So, for instance, with our dataset, a 10 percent trim allows for break dates at, say, 1740 and 1747 (10 percent of the observation set is 6.8); however, when trimmed to 15 percent, the dates are too close together for them both to be considered breaks.

Further, a break is considered significant if its scaled F-statistic is higher than the Bai-Perron critical value.

Table 3D.1 Test results for structural breaks

Trimming Percentage	Break Test	F-Statistic	Scaled F-Statistic	Bai-Perron Critical Value	Break Date Indicated
10	0 vs. 1	38.30	114.90	14.60	1768
	1 vs. 2	35.47	106.41	16.53	1746
	2 vs. 3	4.76	14.28	17.43	
15	0 vs. 1	36.85	110.54	13.98	1746
	1 vs. 2	4.96	14.87	15.72	

A caveat here is that the Bai-Perron test performed applies only to linear models. So, it cannot be conducted using the log-difference Gompertz specification (which is nonlinear) discussed earlier. As such, the above test is conducted against the linear specification *Aggregate HP* = $\alpha + \beta_1$ (*Trend*) + β_2 (*Trend*^{2}).

In general, results of our breakpoint tests (including Bai-Perron, Chow, and Quandt-Andrews) have seemed to vary based on seemingly minor assumptions (e.g., see the difference at 10 percent versus 15 percent trimming above). So, it is perhaps best to view the breakpoint analysis as a supporting piece of evidence for conclusions drawn from historical data and the literature. Our results should not be interpreted as supporting a case for a structural break all by themselves.

Notes

1 Nuvolari et al., "Early diffusion", pp. 292–3.
2 Ibid., p. 296. See also Harris, "The employment of steam power", p. 138; Allen, "The introduction of the Newcomen engine", p. 170; Kanefsky and Robey, "Steam engines", p. 185; Flinn, *British coal industry*, p. 119.
3 Nuvolari et al., "Early diffusion", pp. 300–8, 316–17; quote from p. 300.
4 The author contemplated initially asking for permission from John Kanefsky to reproduce the part of the database which covers the time period of this monograph. However, it was mutually decided to abstain from this action because Dr. Kanefsky is engaged in an ongoing effort to update his own original work and plans to publish the revised version of it in the near future.
5 The data-gathering method of the database and the gaps in the evidence are described in Kanefsky and Robey, "Steam engines", pp. 163–82 and in Kanefsky, *Diffusion of power technology*, pp. 260–2, 268, 270–1, 273, 434–5, 437–9, 442. One particularly useful source of the secondary literature was the so-called Brown list. William Brown, viewer of Throckley colliery and erector of engines, compiled a list of 99 engines erected in collieries by 1769 (57 of which were still in operation); his list was also utilized by Smeaton. It is not clear whether he intended this list to be inclusive of all engines erected in collieries until that year (well over 300 by then) or just in the Newcastle coalfield. The fact of the matter is that the list focuses mainly on the coalfields of Northumberland and Durham with few outliers in Scotland. See Duckham, *Scottish coal industry*, p. 83; Flinn, *British coal industry*, pp. 122–3; Rolt, *Thomas Newcomen*, pp. 120–1.
6 *Cornish beam engine*, pp. 18, 22. Granted these problems, it should be stressed that some claims found in the secondary literature should be treated with caution. For

instance, Pryce was a resident of Cornwall, and thus presumably an authority on local matters, leading Rogers (*The Newcomen engine*, p. 17), for instance, to the conclusion that his claims were "perfectly plausible." And Pole (*Cornish pumping engine*, p. 12) conveys uncritically Pryce's claim that in the 36 years prior to the time he wrote (1740) there was only one engine erected in Cornwall; however, the database cites six of them.

7 The author wishes to thank Dr. Kanefsky for the information, provided in a personal communication, regarding the new engines he added recently. When it comes to the engines added by the author, their inclusion in a revised database is a bit problematic for some of them: first, the evidence is not always strong enough; second, a few of these engines are cases of re-erecting an engine pulled from a previous location by utilizing its components to an undetermined degree which raises the question as to whether they should be counted as new. Finally, it should be noted that the exchange of information between the author and Dr. Kanefsky about the engines missing from the original database reached the former right before the manuscript was about to enter the production stage and thus could not be taken into account. This unfortunate event translated to creating a very small discrepancy between the two sets of figures when it comes to the aggregate number of engines, as well as their sectoral and regional allocation. However, the differences in the figures are trivial and thus the author very much doubts they make any substantial impact on the results of the econometric analysis.

8 The author would be happy to share this information upon request.

9 See next paragraph regarding the derivation of the data.

10 The methods used in the last type of derivations are described in Appendix 3B. The harvest of information they provided was not bountiful but they comprise a promising venue for expanding the list of engines with known hp, particularly for researchers with stronger knowledge on the technical features of engines.

11 This figure is the mean of all 1,000 iterations on the Monte Carlo/rolling bins simulation.

12 There are three definitions of hp. First, *nominal hp* which is a function of two technical features of an engine: the diameter of its cylinder and length of the stroke. Second, *the indicated hp* which takes into account two additional features, the number of strokes per minute or feet traveled by the piston per minute (also known as velocity), and the pressure or load on the piston expressed in lbs per square inch. Indicated hp is closely related to the duty of an engine. Finally, *effective hp* (also called *actual* or *net hp*) deducts the amount of friction lost from the indicated hp due to its moving parts. See Hawkins, *Hand book of calculations*, p. 101; Perry, *An elementary treatise*, p. 62; Roper, *Hand-book of land and marine engines*, p. 61.

13 Hawkins, *Aids to engineers' examinations*, p. 79; Burn, *The steam-engine*, p. 99; Roper, *Hand-book of land and marine engines*, p. 61; Allen, *The science of mechanics*, pp. 337–8.

14 Such adjustment is not made by NVT, constituting a major difference with the methodology of the present study.

15 *Diffusion of power technology*, p. 260.

16 *The industrial revolution in Shropshire*, p. 48.

17 Dunn, *The coal trade*, pp. 23–4; Rolt, *Thomas Newcomen*, pp. 120–1; Galloway, *Annals*, pp. 261–2; Galloway, *The steam engine*, pp. 127, 129; Farey, *Treatise on the steam engine*, pp. 233–4. It should be noted that, contrary to every other authority the author is aware of, Flinn claims that every engine in the Brown list was at work in 1769; see Flinn, *British coal industry*, p. 122.

18 *The Newcomen engine*, p. 16.

19 Another method that could have been used is to find hp in use based on depreciation rates. However, the evidence on the latter, summarized in the next chapter, is much more limited compared to the adopted method which is based both on more extensive data and is backed by Kanefsky's estimates.

20 Rolt, *Thomas Newcomen*, pp. 58–9. Newcomen himself had a keen interest in having his engine adopted in Cornwall and, in fact, two of the earliest engines were erected there but the failure of the Wheal Vor engine focused his attention on the Midlands through his connections with the local Baptist community. An engine was erected in the property of William Bache of Wolverhampton but Bache died shortly thereafter and the engine was re-erected at Tipton in the estate of Lord Dudley; see Allen, "The 1712 and other Newcomen engines", p. 8. For the location and supporting evidence regarding some of the early Newcomen engines see Galloway, *Annals, Vol. 1*, pp. 240–4; Flinn, *British coal industry*, pp. 119–20.

21 Arago, *Life of James Watt*, p. 54 falsely claims there was only one Savery engine erected in the mining sector. See Jenkins, "The early history of the steam engine", pp. 115–16. There was some debate as to whether the first Cornish engine at Wheal Vor was a Savery model but most certainly it was one by Newcomen since Savery ceased his efforts to introduce his engines in mines by 1705; see Rolt, *Thomas Newcomen*, p. 59.

22 The total of 567 engines identified by the author following the additions he made to the Kanefsky database is slightly different from the figure Dr. Kanefsky has come up with based on his latest update. Specifically, he has identified 565 engines up to 1773, five of which are doubtful. But he adds another nine engines whose year of erection is not known but they certainly fall in the pre-1774 period. Hence, his total figure of aggregate diffusion, not counting the "doubtful" engines, comes to 569. The author wishes to thank Dr. Kanefsky for the update on his findings in a personal communication.

23 The methods used to test for structural breaks are discussed in Appendix 3D.

24 Kanefsky and Robey were the first ones to view 1733 as a critical date and the endpoint of the first phase of diffusion followed by a second phase running throughout the period 1734–80. Flinn used the same dividing line, reasoning that the "expiry of the patent in 1733 removed a major inhibition." Nuvolari et al. followed suit based on a historical outline they provide emphasizing the expiration of the patent as a critical event (their second phase is 1734–74). None of these authors, however, subject aggregate data to some kind of testing procedure hence the contrast with my dates regarding structural break points. See Nuvolari et al., "Early diffusion", p. 296; Flinn, *British coal industry*, pp. 120–1 (quote from former page); Kanefsky and Robey, "Steam engines", p. 174. Even when the aggregate diffusion graph is drawn based on engines (not reproduced here) there is a clear visual impression that the trend does not break right after the expiration of the patent.

25 Several collieries erected multiple engines, often moved around from pit to pit as one got exhausted and others opened up. A contemporary technical report referring to Heaton colliery recommended the use of three engines over the extent of 20 acres from depths of 70 fathoms. See Flinn, *British coal industry*, pp. 120–2; Raistrick, "The steam engine on Tyneside", p. 140.

26 The amount of research effort put into identifying engines installed in industrial sectors is far less compared to the effort put in relation to mining and ironworks. It follows that the relevant figures included in the database may be an underestimate of the true figures. However, given the high purchase price of the engines and the fairly small size of firms in these industrial sectors, it is very doubtful that the figures cited are very different from the true figures. The author wishes to thank Dr. Kanefsky for bringing this point to his attention in a personal communication.

27 It is difficult to make comparisons between my regional assessment and those of other authors since our analyses are broken down into different sub-periods and, in some cases, use different regional units of assessment (counties vs. wider regions). But, notwithstanding differences in tone, the assessments are in sync and they certainly confirm NVT's findings of high spatial clustering through the 1730s and a wider dispersion afterwards. See Nuvolari et al., "Early diffusion", pp. 297–300, 315; Kanefsky and Robey, "Steam engines", pp. 176–9; Flinn, *British coal industry*, pp. 120–2.

28 For the earliest (and subsequent) engines in Cornwall see Barton, *Cornish beam engine*, pp. 15–16, 19–20.

29 Figure 3.3 is drawn on the basis of figures of the cumulative hp installed without taking into account engines falling out of use because the latter information is impossible to estimate in the case of individual counties. Incidentally, the results of testing reported in Appendix 3C indicate that the logistic growth curve fits better the data at the county level.

30 Hamilton, *Economic history of Scotland*, p. 207; Whatley, "The introduction of the Newcomen engine to Ayrshire", p. 69. For references to some Scottish engines, see Duckham, *Scottish coal industry*, pp. 82–3.

31 For instance, see Atack et al., "The regional diffusion of the steam engine", p. 284.

32 Nabseth and Ray, eds., *Diffusion of new industrial processes*, p. 8; Radnor et al., *Diffusion of innovations*, pp. 46–7; Metcalfe, "Impulse and diffusion", pp. 349–50; Metcalfe, "Diffusion of innovation", pp. 148–9; Karshenas and Stoneman, "Technological diffusion", p. 267.

33 Hurter and Rubenstein, "Market penetration", pp. 205–6; Gold, "On the adoption of technological innovations", p. 107; Rosegger, *Economics of production and innovation*, p. 210; Radnor, et al., *Diffusion of innovations*, pp. 46–7; Metcalfe, "Impulse and diffusion", pp. 349–50; Nabseth and Ray, eds., *Diffusion of new industrial* processes, p. 297.

34 Hatcher, *British coal industry,* pp. 217–33; Flinn, *British coal industry*, p. 113; Galloway, *Annals of coal mining*, p. 78.

35 *Annals of coal mining*, pp. 52, 76–7.

36 Rolt, *Thomas Newcomen*, pp. 131–2; Farey, *Treatise on the steam engine*, p. 275.

37 The database records only one engine for that purpose, the only such returning engine in any type of mine.

38 Farey, *Treatise on the steam engine*, p. 297; Musson and Robinson, *Science and technology,* pp. 398–9; Flinn, *British coal industry,* pp. 100–2, 112; Galloway, *Annals of coal mining*, pp. 113–15. Contemporary publications, such as Leupold's *Theatrum Machinarum* (1727), often depicted the use of water-power in driving machinery; see Musson and Robinson, *Science and technology*, p. 398.

39 The figure is derived by multiplying the total hp in use by 1773 (7,503.2) by the share of the mining sector (86.88 percent); see previous section.

40 *Diffusion of power technology*, pp. 148, 201; Flinn, *British coal industry,* pp. 100, 110–11; Hatcher, *British coal industry,* p. 214. Water power made some inroads in winding after 1770, until then horse gins being the predominant form of power.

41 But even in Cornwall there were 50 water wheels used in drainage averaging 20 hp and thus producing 1,000 hp; see Kanefsky, *Diffusion of power technology*, pp. 148, 200–2, 231. In contrast, the cumulative hp provided by steam in 1773 was 1,473; but only 840 hp was in use given the 57 percent rule which, however, should be viewed as a rough estimate.

42 *Diffusion of power technology*, p. 200.

43 Ibid., pp. 221, 225–7.

44 Flinn, *British coal industry,* pp. 110–11.

45 The proportion counted by steam would change only by a percentage point or so when the standard deviation of hp in use in 1773 is taken into account.

46 Farey, *Treatise on the steam engine*, pp. 296–7; Hyde, *Technological change*, p. 70; Trinder, *The industrial revolution in Shropshire,* p. 48.

47 Of the 23 steam engines cited in the database in relation to this sector installed by 1773 all but two are designated as "returning engines." The first engine used to blow a cylinder was installed in 1767 at the Bradley Ironworks (Staffordshire) followed by one in Coalbrookdale in 1772.

48 In supporting his statement, he adds that as late as 1790, 12 out of 83 coke blast furnaces did not utilize any steam power while all 25 charcoal furnaces were water-powered; Hyde, *Technological change*, p. 71.

49 *Technological change*, pp. 11, 71.
50 Ibid., p. 72; Schumbert, *British iron and steel industry*, p. 243; Davies and Pollard, "The iron industry", p. 79; Rolt and Allen, *The steam engine of Thomas Newcomen*, p. 122.
51 *Dynasty of ironfounders*, pp. 107–13, 115–18, 144.
52 *Diffusion of power technology*, pp. 139–40.
53 Farey cites two engines erected in Yorkshire and Wales in 1779–80 whose power were c. 12 and 18 hp respectively; see his *Treatise on the steam engine*, pp. 279–81. See also Kanefsky, *Diffusion of power technology*, p. 200.
54 Davies and Pollard, "The iron industry", pp. 77–8; Riden, "The output of the British iron industry", p. 448.
55 Farey, *Treatise on the steam engine*, pp. 212, 296; Kanefsky, *Diffusion of power technology*, pp. 201–2.
56 More detailed analysis, however, is needed for these sectors. Paper mills, for instance, had very low power requirements (7–8 hp/mill) and thus water power may have been largely adequate in most, if not all, paper mills.
57 That is not to say that Newcomen engines made a significant contribution to such growth or that they had the potential to do so for the economy as a whole, given their technological limitations.
58 And, to reiterate, the author revised some, though few, of the hp figures found in Kanefsky and Robey by replacing them with figures found in the secondary literature or based on the technical characteristics of individual engines.
59 *Treatise on the steam engine*, p. 237.
60 "The Newcomen engine", p. 70.
61 It should be borne in mind, however, that there are discrepancies in the figures quoted in the Brown list and other sources. See Kanefsky and Robey, "Steam engines", p. 183; Kanefsky, *Diffusion of power technology*, p. 442; Galloway, *The steam engine*, pp. 128–30; Galloway, *Annals of coal-mining, Vol. 1*, pp. 261–2; Rolt, *Thomas Newcomen*, pp. 120–1; Farey, *Treatise on the steam engine*, p. 234; Rogers, *The Newcomen engine*, pp. 51–2; Dunn, *An historical, geological, and descriptive view of the coal trade*, pp. 23–4.
62 Rolt, *Thomas Newcomen*, pp. 126–7. As cylinder diameters increased, along with the amount of steam generated, it prompted the use of multiple boilers beginning in the middle of the century. According to a sample put together by Kanefsky and Robey ("Steam engines", pp. 183–4) diameters increased from 21 inches in the 1710s, to 32 inches by the 1730s, 42 inches by the 1740s, peaking at 49 inches in the 1760s. The diameter of 67 engines from the Brown list was 45.8 inches; Galloway, *The steam engine*, p. 129. On this trend as well as large lists of cylinder sizes, see Barton, *Cornish beam engine*, pp. 20, 270; Briggs, *The power of steam*, p. 51; Flinn, *British coal industry*, p. 123; Rogers, *The Newcomen engine*, pp. 51–2.
63 *Treatise on the steam engine*, p. 234.
64 Kanefsky argues that, if an engine is driven hard, nominal and indicated hp could deviate from each other but not by much; *Diffusion of power technology*, pp. 23, 28. See also Bourne, *Handbook of the steam-engine*, pp. 208–10.
65 Rigg, *Practical treatise on the steam engine*, p. 14.
66 Bourne, *Catechism of the steam engine*, p. 103; Hodge, *The steam engine*, pp. 43, 161; Farey, *Treatise on the steam engine*, p. 440; Benjamin, *The steam engine,* p. 2; Perry, *Elementary treatise on steam*, pp. 61–2; Burn, *The steam-engine*, p. 99.
67 Farey, *Treatise on the steam engine*, p. 165.
68 Bourne, *Treatise on the steam engine*, p. 247. For other formulas utilized, some less straightforward, see Allen, *The science of mechanics*, pp. 337–40; Farey, *Treatise on the steam engine, Vol. II*, p. 230.
69 Kanefsky, *Diffusion of power technology*, pp. 22–3; Galloway, *Annals of coal mining*, pp. 261–2; Galloway, *The steam engine*, pp. 129–30; Rolt, *Thomas Newcomen*, p. 126;

Bourne, *Handbook of the steam-engine*, p. 211; Rigg, *Practical treatise on the steam engine*, p. 14; Allen, *The science of mechanics*, pp. 337–8; Scott, *The engineer's and machinist's assistant*, p. 48; Farey, *Treatise on the steam engine*, p. 234; Stuart, *Historical and descriptive anecdotes*, p. 292; Hawkins, *Hand book of calculations*, p. 79. Additional data were utilized from the revised database.
70 The discrepancy in the mean figures stems from the fact that Farey states the velocity of the 15 Brown engines as 50.1 whereas Stuart as 100.2 ft and that affects the weighted mean figure. Kanefsky, *Diffusion of power technology*, pp. 22–3; Bourne, *Handbook of the steam-engine*, p. 211; Rigg, *Practical treatise on the steam engine*, p. 14; Farey, *Treatise on the steam engine*, p. 234; Stuart, *Historical and descriptive anecdotes*, p. 292. Additional data were utilized from the revised database.
71 Pearl and Reed, "On the Rate of Growth of the Population."
72 Franses, "Fitting a Gompertz Curve"; idem, "A Method to Select Between Gompertz and Logistic Trend Curves."
73 Lien and Vuong, "Selecting the best linear regression model"; Vuong, "Likelihood Ratio Tests."
74 Bai and Perron, "Estimating and testing linear models."

Bibliography

Allen, J. S., "The 1712 and other Newcomen engines of the earls of Dudley", *Transactions of the Newcomen Society*, 37 (1964–5), pp. 57–84.

Allen, J. S., "The introduction of the Newcomen engine from 1710 to 1733", *Transactions of the Newcomen Society*, 42 (1969–70), pp. 169–90.

Allen, J. S., "Addendum to the introduction of the Newcomen engine from 1710–1733", *Transactions of the Newcomen Society*, 43 (1970–1), pp. 199–202.

Allen, J. S., "The introduction of the Newcomen engine from 1710 to 1733: second addendum", *Transactions of the Newcomen Society*, 45 (1972–3), pp. 223–6.

Allen, Z., *The science of mechanics* (Providence: Hutchens & Cory, 1829).

Arago, M., *Life of James Watt*, 3rd ed. (Edinburgh: A. & C. Black, 1839).

Atack, J., F. Bateman, and T. Weiss, "The regional diffusion and adoption of the steam engine in American manufacturing," *Journal of Economic History*, 40 (1980), pp. 281–308.

Bai, J. S., and P. Perron, "Estimating and testing linear models with multiple structural changes," *Econometrica*, 66, 1 (1998), pp. 47–78.

Barton, D. B., *The Cornish beam engine* (Exeter: Cornwall Books, 1989).

Benjamin, C. H., *The steam engine; a concise treatise for students and engineers* (Brattleboro, Vt.: Technical Press, 1909).

Bourne, J., *A treatise on the steam engine in its application to mines, mills, steam navigation, and railways* (London: Longman, Brown, Green and Longmans, 1846).

Bourne, J., *A catechism of the steam engine*, 5th ed. (New York: D. Appleton & Co., 1864).

Bourne, J., *Handbook of the steam-engine: containing all the rules required for the right construction and management of engines of every class . . . constituting a key to the "Catechism of the steam-engine"* (New York: D. Appleton & Co., 1870).

Briggs, A., *The power of steam: an illustrated history of the world's steam age* (Chicago: University of Chicago Press, 1982).

Burn, R. S., *The steam-engine, its history and mechanism: being descriptions and illustrations of the stationary, locomotive, and marine engine, for the use of schools and students*, 6th ed. (London: Ingram, 1854?).

Davies, R. S. W., and S. Pollard, "The iron industry, 1750–1850", in Feinstein and Pollard, eds., *Studies in capital formation*, pp. 73–104.

Duckham, Baron F., *A history of the Scottish coal industry, volume I: 1700–1815* (Newton Abbot: David & Charles, 1970).

Dunn, M., *An historical, geological, and descriptive view of the coal trade of the north of England* (Newcastle upon Tyne: W. Garrett, 1844).

Farey, J., *A treatise on the steam engine, historical, practical and descriptive* (London: Longman, Rees, Orme, Brown, and Green, 1827).

Farey, J., *A treatise on the steam engine, Vol. II*, (Newton Abbot, 1971, reproduced from an undated typescript).

Feinstein, C. H., and S. Pollard, eds., *Studies in capital formation in the United Kingdom, 1750–1920* (Oxford: Clarendon Press, 1988).

Fletcher, J. M., and A. J. Crowe, *An early steam engine in Wednesbury: some papers relating to the coal mines of the Fidoe family, 1727–9* (Wednesbury: Central Library, 1966).

Flinn, M. W., *The history of the British coal industry, Vol. 2, 1700–1830: The industrial revolution* (Oxford: Clarendon Press, 1984).

Franses, P. H., "A method to select between Gompertz and logistic trend curves," *Technological Forecasting and Social Change*, 46, 1 (1994), pp. 45–9.

Franses, P. H., "Fitting a Gompertz curve," *Journal of the Operational Research Society*, 45, 1 (1994), pp. 109–13.

Galloway, R. L., *The steam engine and its inventors; a historical sketch* (London: Macmillan, 1881).

Galloway, R. L., *Annals of coal-mining and the coal trade: the invention of the steam engine and the origin of the railway, 2 vols.* (London: Colliery Guardian, 1898–1904).

Gold, B., "On the adoption of technological innovations in industry", in MacDonald et al. eds., *The trouble with technology*, pp. 104–21.

Goodchild, J., "On the introduction of steam power into the West Riding", *South Yorkshire Journal*, III (1971), pp. 6–14.

Hamilton, H., *An economic history of Scotland in the eighteenth century* (Oxford: Clarendon Press, 1963).

Harris, J. R., "The employment of steam power in the eighteenth century", *History*, LI (1967), pp. 133–48.

Hatcher, J., *The history of the British coal industry, Vol. 1, Before 1700: towards the age of coal* (Oxford: Clarendon Press, 1993).

Hawkins, N., *Aids to engineers' examinations. Prepared for applicants of all grades, with questions and answers. A summary of the principles and practice of steam engineering* (New York: T. Audel & Co., 1901).

Hawkins, N., *Hand book of calculations for engineers and firemen. Relating to the steam engine, the steam boiler, pumps, shafting, etc.* (New York: T. Audel & Co. 1901).

Hodge, P. R., *The steam engine; its origin and gradual improvement, from the time of Hero to the present day* (New York: D. Appleton & Co., 1840).

Hurter, A. P., and A. H. Rubenstein, "Market penetration by new innovations: the technological literature", *Technological Forecasting and Social Change*, 11 (1978), pp. 197–221.

Hyde, C. K., *Technological change and the British iron industry, 1700–1870* (Princeton NJ: Princeton University Press, 1977).

Jenkins, R., "Savery, Newcomen, and the early history of the steam engine", *Transactions of the Newcomen Society*, 3 (1922–23), pp. 96–118.

Kanefsky, J. W., *The diffusion of power technology in British industry 1760–1870* (Ph. D. thesis, University of Exeter, 1979).

Kanefsky, J., and J. Robey, "Steam engines in eighteenth century Britain: a quantitative assessment," *Technology and Culture*, 21 (1980), pp. 161–86.

Karshenas, M., and P. Stoneman, "Technological diffusion", in Stoneman, ed., *Handbook of the economics of innovation*, pp. 265–97.

Lien, D., and Q. H. Vuong, "Selecting the best linear regression model: a classical approach", *Journal of Econometrics* 35, 1 (1987), pp. 3–23.

Lord, J., *Capital and steam-power, 1750–1800*, 2nd ed. (London: Cass, 1966).

Louis, H., "Early steam engines in the north of England", *Transactions of the Institute of Mining Engineers*, 82 (1931–32), pp. 526–30.

MacDonald, S., D. L. Lamberton, and T. Mandeville, eds., *The trouble with technology: explorations in the process of technological change* (New York: St. Martin's Press, 1983).

Metcalfe, J. S., "Diffusion of innovation in the Lancashire textile industry", *Manchester School of Economics and Social Studies*, 2 (June 1970), pp. 145–62.

Metcalfe, J. S., "Impulse and diffusion in the study of technical change", *Futures*, 13 (1981), pp. 347–59.

Mott, R. A., "The Newcomen engine in the eighteenth century", *Transactions of the Newcomen Society*, 35 (1962–3), pp. 69–86.

Musson, A. E., and E. Robinson, *Science and technology in the industrial revolution* (Manchester: Manchester University Press, 1969).

Nabseth, L., and G. Ray, eds., *The diffusion of new industrial processes: an international study* (Cambridge: Cambridge University Press, 1974).

Nixon, F., "The early steam engine in Derbyshire", *Transactions of the Newcomen Society*, 31 (1957–9), pp. 1–28.

Notched Ingot, The, "After Newcomen" (July 1966), pp. 17–19.

Nuvolari, A., B. Verspagen, and G. N. von Tunzelmann, "The early diffusion of the steam engine in Britain, 1700–1800. A reappraisal", *Cliometrica*, 5 (2011), pp. 291–321.

Pearl, R., and L. Reed, "On the rate of growth of the population of the United States since 1790 and its mathematical representation", *Proceedings of the National Academy of Sciences of the United States of America*, 6, 6 (1920), pp. 275–88.

Perry, J., *An elementary treatise on steam* (London: Macmillan, 1874).

Pole, W., *A treatise on the Cornish pumping engine* (London: John Weale, 1844).

Pollard, S., *The genesis of modern management: a study of the industrial revolution in Great Britain* (Cambridge, MA: Harvard University Press, 1965).

Radnor, M., I. Feller, and E. M. Rogers, *The diffusion of innovations: an assessment* (Evanston, Ill.: Center for the Interdisciplinary Study of Science and Technology, Northwestern University, 1978).

Raistrick, A., "The steam engine on Tyneside, 1715–1778", *Transactions of the Newcomen Society*, 17 (1936–7), pp. 131–63.

Raistrick, A., *Dynasty of ironfounders: the Darbys and Coalbrookdale* (London, New York and Toronto: Longmans, Green & Company, 1953).

Riden, P., "The output of the British iron industry before 1870", *Economic History Review*, 2nd ser., XXX (1977), pp. 442–59.

Rigg, A., *A practical treatise on the steam engine* (London, New York: E. & F. N. Spon, 1878).

Rogers, K. H., *The Newcomen engine in the west of England* (Bradford-on-Avon: Moonraker Press, 1976).

Rolt, L. T. C., *Thomas Newcomen: the prehistory of the steam engine* (Dawlish, Eng.: David and Charles, 1963).

Rolt, L. T. C., and J. S. Allen, *The steam engine of Thomas Newcomen* (New York: Science History Publications, 1977).

Roper, S., *Hand-book of land and marine engines, including the modeling, construction, running, and management of land and marine engines and boilers* (Philadelphia: Claxton, Remsen & Haffelfinger, 1875).

Rosegger, G., *The economics of production and innovation: an industrial perspective* (Oxford and Boston: Butterworth Heinemann, 1996).

Russell, J. S., *A treatise on the steam engine: from the seventh edition of the Encyclopaedia Britannica* (Edinburgh: A. & C. Black, 1846).

Schafer, J. L., "Multiple imputation: a primer." *Statistical Methods in Medical Research*, 8, 1 (1999), pp. 3–15.

Science Museum, *Catalogue of Watt centenary exhibition* (London, 1919).

Science Museum, *Catalogue of the mechanical engineering collection in the Science Museum, South Kensington, with descriptive and historical notes*, 6th ed. (London, 1919).

Schumbert, H. R., *History of the British iron and steel industry from c. 450 B.C. to A.D. 1775* (London: Routledge & Kegan Paul, 1957).

Scott, D., *The engineer's and machinist's assistant* (Glasgow, Edinburgh, London: Blackie and Son, 1847).

Stoneman, P., ed., *Handbook of the economics of innovation and technological change* (Oxford, UK and Cambridge, US: Blackwell, 1996).

Stowers, A., "The development of the atmospheric steam engine after Newcomen's death in 1729", *Transactions of the Newcomen Society*, 35 (1962–3), pp. 87–96.

Stuart (Meikleham), R., *Historical and descriptive anecdotes of steam engines* (London: Wightman and Cramp, 1829).

Trinder, B. S., *The Industrial Revolution in Shropshire* (Chichester: Phillimore, 2000)

Von Tunzelmann, G. N., *Steam power and British industrialization to 1860* (Oxford: Clarendon Press, 1978).

Vuong, Q. H. "Likelihood ratio tests for model selection and non-nested hypotheses", *Econometrica*, 57, 2 (1989), pp. 307–33.

Whatley, C. A., "The introduction of the Newcomen engine to Ayrshire", *Industrial Archaeology Review* 2 (1965), pp. 69–77.

White, A. W. A., "Early Newcomen engines on the Warwickshire coalfield, 1714–1736", *Transactions of the Newcomen Society*, 41 (1968–69), pp. 203–16.

Willies, L., J. Rieuwerts, and R. B. Flindall, "Wind, water and steam power on Derbyshire lead mines: a list", *Bulletin of the Peak District Mines Historical Society*, 6, 6 (December 1977), pp. 303–20.

4 The cost of steam vs. other power sources in the British economy, 1706–73

Previous analyses of steam power by von Tunzelmann, Kanefsky, Nuvolari, and Verspagen have shed light on how the unevenness in the diffusion rate was conditioned by economic and non-economic factors, playing out both on the demand and supply sides, marked by complexity and feedback mechanisms.[1] But not much has been written about the cost of steam power in relation to other power sources while the Newcomen model was the only option up to 1774. One does find simple comparative statements regarding the cost of power sources in the literature of the eighteenth and nineteenth centuries. But in an era in which notions such as the cost of capital in the form of interest or the depreciation rate of machinery were imperfectly understood and erratically applied, it was natural to lack precise figures. Von Tunzelmann delved into the subject but focused on later periods when data availability becomes more abundant.[2] However, a more thorough scouring of the older and the more recent secondary literature reveals that the data for the pre-Watt era, though far from jumping out from a horn of plenty, is also far from being scarce.

To state the obvious, the cost of steam power in relation to alternative techniques is a key factor in understanding the contours of diffusion of the former during this early phase and thus provides a natural entry point into the explanatory framework which will come together in this and the remaining chapters of the book. However, this subject is also important for business historians since the choice of power inputs was bound to affect the profitability of firms, especially in the mining industry where nine out of ten engines were adopted up to 1773. Even more importantly, by comparing the costs of the various power inputs, this chapter provides a foundational understanding of the "energy transition" phase, centered in the eighteenth century, that has been described by Wrigley and by Kander, Malanima, and Warde in their recent publications.[3]

The chapter is divided into four main sections. The first one looks at the components of the annual fixed and operating costs of Newcomen engines on a per hp basis, the only meaningful way to engage in a comparative analysis. This section uses a comparative statics approach to distinguish two main periods (one up until the end of the 1730s, the other one thereafter) based on the power of engines which had an effect both on labor and capital costs, especially on fuel consumption. The second part engages in the same discussion in regard to other power sources (horses, water power and wind power, and adits) but without such chronological differentiation being necessary.[4] The third section provides a synthesis of the evidence and interpretation of it; it will be shown that a particular use of the threshold concept was not terribly relevant in comparing different power sources; their costs remained fairly apart, in most cases, thus facilitating the decision making process of adopting agents.[5] The final section points out several limitations of technologies alternative to steam in terms of their geographical dispersion and technical capabilities which are important to point out in order to appreciate why steam power was often preferred despite being more expensive in relation to some of these alternatives.

The cost of steam power

The fixed cost of Newcomen engines

The fixed cost of steam engines was comprised of two main components: capital cost (interest and depreciation) and the patent premium. The calculation of the former hinges on the purchase price of engines for which there is a considerable number of observations. But the deduction of capital cost per hp is not straightforward because of the ambiguity as to whether prices include ancillary costs, such as the engine house and the sinking of shafts; not to mention there is scarcity of data on the power of particular engines posing problems with the calculation of cost on a per hp basis. Nevertheless, the evolution of such cost can be traced and the results will be contrasted with general estimates by various authors.

The typical size of a steam engine throughout the 1730s was 10 hp, roughly corresponding to a cylinder diameter of c. 30 inches, or somewhat above.[6] According to testimony given before Parliament, purchase prices ranged from as low as £800 for poor-quality engines to as high as £1,200. A modern estimate, by Rolt, matches the mean of this range (£1,000). But these figures refer only to the purchase of an engine; another £100 or so has to be added for the cost of "contingent works" which mainly referred to the cost of the engine house.[7]

These figures found in older and more recent literature seem to be right on target in light of a good amount of evidence on individual engines found by the author. The top 16 observations of Table 4.1, referring to the period up to 1740,

Table 4.1 Purchase price of engines and total cost of erection (in £)

Engine I

Year	Engine	Cylinder diameter (inches) or hp	Stated cost	Total cost	Comments
1715	Woods mine	22 in.	over £1,000	over £1,000	"erection and setting up" cost
1717	Howgill	5 hp	200	350?	added the estimated labor cost of erection and of the engine house
1718	Griff	?	2,000	2,000?	

1719	Whiston	?	"at least" 1,500	"at least" 1,500	"permission to erect together with the expense of erection"
1725	Park colliery	25 in.	500	600?	Added estimated cost of engine house
1726	Edmonstone	28 in.	1,007.56	c. 1,200	
1727	Whitehill	29 in.	1,200	1,350?	added the estimated labor cost of erection and of the engine house
1728?	Mr. Gun-Jones engine	?	300	300?	
1730	Coneygree	30 in.	700	700?	
1730	Bushblades	?	800	1,827	Extra cost of civil engineering work
1733	Ridley	33 in.	849.8	849.8	
1733	Heaton	15 hp	700	700?	
1734	Bo'ness	?	1,500	1,600	Pre-erection estimate, added the estimate for the cost of the engine house
1737	Saltom Pit	42 in.	1,201.95	1,300?	added the estimate for the cost of the engine house
1737	Dudley Wood	36 in.	700	800?	added the estimate for the cost of the engine house
1738	Long Benton	42 in.	1,200	1,300?	added the estimate for the cost of the engine house

Engine II

1743	Jarrow	40 in.	1,200	1,200?	
1744	Walbottle	70 in	1,691.77	1,691.77	
1745	Coalbrookdale	?	854.17	854.17?	
1749	Warmley Brass	14 hp	2,000	2,000	
1753	North Wood	?	1,000	1,000?	
1753	?	?	1324.25?	1324.25?	Pre-erection all-inclusive estimate made by Brown
1754	Saltwellside	32 in.	410.12	410.12	
1754	Coalbrookdale	48 in.	751.32	751.32?	
1755	Tanfield Lea	?	1,200	1,200?	
1758	?	?	846.32	846.32?	
1761	Dawley	60 in.	710.58	710.58?	

(continued)

Table 4.1 (continued)

1763	Walker	98 hp	"nearly" £5,000	£5,324?	added the estimate for the cost of the engine house
1764	Bo'ness	?	1,637	1,961?	added the estimate for the cost of the engine house
1764	Placket Winster	?	c. 5,000	c. 5,000?	
1767	New River Head	5 hp	800?	800?	Pre-erection estimate
1768	Dolcoath, Bullengarden	17 hp	2,200?	2,200?	Pre-erection estimate
1770?	Griff	60 in.	2,500	2,500?	

Notes: Whenever possible, the hp of an engine is stated or, in the absence of such figures, the diameter of the cylinder. However, contrary to the belief of some authors, the two variables do not show a consistent correlation and thus the diameter figures should be treated with caution as an indicator of power. The stated cost refers to the figures found in the secondary literature. Some guesswork was involved on the part of the author as to whether they included ancillary expenses such as the labor cost of erecting the engine, the sinking of shafts, and the erection cost of the engine house. If these were certainly, or most likely, omitted figures, they were added to the stated cost based on general estimates or mean values. The labor cost of erecting the engine in the middle of the eighteenth century was £40–60; the mean value of £50 was added. The cost of an engine house prior to 1740 was c. £100 based on the mean of two figures. Such cost increased after 1740, the figures varying depending on how well was made, whether it was simply functional as opposed to paying attention to aesthetic details and whether outside labor was hired as opposed to employing one's workers. According to Kanefsky the range was £200–500 or more; for the purposes of the present calculations £324 was added based on the mean of two observed values. For sources on these particular costs, see Kanefsky, *Diffusion of power technology*, pp. 150–1; Dickinson, *Short history of the steam engine*, pp. 59–61; Raistrick, "The steam engine on Tyneside," pp. 146, 156–8; Tann, "The steam engine on Tyneside," p. 55; Allen, "The 1715 and other Newcomen engines," p. 246.

Sources: Allen, "The introduction of the Newcomen engine," pp. 173, 179–80, 182; Allen, "Some early Newcomen engines," p. 199; Barker and Harris, *A Merceyside town*, p. 24; Allen, "The 1715 and other Newcomen engines," p. 59; Bald, *General view of the coal trade of Scotland*, pp. 20, 22–3 158; Farey, *Treatise on the steam engine*, p. 229; Tann, "The steam engine on Tyneside," p. 55; Allen, "The 1715 and other Newcomen engines," pp. 254–5, 266–7; Hills, *Power from steam*, p. 35 Dickinson, *Short history of the steam engine*, pp. 59–61; Raistrick, "The steam engine on Tyneside," pp. 137, 142, 146, 156–8; Nef, *The rise of the British coal industry, vol 2*, p. 191; Stuart, *Historical and descriptive anecdotes* p. 303; Raistrick, *Dynasty of ironfounders*, pp. 139, 143, 145, 287–9; Davey "The Newcomen engine", p. 676; Rogers, *The Newcomen engine*, pp. 28–9; Flinn, *History of th British coal industry*, p. 192; Stowers, "The development of the atmospheric steam engine," p. 88 Duckham, *History of the Scottish coal industry*, p. 86; Willies et al, "Wind, water and steam power," p. 310; Scott, "Smeaton's engine of 1767 at New River Head," p. 120; Barton, *Cornish beam engine* p. 137; White, "Early Newcomen engines," p. 209.

generate a mean value of £1,086, rounded up to £1,100. The cost per hp of those early engines, henceforward generically labeled *Engine I* (referring to a typical specimen of the group), comes to £110.[8]

Beginning in the 1740s, and through the end of the period, there is a pronounced increase in the power of engines and, at the same time, the range of deviation of the mean decadal values becomes more narrow; the typical engine at the time being c. 25 hp, having a 40–45 inch cylinder diameter. General estimates found i the literature differ on how much an engine of that size would cost.[9] Raistrick and Kanefsky provide low-end figures suggesting that an engine of such cylinder size would cost c. £1,200. In contrast, according to Dickinson, purchase prices already reached £1,700 by the mid-1740s, and thus presumably more later on, a figure that probably refers to a typical size engine and is all inclusive. There is also an account by an expert (Robert Mylne) given in 1775 before a Parliamentary committee based on his experience over the previous three to four years; according to him, an engine of 18 inch diameter would cost in London £1,400 inclusive of all the pump work but not the cost of the engine house; this figure suggests that more powerful engines would have been more expensive.

There are a couple of samples provided by other authors which seem to support the more modest figures. Raistrick refers to four unidentified engines built in the 1750s or 1760s whose costs average c. £967. Flinn uses a sample of eight engines, most of them built since the 1740s, with a mean cost of £1,140.[10] However, the more robust sample put together by the author (seventeen observations) for the post-1740 period (Table 4.1/Engine II, the latter referring to an engine of a size typical for the period) gives a mean value of £1,751.38, rounded to £1,750 and corresponding to £70 per hp for these larger engines. It would be stating the obvious to note that the cost of larger engines did not have to increase proportionally to their power. But another reason for the slower increase of purchase prices was the cost reduction in two key components of the engine, the boiler and the cylinder (see Appendix 4A).

Given these purchase prices, the first capital cost charge would be interest on invested capital. No series of interest rates is available for the period, the nearest proxy being the yield on Consols which was lower compared to interest rates prevailing in industry; their yield stood at 3.5 percent in the period 1756–70. The author has decided to follow Allen who assumed a 5 percent rate translating, on an annual basis, to £55 for *Engine I* and £87.5 for *Engine II*.[11]

Calculations of depreciation rates are not straightforward because it was a notion that was "imperfectly understood and inconsistently applied";[12] even when the latter was the case, the rates adopted varied quite widely reflecting the fact that the lifetime of engines oscillated within a very wide margin.[13] Some steam engines were abandoned or discontinued within a short time following their installation either because the potential of increasing output was exhausted and/or due to cost considerations;[14] but in other cases their lives extended up to one and a half centuries.[15] After all, colliery owners had every incentive to keep them in good condition since selling a used engine whose maintenance had not been up to par would fetch a small portion of the original total cost.[16] For some of these engines the depreciation rate can be deducted based on estimates of their market values in years following their installation while still working, in other cases from information referring to their entire operating lives. The mean depreciation rate of eleven such engines was 7.5 percent indicating a useful life slightly exceeding thirteen years.[17] The annual depreciation for *Engine I* would be £82.5, and £131.25 for *Engine II*.

The last component of fixed cost was the patent premium. It is well known that Newcomen came to an agreement with Savery, probably in 1705, which included the former as part of the latter's patent. It was the most rational choice since attempting to secure his own patent would probably have invited Savery's opposition and the patent would not have lasted for more than fourteen years. Newcomen enjoyed the benefits of the patent until his death in 1718, though from 1715 on he was a mere member of the syndicate which took over the patent through its expiration in 1733. Newcomen was personally involved in the erection of some engines but its marketing became more aggressive once the syndicate took over, in the process using the expertise of key figures such as Calley, Potter and Beighton.[18]

The syndicate's policies on the premium were seemingly erratic: extreme variability, in some cases charging no fees, and arbitrary refusal to do business with some mine owners or to allow the erection of the engine in certain places such as London with the exception of the York Building.[19] The sense that the fees charged were fairly capricious seems to be reinforced when looking at Figure 4.1. There was no discernible pattern, for instance, in relation to the power of engines. The 1714 Griff engine and the one at Broseley (1715) were of the same power (3 hp) but the annual premium per hp in the former was £121.33 through 1720 (reduced to £50 thereafter) but only £6.66 for the latter. The respective figures stood at £36.4 for the Howgill engine (1717), and just £2.62 for the one at Trelogan (1732).[20] The same inconsistencies apply when we take into account the cylinder diameter. For instance, the total annual premiums for the Bilston engine (1714, 13 inches) were in the range of £150–208 during different periods of the patent but only £20 for the engine at Pelsall (1717, 16 inches). The engines at Byker, Stevenston, Fidoe's, and Heaton had comparable cylinder sizes (24–33 inches) but the annual premiums ranged from £65 to £420. There was one, fairly weak, correlation between premium levels and location, with engines in Wales and, especially, Scotland being charged lower amounts, though such instances also occur in English counties. There is also a fairly clear trend in terms of charging either lower premiums as the expiration of the patent approached or a lump sum, beginning in 1726 or so, which translated to lower annual amounts for the remaining years (e.g., Howgill, Edmonstone, Houghton-le-Spring, Trelogan, Saltom Pit).

Smith believes that the premium policy of the syndicate was not arbitrary but favored certain locations and types of duties that offered the likelihood of giving the best results.[21] But it appears that the main criteria were the power of the syndicate vs. potential adopters which weakened as the patent came close to expiration; and the willingness to charge lower amounts in regions where the presence of other high-cost elements (to be discussed below) rendered adoption more difficult (e.g., Scotland). In the end, the mean value of twenty premium observations was £138 (of a range spanning £20–420) adding the biggest component to the annual fixed cost of *Engine I* through 1733.

Operating cost of Newcomen engines

Operating cost comprised three components: repairs and replacement parts, labor cost, and fuel. The cost of repairs and replacement parts would add a small amount

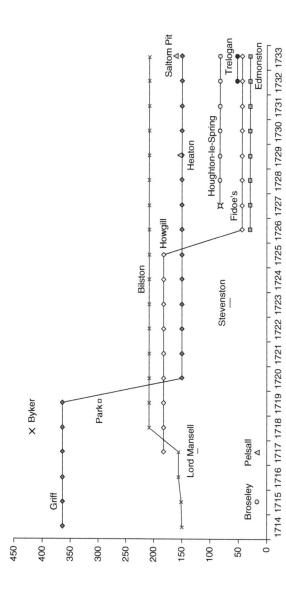

Figure 4.1 (continued)

Notes: The continuous lines represent engines for which the premiums are known for a number of years. The single marks represent engines for which the premium is known for just one year, in most cases the year of installation, though there is a good chance the premium figures of these engines remained stable for a number of years. In the case of one engine (Woods mine, Flint) the deal struck with Newcomen in 1715 was to entitle him to 1/3 of the profits, implying the absence of a fixed premium, but this engine was not included in the graph in the absence of profit figures.

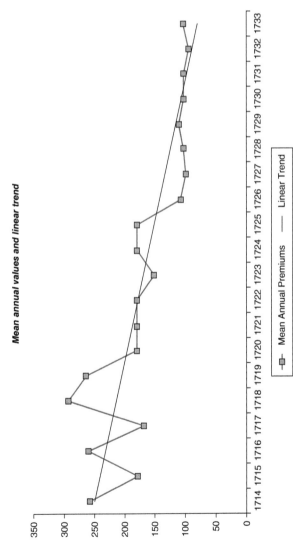

Figure 4.1 Annual premiums of Newcomen engines

Notes: The line connecting the squares represents the annual mean premium of engines with known premiums. The straight line is the linear trend corresponding to the average premiums.

Sources: Allen, "The introduction of the Newcomen engine," pp. 173-4, 180, 187, 189; Allen and Elton "Edward Short" pp. 284, 289; Rolt and Allen, *The steam engine of Thomas Newcomen*, pp. 54-5, 64, 146, 151, 153; Allen, "Addendum", p. 200; Allen, "The 1715 and other Newcomen engines," pp. 253-5; Rowlands, "Stonier Parrott and the Newcomen engine", pp. 52, 55; Allen, "Some early Newcomen engines," p. 198; Whatley, "The introduction of the Newcomen engine to Ayrshire", p. 72; Bald, R., *A general view of the coal trade of Scotland*, pp. 20, 22-3, 158; Farey, *A treatise on the steam engine*, p. 229; Allen, "John Fidoe's 1727 Newcomen engine," p. 150; White, "Early Newcomen engines," pp. 209, 211-2; Rhodes, "Early steam engines in Flintshire", p. 219.

to the operating cost of an engine but, unfortunately, it is difficult to assign figures due to the scarcity of data.[22] Labor cost was also, by and large, not exorbitant. The annual salary of the engineer at Trelogan (1732) was £39 but excludes an unknown amount for five assistants. Economies of scale were realized in this colliery when, by 1762, one engineer was responsible for two engines adding £19.5 to the labor cost of each engine but excluding an unknown amount for seven assistants. Savings were probably more substantial in the case of the six engines at Heaton which employed eight men in 1741 for an annual labor cost per engine at £24.7. But in Scotland labor cost was often far more exorbitant in lieu of the scarcity of local engineering skills necessitating the use of "imported" English expertise. At Edmonstone and Whitehill, in 1726 and 1727 respectively, the chief engineers were getting paid £200 plus half of the net profits of the collieries.[23]

Despite the spotty data on these two types of cost, we are fortunate to have combined figures for both of them for a number of collieries which are consistent with the evidence above. Based on these figures, the annual cost of repairs, parts, and labor for both *Engines I* and *II* would be taken as £126.7. However, labor cost in Scotland continued to be exorbitant throughout the period and thus the combined operating labor and capital cost would be defined at £231 for Scottish engines during both periods.[24]

The fuel consumption bill scored the widest variability and, depending on location, had the potential of imposing the heaviest financial burden. The evidence is consistent enough to provide fairly robust estimates. During the 1730s the fuel consumption of six engines having disparate hp but averaging c. 10 hp was 38.25 lbs/hp/hour.[25] Making the assumption that engines would operate for 12.26 hours/day, this rate translates to an annual consumption of 20,377 bushels (equivalent to 764 tons weight). The financial burden would be fairly small in collieries. Several pithead prices from northern and Scottish collieries (1710–25) indicate that sleck would be valued at c. 0.05s/bushel, ordinary coal at 0.08–0.14s, whereas "sea" coal would fetch c. 0.18–0.20s (see Figure 4.2 for all coal prices cited). Collieries would use mainly sleck but some "good coal, the market article" would have to be thrown in to get the sleck going. Given the aforementioned figures the annual fuel bill for *Engine I* in collieries would be £51.[26] However, coal prices elsewhere were much higher. The mean price of coal in London during the period 1706–39 was 0.86s/bushel translating, at the annual rate of consumption mentioned above, to £876.[27] Fuel cost in Cornwall would not be far lower. A ton of coal would cost 15s to land in Cornwall in 1760 and land carriage would add another 5s. Cornish prices are hard to get for earlier years but if the London price ratio for 1760 vs. 1706–39 applied to Cornwall (c. 20 percent lower in the latter period) then the Cornish price would be 16s/ton.[28] The infamous duty imposed by the government, abolished in 1741, added 3.25s/ton resulting in an annual fuel bill of £735.4.[29]

Similar regional variations emerged regarding *Engine II*. Utilizing 54 observations from 47 engines (those with known hp have a mean of 21.3 hp, hence similar to *Engine II*), the fuel rate was 29.5 lbs/hp/hour.[30] The annual consumption would be 39,288 bushels (or 1,473 tons); at 0.177s/bushel in collieries, the annual bill

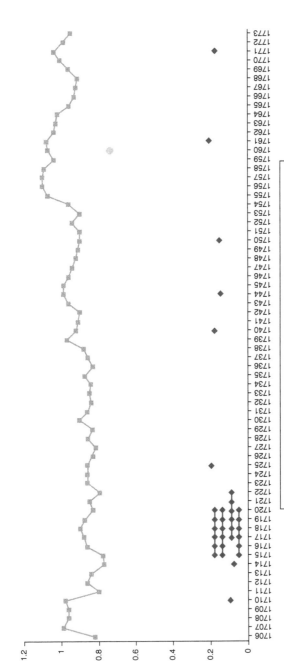

Figure 4.2 Current coal prices, 1706–73 (in shillings/bushel)

Note on sources: London prices were derived as a simple arithmetical mean of several values for each year from various sources gathered by Beveridge in the wider London area: Eton college, Westminster school and abbey, Greenwich hospital, Chelsea hospital, Lord Stewart's department, and Navy victualling; see his *Prices and wages in England*, pp. 146–7, 194–5, 294, 313, 434–6, 577–8, 684. Pithead prices for Engine I are from Nef, *The rise of the British coal industry*, *vol. II*, pp. 390,394, and for Engine II from Ashton and Sykes, *The coal industry*, p. 252. The four straight lines represent means for a particular range of years. The 1760 Cornish price is from Barton, *The Cornish beam engine*, p. 20 and Kanefsky, *The diffusion of power technology*, p. 172. All prices are in shillings/bushel, converted from different measures used by the various authors. Some of the price series (e.g., Beveridge, Nef) reflect coals of different qualities and/or are wholesale or contract prices. They were not flexible in the short run though they were bound to reflect price movements in London tied to prices in the northeastern coalfield (where coal mostly came from) beyond the very short run; Flinn, *The history of the British coal industry*; *vol. 2*, p. 306.

Note on transportation costs: There are discrepancies in the literature on the cost of overland transportation ranging from the cost of coal doubling every two miles (but quadrupling in the Lancashire coalfield) to doubling every ten miles. In the case of a Glamorgan estate, it was more expensive to transport coal to the dock from various pitheads of an estate than to produce it. According to a general estimate (without reference to specific goods), the cost was not much less than 1s/ton/mile translating to doubling the price of ordinary coal in the early part of the century every six miles. The same would reach £347.7.[31] The London version of *Engine II*, at a mean price of 0.97s/ bushel during the period 1740–73, would have an annual bill of £1,905.5 whereas the Cornish version, at a price of £1/ton (in 1760), would have a bill of £1,473.[32]

My overall figures regarding operating cost are in broad agreement with general estimates and comparable figures referring to specific engines such as the one erected at Griff colliery.[33] We are on even firmer ground when it comes to the estimates regarding operating cost for *Engine II/collieries* (£474.4). Raistrick cited £400 as a general estimate referring to the 1750s-60s. This figure is identical to one provided by Stowers referring to a specific (but unnamed) engine and another one for the Walbottle colliery engine in 1744; the operating cost of the Tanfield Lea engine stood at £416 in 1755.[34]

The total cost of steam power

The combined figures on fixed and operating costs are summarized in Table 4.2. The table splits the period 1706–39 into two subperiods (*Engine IA* and *Engine IB*) in order to take into account the impact of the patent premium and its expiration in 1733; and it provides figures for four different locations/sectors (English collieries, their Scottish counterparts, London, and Cornwall) for which the data are sufficiently robust to reproduce this exercise.

It would be interesting to contrast my total cost estimates to statements made by Crafts and Allen, both of them relying on the very limited data for this period provided by von Tunzelmann. Crafts calculated the annual cost per steam hp of a

Table 4.2 Total annual cost and annual cost per hp (in £) of steam power, 1706–73: an accounting perspective

	Engine IA, 1706–33	Engine IB, 1733–39	Engine II, 1740–73
Fixed cost			
Interest	55	55	87.5
Depreciation	82.5	82.5	131.25
Premium	138		
Operating cost			
Labor+parts+repairs	126.7	126.7	126.7
(but in Scotland)	231	231	231
Coal/collieries	51	51	347.7
Coal/London	876	876	1,905.5
Coal/Cornwall	735.4	735.4	1,473
Total annual cost and annual cost/hp			
English collieries	453.2/45.32	315.2/31.5	693.1/27.7
Scottish collieries	557.5/55.75	419.5/42	797.4/31.9
London	1,278.2/127.82	1,140.2/114	2,251/90
Cornwall	1,137.6/113.7	1,000/100	1,818.4/72.7

Sources: see text.

"typical" Newcomen engine in "mining" in 1760, without specifying these terms, at £33.5. This figure is somewhat above mine for *Engine II* referring to Scottish and English collieries (£31.9 and £27.7 respectively) but well below the figure for the Cornish version (£72.7).[35] In other words, "one figure fits all" type of statement is clearly erroneous; the type of mine and its location did matter.

There are also some estimates by Allen on the evolution of costs per hp showing a decline of the overall cost driven by a modest reduction in capital cost and a far more drastic one in fuel cost.[36] My exercise clearly justifies this pattern. However, his statement that fuel and capital costs accounted for 45 percent each, with labor filling the residual 10 percent, is borne out by my data, more or less, only for the collieries version of *Engine II*. The principal components of costs in collieries for *Engine I* were the cost of labor, raw materials, and replacement parts as well as the premium payments through the expiration of the patent. In contrast, by far the most dominant component of cost in locations such as London and Cornwall was the cost of fuel (c. 65–85 percent), its weight increasing as time went by.[37]

The above calculations can also be reproduced regarding the Savery engine albeit based on more limited data (see Appendix 4B). But we turn next to the cost of alternative power sources.

The cost of alternative methods

Horses

Using horses attached to gins was the traditional method of lifting water prior to the steam era and this continued intermittently during the eighteenth century. A large number of horses were needed since they could work for only a few hours a day. The engine that was erected at Elphingstone, East Lothian, in 1720 came to replace no less than 50 of them. Still, their purchase cost was lower compared to steam engines, their main drawback lying in their high operating cost because they were expensive to feed. The expense of winning Walker colliery in 1711 was £5,011.9 including the use of horses for drainage; two horse gins were used, working night and day, the sinking going down to a depth of 30 fathoms. An expert, John Barnes, stated in an affidavit in 1722 that if the same process was undertaken with a steam engine the cost would have been "much cheaper". A heavy financial burden was also incurred once new pits were sunk. The operating cost of horse gins at Gregory lead mine was £390 in 1765 but at Bedworth colliery right before the dawn of the steam era and at Hawkesbury mines later on, the figure reached over £2,000 annually.[38]

The other drawback of horses in their lifting capacity. A typical steam engine at the time could lift 28,548 ft lbs/minute, given a rate of 21 mil/day (see Appendix 4B). Watt defined hp as being equal to 33,000 lbs but this figure is unrealistic. Smeaton and other engineers argued that a good horse can raise 22,000 lbs one foot high per minute if the objective is to have it working for eight hours a day. The latter figure was considerably lower than the one of steam.[39] But while experts unanimously agree that the Newcomen engine "was considerably cheaper per gallon of water raised than the old methods of horse-gins," precise data on cost and lifting capacity are hard to find.[40] Nevertheless, the task is feasible.

One of the earliest and most comprehensive accounts refers to Howgill colliery, Cumberland. It is an extremely detailed report prepared in 1713 laying out the cost of horses when it comes to reclaiming three abandoned sections of the mine while weighing also the option of purchasing a steam engine (installed in 1717). According to the report, the use of horses would take 147 days to lift the specified quantity of water and would cost £233.3 (including the cost of ropes, buckets, and other miscellaneous expenses). I have raised this sum to £247.2 to include the estimated interest and depreciation charges missing from the report. In contrast, the 5 hp steam engine that was installed could have completed the task in 90.85 days and would have cost £56.4, i.e., 22.8 percent of the cost of horses while draining the same quantity of water.[41]

Another comparison can be made for Griff colliery where more than 50 horses were used at the beginning of the century with an annual operating cost of £900. Labor cost was estimated at £300 while interest and depreciation charges added an estimated £26 and £43.3 respectively. The total annual cost comes to £1,269.3 or £3.47 daily. We have sufficient information to reconstruct the annual cost of the steam engines that were installed subsequently (1714, 1718, 1725). The first one was of 3 hp but the others were probably more powerful and thus a purchase price of £1,100 would be a reasonable guess translating to £55 interest charges, while depreciation added £75 and the premium was £150. The operating cost per engine (mean of two engines in the late 1720s) was £94.65 (but excluding an unknown amount for the cost of new parts), a figure that conforms to Desaguliers's statement that annual operating expenses at Griff never exceeded £150. The total cost of an engine was £374.65 rounded up to £400 to include the cost of new parts. The daily cost was £1.09, i.e., 31.5 percent of the cost of horses drawing the same quantity of water.[42] The cost ratio of the two methods regarding these two collieries in the early part of the century stands at a mean of c. 27 percent.

Finally, there is another detailed estimate referring to an unnamed colliery in 1752 which points out that the cost of drawing 67,200 gallons of water per day with horses would amount to £438 annually, a figure that was raised by the author to £448.6 to include interest and depreciation cost. The cost of a steam engine, of c. 12 hp, is also provided by the report but without depreciation. When the latter is included the annual cost comes to £450, virtually identical to that of horses, but drawing 250,560 gallons/day. The annual cost of extracting the latter quantity with horses would have been £1,672.8 or £4.58 daily compared to a daily cost for the engine at £1.23. The cost of steam was 26.8 percent to that of horses.[43]

It is quite remarkable that the cost ratio of horses vs. steam remained fairly stable in collieries over a good part of the eighteenth century. But it is also quite surprising since steam scored improvements in efficiency and thus a reduction of cost per hp. The relative stability of the ratio indicates that horses scored a proportional improvement in efficiency and raises the question regarding its cause. Wrigley, referring to road transportation during the eighteenth century, outlined the impressive growth in the efficiency of horses attributing it to dietary improvements stemming from the expansion in the production of oats.[44] It is not unreasonable to expect that such efficiency gains in the use of horses were not limited to transportation but spread throughout the economy. In addition, the utilization of better equipment and pumping devices contributed, to an undetermined extent, to this trend.

Finally, it is important to stress that in locations other than collieries the cost gap between the two energy sources was much narrower. Smeaton supplied estimates in 1766 for the comparative cost of horses vs. steam for the New River Head company, London. The engine would draw 1,307.7 tons/day and cost 24.65s. In contrast, horses would draw 490.4 tons/day and cost 12.54s; but the cost of drawing the same quantity as the steam engine would be 33.43s. In other words, the cost of steam amounted to 73.7 percent of that of horses.[45] In the end, a 5 hp engine was installed in 1769.

Water power

Water wheels were one of the most sought after methods of draining mines, though their use was feasible only in areas that were well endowed with sources of water. Cornwall, being one of them, received a visit c. 1700 by John Costar, a well-regarded engineer, who attempted to convince his local counterparts that utilizing water wheels of 30–40 feet diameter provided the ideal amount of power. But the use of smaller water wheels persisted. According to Pryce, writing in 1778, the preferred method of draining in Cornwall was to use pumps driven by water wheels of 12–15 feet diameter; and if the depth was considerable to use them one on top of the other, in one case seven of them being placed in such manner.[46]

The cost of water wheels was not particularly exorbitant. One such wheel of the bob type, the most efficient of its kind, was erected at Strathore, Fife, in 1738 or 1739. Its size was pretty typical in that it had a 21 ft wheel diameter, operated twin beams and was capable of performing nine strokes a minute raising 185 hogsheads of water per hour from an unspecified depth. The total cost of the engine, mounting, pit and pumps was over £200. But, on average, wheels would cost less than £100 and the inclusion of the transmission mechanism would increase this amount by c. 50 percent.[47] However, "the building of dams, ponds, aqueducts and so on might incur a coal master in great expense even where a suitable stream lay not too far distant from the colliery." The cost of building water courses for a Lancashire spinning mill in 1786 was £223.15 while Smeaton estimated that a two-mile leat driven through hard rock would cost £400.[48]

When it comes to annual cost only rough estimates can be provided. The erection cost of a typical size wheel (20–25 ft diameter, c. 14.25 hp) and its related infrastructure was c. £367, conforming to Kanefsky's assessment that total installation cost was £20–30/hp. Annual interest charges would be £18.35. Depreciation rates would be higher than steam engines evident by the fact that insurance valuations found by Tann placed the value of small wheels at £40–60, for larger ones at c. £100, i.e., at about half the cost of a new wheel. At a 10 percent rate, depreciation charges would add £36.7. Finally, £10 was added for replacement parts and maintenance work, which could be done cheaply by carpenters and clockmakers, bringing the annual total cost to £65, and the cost per hp to £4.5.[49]

Adits

There is speculation that adits may have been used for drainage as early as the Middle Ages. They were certainly common by the sixteenth century, although in Scotland an account written in 1672 speaks of them as being a fairly new innovation. Their feasibility hinged on the nature of the terrain, rocky or soft and crumbly strata making the task impossible. But when feasible they could be extended gradually to run over several miles; in Fife the average length of 27 adits was 1.25 miles. Considering this length as typical and given a rate of £1.11/yard based on an estimate for Barnsley Moor (South Yorkshire) in 1716, the total cost would amount to £2,444.4, though lower figures have been found such as the sough erected by Parrott in Felling Grounds (Worcestershire) costing £500 in 1717–18. The annual interest charge would amount to £122.2. In terms of operating cost, ventilation shafts had to be sunk from time to time, in some occasions exceeding the entire cost of the adit. Passages could be blocked by falling roofs and debris following heavy flows and to make them operational again could be fairly expensive. I will assume that £32.5 was spent annually to clean damaged sections as was the case at the Gregory lead mine in Derbyshire in 1766; this section was 130 yards long, i.e., c. 6 percent of 1.25 miles. The total annual cost would amount to, roughly, £155.[50]

Windmills

Windmills were mainly erected in Scotland, their effective application to mines dating shortly after 1708 when the town of Montrose sent John Young to Holland to study superior Dutch construction techniques. It is not clear how instrumental was Young's trip but several windmills were erected subsequently in Scotland, especially close to the windy Firth of Forth. There is a surviving estimate from c. 1738 for the erection of a windmill with pumps going down 20 fathoms in Strathore, Fife citing a figure of £57.35 for the wright's workmanship. A slightly later estimate raises the cost to £115.25 but this assumed that the pumps would sink to a depth of 30 fathoms. Given such figures, interest charges would be c. £4–5 a year. Depreciation rates, however, could add a more substantial amount since windmills were often blown away by strong winds such as the one erected in 1737 on the property of John Gray, owner of Westmuir colliery near Glasgow who saw his investment blown to pieces in 1740. Such a short life span would add another £28–29 for a total of c. £33, a figure that would be taken as the upper limit of the annual total cost of windmills. Given that the typical drainage windmill would generate 5 hp, the annual cost per hp was £6.6.[51] However, since this is an upper limit, the cost of wind power would be taken as equal to that of water power (£4.5).

The total cost of steam power vs. alternative methods

Before summarizing the empirical evidence some reflections are in order regarding its robustness and reliability. When it comes to steam power, the amount of data gathered by the author on the various components of capital and operating cost far exceed any previous attempts and provide a sound basis of analysis especially when contrasted against general estimates often provided by the existing literature. The main drawback lies in our inability to trace the evolution of such costs based on the gradual increase in the power of engines. This caveat prevents us from calculating such costs on a per hp basis, the only meaningful way of making comparisons, say per decade. But there is certainly a high level of reliability in adopting the comparative statics approach of this chapter by dividing our period into two main parts since the typical power of steam engines was clustered around two figures (10 hp and 25 hp) through the 1730s vs. thereafter.

The evidence on the cost of horses is certainly more narrow, relying on only three observations, though very detailed ones. But the author feels confident of their reliability because the figures cover an extended time span and, more importantly, they oscillate within a narrow range when compared with the cost of steam. The real scarcity of data lies in the case of adits, water power, and wind power. There are few and scattered data that have to be collated, capable of providing only an impressionistic picture in terms of the typical power and cost of such technologies during this period of time, i.e., without supporting a refined evolutionary analysis. But the degree of pessimism should not be overstated. The figures utilized are in line with general estimates provided by other historians (e.g., Kanefsky) and with the universal consensus that, judging only on the basis of cost, these technologies were preferable to steam where feasible and/or available.

Figure 4.3 pulls together the entire evidence on the cost evolution of various methods used to lift water. The most obvious general conclusion is that the concept of the threshold is largely irrelevant since the cost structures of the various power sources were such as to place them fairly apart from each other. A more refined sectoral and regional analysis allow us to draw a number of additional inferences as follows.

First, horses were decidedly the most expensive power source in collieries despite their substantial efficiency improvement over time; this disadvantage applies also to Scottish collieries despite the higher labor cost of steam. Steam power, however, remained initially less competitive to adits as well as wind and water power. But the elimination of the patent premium and the improved efficiency of larger engines in the post-1740 period meant that engines with very low fuel consumption would operate along the Smin line and thus pose a challenge to the utilization of adits, though water and wind power remained unbeatable alternatives. These expectations are met fairly well when contrasted to actual patterns of diffusion. Water was not readily available in collieries and thus its use was largely absent. Adits were constructed when the morphology of the terrain allowed it. But steam had the widest potential applicability and came to dominate this sector.[52]

Second, the situation in London was considerably different. The cheapest methods either could not be utilized (adits) or were of limited applicability (water and wind). The costs of steam and horses were probably along similar lines through the 1730s but the decline in the cost of the former subsequently meant that horses could compete only if the utilization of steam involved engines whose fuel consumption was well above the mean. These expectations are validated by the existing evidence since the adoption of engines in London took place mainly

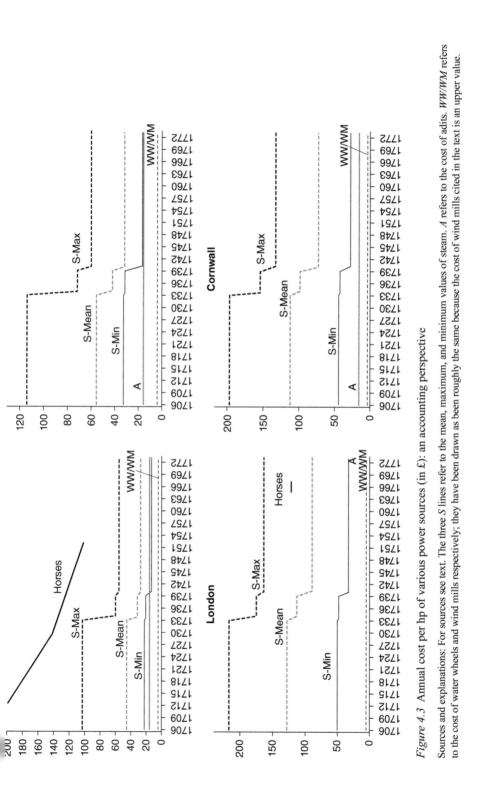

Figure 4.3 Annual cost per hp of various power sources (in £): an accounting perspective

Sources and explanations: For sources see text. The three *S* lines refer to the mean, maximum, and minimum values of steam. *A* refers to the cost of adits. *WW/WM* refers to the cost of water wheels and wind mills respectively; they have been drawn as being roughly the same because the cost of wind mills cited in the text is an upper value.

in the post-1740 period although their anemic prior diffusion was also due to restrictions imposed by the syndicate.

Third, in the metal mines of Cornwall the cost structures of horses and steam were comparable to those in London and thus horses were fairly competitive through the 1730s. On the other hand, adits, water and wind power clearly offered the best options throughout the period even if engines achieved the lowest levels of fuel consumption. That is precisely what one observes when looking at actual patterns of diffusion, i.e., widespread use of water power, which was more readily available in the county, matching (if not exceeding) the hp generated by steam.

One major note of caution is in order. The conclusions described above would have been drawn by potential adopters of the various power sources in the eighteenth century assuming they had the sophistication to engage in the sort of calculations outlined up to that point. But it has been noted earlier that often charges referring to interest and depreciation were not taken into account. Hence Figure 4.3 provides an accounting perspective that may not have been universally relevant at the time. Figure 4.4 addresses this issue by providing a comparative perspective from the viewpoint of a less sophisticated contemporary entrepreneur, i.e., someone who may have failed to take into account interest and depreciation charges both for steam and other power sources. It is evident that the perspective of such potential adopters would have been the same as that of their more sophisticated counterparts: the costs of the various power sources remained apart from each other and thus their decision-making process was equally simplified.

Spatial and technological limitations of alternative methods

Based on a cost comparison alone, the diffusion of steam should have not taken off during this period. However it did so, in part, for reasons that have to do with the technical capabilities of the alternative technologies and their lack of feasibility in many locations. This point can be illustrated in reference to collieries.

At the dawn of the steam era the very survival of individual collieries was at stake.[53] The introduction of the Savery model did not offer much of a solution despite the boastful statements of its inventor.[54] In contrast, the technological capabilities of the Newcomen model were far more substantial; drawing from a sample of seventeen engines installed in mines, the mean depth achieved was a little over 69 yards (the range being 24–190 yards).[55] On the other hand, the technological and seasonal limitations of alternative energy sources prevented the sinking of mines in such great depths, hence stalling the expansion of output.[56]

Water wheels could provide, in exceptional cases, up to 50 hp though most of them were of less than 15 hp; and they were able to draw from as deep as 40–80 yards, even deeper in some exceptional cases, hence they were not much inferior to steam engines in this regard despite occasional complaints.[57] But their main drawback lay in posing the risk of flooded mines during summer draughts. Given their lower cost, collieries held on to them as long as they could, Lumley waiting until 1727 to install its first steam engine, Heaton until 1729, and Jesmond until 1731. However, procrastinating was often not an option in collieries facing severe

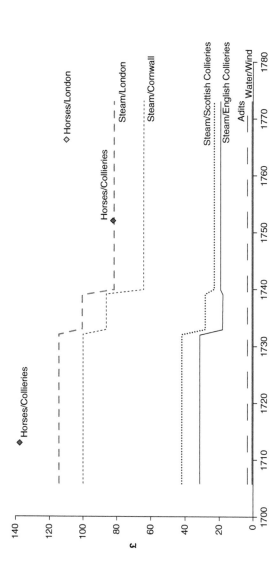

Figure 4.4 Comparative costs of various power sources, 1706–73: an alternative entrepreneurial perspective

Notes and Sources: The figures used to construct this graph are the exact same ones as in Figure 4.3 minus interest and depreciation charges for all power sources. The steam cost lines reflect mean values; the ones incorporating minimum and maximum values for the four different locations/sectors have not been drawn for the sake of making it easier to read the graph.

conditions; the mines of James Lowther ceased operating by 1705 due to the inadequacy of watermills and windmills in coping with the drainage task, thus forcing the installation of an engine at Howgill in 1717.

Windmills could not present a credible alternative to steam engines even in Scotland.[58] Having winds for a few hours a day could suffice to lower the water level in a pit of moderate depth. The windmill erected by John Gray, owner of Westmuir colliery, near Glasgow, in 1737 did have tolerable efficiency until it was blown to pieces by strong winds three years later; and one of the windmills erected in the Fife shortly after 1746 is stated to have drained the mine sufficiently. But wind inactivity for a period of time meant that a mine could be flooded within a short period of time. However, the owners of small mines facing transportation constraints and limited markets could be willing to take the risk especially since the fixed capital investment was so low.

Adits did offer a couple of advantages: they could be used in conjunction with pumps, the latter being limited to raising water to a maximum of 40 yards; and they could be used to drain several pits thus offering the potential of colliery owners sharing its cost. But they needed hilly terrains to be constructed and were more limited than water wheels or steam engines in reaching great depths; Parrott did construct a sough in 1717–18 in Felling Grounds when he leased the property but it proved inadequate and he subsequently erected an engine.[59]

Horses were an even less attractive alternative due partly to their exorbitant cost but also because of limitations in the amount of power they could generate; whenever power above 3–4 hp was needed problems with harnessing them would arise. On the other hand, they did not present the problem of indivisibilities and thus diminutive collieries opted to use them, such as one at Doura, Ayrshire drawing water from merely 18 yards.[60]

Issues of cost and/or operational problems of alternative methods prompted an expert writing in the 1770s to observe that "Mr. Newcomen's invention of the fire engine enabled us to sink our mines to twice the depth we could formerly do by any other machinery."[61] Hence it becomes apparent that in locations where alternative techniques were either not feasible or inadequate, the diffusion of steam power was driven solely based on the behavior of its own cost.

Some concluding remarks

The "energy transition" was well under way during the period covered by this study. Between the first and sixth decades of the eighteenth century coal consumption per head increased substantially (from 14,719 to 21,403 megajoules). Part of this growth has been attributed to household consumption, particularly through the supplies drawn by London from the Newcastle coalfield. But most of the increase was due to the use of coal in production processes, with mining playing a leading role in this regard. During the same time the consumption of water power also scored an increase, albeit less dramatic (from 173 to 198 megajoules). On the other hand, power provided by draught animals declined (from 5,744 to 5,117 megajoules).[62] The present chapter provides the rationale for these shifts by looking at the configuration of relative factor prices when it comes to various power sources. Water power remained the least expensive generator of energy; however, its expansion was bound to be restrained by physical limitations. On the other hand, draught animals were rendered very expensive in relative terms the moment the Newcomen engine was introduced, leading from that point on to a precipitous decline of the energy they generated on a per capita basis.

More importantly, in terms of the author's research agenda, the relative cost of power sources is one of the key elements in appreciating the pace of steam power diffusion in the pre-Watt era. But the conclusions of this chapter are just a starting point. The analysis begs several questions, some of which have been investigated by the existing literature, though at different depth levels: the distribution of firm sizes and the constraints this factor imposed on the purchase of steam engines; the extent to which their adoption could increase output; whether there was the potential for market expansion given limitations imposed by the transportation network; and how the increase in marginal product related to marginal cost and profitability.[63] Another set of questions relate to the spatial diffusion of engineering skills and its concomitant impact on labor as well as capital costs, particularly on fuel efficiency.

In the end, the author concurs with Nuvolari, von Tunzelmann, and Verspagen that models emphasizing the relative profitability of two competing technologies based on current factor prices or the threshold approach are largely simplistic. A formal model is needed to look into what these authors call the "microbiology" of the diffusion process "seen as the emerging outcome of micro-processes of techno-logical learning and market selection among boundedly rational agents" suggested by evolutionary theory.[64] The analysis proceeds in the next chapter by focusing on the aspect of "technological learning" through the evolution of engineering skills.

Appendix 4A: A note on the cost of boilers and cylinders

The Newcomen engine had a large number of wooden parts, e.g., the beam that was made out of a continuous oak log and the pumps for the pit that were originally made of elm (but later of cast iron). But metal parts (brass and copper originally) dominated the cost structure.[65]

When it comes to boilers, the top would be covered by a sheet of lead under the presumption that plates of iron riveted together could not be made tight enough to withstand the pressure of steam. Typical examples of boilers were a copper one made in Wales in 1717 costing £150 and another one made of brass for the Ketley company in 1760 which cost £402. But as early as 1717 wrought iron plates were used to make them; by the 1760s they were common, leading to a substantial reduction in cost. Prices of iron boilers recorded by the author were in the £43.5–126 range. But the amount spent could easily reach a few hundred pounds in the case of powerful engines which used a number of them such as the 98 hp Walker colliery engine (1763) which had three of them in service and one on standby.[66]

The construction of cylinders also witnessed a significant reduction in price.[67] The very first ones were made of brass by using the expertise of bell founders or, in the south of England, mostly of gun founders. According to one account, they "were faulty in workmanship, and of great expense."[68] Indeed, at 1s 4d per lb, brass was very expensive although it could be sold for scrap at 8d per lb. As a result, it would fetch prices as high as £250 in the south where the syndicate experienced problems finding foundries; but the greater presence of brass founders and the increased competition on Tyneside, which stuck to the material the longest, meant that they could be purchased locally for as little as £150. Desaguliers recommended them as late as 1744 based on sound theoretical principles, i.e., that they could be cast with walls thinner than iron and thus heat and cool more rapidly, speeding up the engine's working cycle by 1–2 strokes/minute; their higher efficiency would counterbalance their higher cost. In practice, however, brass cylinders cast 1/3 inch thick could not withstand the mechanical stresses and the ones constructed were nearly one inch thick. In addition, brass cylinders had limitations in terms of increasing their size (no more than 28–29 inches diameter) and thus the engine's power, evident by the multiple small engines erected in several collieries (e.g., Jesmond, Heaton, Tynemouth Moor, Long Benton, Byker).

As the need for achieving greater depths in collieries became keen, they demanded bigger cylinders; brass would not only have increased the cost substantially but also would have necessitated thicker walls thus giving up its presumed thermal efficiency. Iron offered a much cheaper alternative at 36s per cwt though it was more corrosive and prone to breaking in which case such cylinders would have zero value. Iron cylinders came to the market as early as 1718 from an unknown source but the most likely culprit was Coalbrookdale given its business with Parrott. The company certainly made them by 1722, constructing 22–27 of them by the expiration of the patent (there are discrepancies regarding the figures found in the literature), but in larger numbers once it utilized better boring equipment in 1734 and came to dominate the market;[69] the company made at least 108 such cylinders by 1760 accounting for over half of those made by that year. Tyneside stuck to its ways until Isaac Thompson, the company's agent in Newcastle, sold an iron cylinder to Brown in 1752 and, in light of the latter's prestige, others followed. A number of iron cylinder prices found by the author were in the range of £20–122; though higher prices can be found, the material was not specified by the primary sources. The price reduction compared to brass cylinders was obviously quite considerable.

Appendix 4B: Annual cost of Savery engines

At least eleven Savery engines were installed during this period, seven of which were experimental, three in mines, and one in waterworks. The power of only three experimental engines is known, all of them being 1 hp. The purchase price of such engines would be c. £80; assuming the same interest and depreciation rates, the combined cost would be £10.[70] The premium, assuming a charge proportional to the 10 hp Newcomen engine, would add another £13.8 to the annual fixed cost. In terms of operating cost, fuel consumption had the potential of being a dominant component. Savery himself was evasive and underplayed the amount of coal necessary to operate his model. There are few data in this regard. In 1774 Smeaton ran a trial of two engines erected in Manchester by Wrigley to work water wheels.[71] The first engine was of 2 2/3 hp and consumed 31.5 lbs/hp/hour; the second engine was nearly 5 hp and consumed 29.4 lbs/hp/hour.[72] These rates are not much higher compared to Newcomen engines at the time. Though they were higher earlier, before Wrigley's improvements, their mean value was used to calculate the fuel consumption at the beginning of the century for a 1 hp engine at 1,622 bushels which translates to an annual cost of c. £4 in collieries, £69.75 in London and £58.5 in Cornwall. Unfortunately no information was found on the labor and capital cost of maintaining these engines. Without it, the total annual cost would be in the range of £27.8–93.5 per hp. In the end, the cost of Savery engines was similar to that of the Newcomen model.[73]

It would be interesting to compare the thermodynamic output of the two atmospheric models. For the Newcomen engine, I have estimated from a sample of firms covering the time periods for both *Engines I* and *II* that the quantity of water capable of being lifted was c. 21 mil ft lbs per hp per day.[74] When it comes to Savery engines, the very early ones had a much lower capacity. Two engines, both of 1 hp installed at Kensington (1712) and Desaguliers's house (1728), had a capacity of slightly over 14 mil ft lbs. But by 1774 the two engines installed in Manchester by Wrigley delivered a mean of almost 24 mil ft lbs per hp per day, that is exceeding the performance of Newcomen engines.[75]

Notes

1 Von Tunzelmann, *Steam power*; Kanefsky, *The diffusion of power technology*; Nuvolari, et al., 'The early diffusion of the steam engine."

2 *Steam power*, pp. 117–41, 149–56, 161–3.

3 Wrigley, *Energy*; Kander, et al., *Power to the people*. However, as noted in the Preface, the implications of how the evolution of costs of various energy sources ties in to this "energy transition" does not fall within the scope of this study.

4 Atack, "Fact or fiction?", and Croft, *Steam-engine principles*, pp. 427–34 have provided simple models on this issue, the latter on the cost of steam, the former on the cost of steam in relation to water power.

5 The literature on technological diffusion often utilizes the concept of the threshold when comparing two alternative technologies. It often happens that the new one scores such technical advances over time that its cost declines to the point of piercing the cost line of the old one, in which case its adoption is suppose to gain speed. See Rosenberg, *Inside the black box*, pp. 26–7.

6 As noted in the previous chapter, this was a mean figure of a wider range, from as low as 5–6 hp during the first decade of diffusion to as high as 15 hp around the time of the expiration of the patent.

7 Rolt, *Thomas Newcomen*, pp. 81–2; Raistrick, "The steam engine on Tyneside", pp. 137–8; Dickinson, *Short history of the steam engine*, p. 61.

8 The standard deviation cannot be calculated since the hp of most engines in the table is not known.

9 Robinson and Musson, *James Watt*, p. 74; Dickinson, *Short history of the steam engine*, p. 61; Kanefsky, *Diffusion of power technology*, pp. 150–1; Raistrick, "The steam engine on Tyneside", pp. 142, 153.

10 Flinn, *History of the British coal industry* p. 193; Raistrick, "The steam engine on Tyneside", p. 146.

11 Allen, *British Industrial Revolution*, p. 174; see also Kanefsky, *Diffusion of power technology*, p. 168.

12 Kanefsky, *Diffusion of power technology*, pp. 149–50,167–9 (quote from p. 167).

13 Kanefsky, on the other hand, stated that engines tended to have substantial longevity; see ibid., pp. 273–4.

14 Parts of the York Buildings engine that stopped working in 1731 were bought and used a year later for the installation of the engine at Trelogan lead mine (Flintshire). The engine proved effective but it quickly became apparent that the cost of fuel was a heavy burden. The coal the mine used was bought for 6s 8d/ton plus another 3s/ton to carry it from the Glasdir pits, just over a mile away. The patent owners tried but failed to help by reducing the premium and its use was virtually discontinued in January 1735 when the main vein was reached and a windmill was put into use; the absence of a fuel bill contributed to raising profit up to £2,250 in 1736, much higher compared to previous years. Another engine was installed in 1752 operating until 1760 and then intermittently for another two years when it stopped working due, once again, to the high fuel bill; eventually it was dismantled and parts of it were sold for c. £88. See Rhodes, "Early steam engines in Flintshire", pp. 219, 222–3.

15 Examples of engines with short lives were the ones at Wheal Vor (1710–14), and the two Trelogan engines (see previous note). There were also a good number of engines that were in operation for many years and eventually sold second hand fetching good prices. The Bagillt Marsh engine, whose size was fairly typical for the pre-1740 period was erected in 1719 and sold in 1733 for £700, recovering a good portion of its original value. Six other engines (Delafield mine, Placket Winster, an unknown "little engine", Lye colliery, Calver Mill Sough, Dolcoath), sold several years after their installation during the post-1740 period, fetched a mean price of £585.6. See Rolt and Allen, *The steam engine of Thomas Newcomen*, p. 153; Allen, "The introduction of the Newcomen engine", p. 186; Willies et al., "Wind, water and steam power", pp. 309–10; Allen, "The Newcomen engine and coalworks at the Hayes", p. 157; Nixon, "The early steam engine in Derbyshire", p. 18; Trevithick, *Life of Richard Trevithick*, pp. 21–2; Rhodes, "Early steam engines in Flintshire", p. 222.

16 Costs relating to erection and that of the engine house were not recoverable; see Flinn, *History of the British coal industry*, p. 122.

17 The range of depreciation rates was 0.66–33.33 percent. The mean adopted here is virtually identical to the one used by Allen (7.1 percent); see Allen, *British Industrial Revolution*, p. 174. The engines in my sample, along with the years of erection and of the year the estimate on their value was made or the year they stopped operating, were: Howgill (1717/1726), Griff (1718/1729), Dudley Wood (1737/1752), Park colliery, Dudley (1725/1748), Tanfield Moor (1750–1876 or 1891), Bedminster colliery (1750–1900), Fairbottom valley, re-erected at Bardsley (1750–1827), South Liberty colliery (1760–1900). To these engines the three previously mentioned with short lives (Wheal Vor and the two at Trelogan) were added. Sources: Allen, "The 1715 and other Newcomen engines at Whitehaven", pp. 254, 266–7; White, "Early Newcomen engines", pp. 209, 211–12; Allen, "The 1712 and other Newcomen engines", pp. 59, 70, 76; *Catalogue of the mechanical engineering collection*, p. 30; *Catalogue of Watt centenary exhibition,* p. 11; Stowers, "The development of the atmospheric steam engine", p. 88.

18 Of particular interest was the agreement struck between Newcomen and Stonier Parrott, his father Richard, and George Sparrow, all three involved in a number of collieries, reaching a more ambitious scope under the syndicate. It was to last 99 years and allow the three partners to build as many engines as they wished in the various collieries they were involved with, in exchange having to pay £150 the first six months and £420 for each engine erected. If a colliery became very profitable and raised above 20,000 stacks of coal per year, an extra payment of £100 for every 5,000 stacks had to be paid. The three partners aspired, through this agreement, to become powerful middlemen between the syndicate and colliery owners. But the relationship soured and by 1725 Parrott took the initiative to petition the House of Commons to annul the patent by making the argument that the Newcomen engine should not have been included under Savery's patent to begin with given their very different working principles. Parrott wished to bring this action on behalf of numerous colliery owners who, he claimed, gave him their full support. In the end, Parrott's efforts failed to gain much

support and the syndicate went on to secure enormous profits given the number of engines installed during the monopoly period at often exorbitant premiums. See Briggs, *Power of steam*, p. 34; Jenkins, "Savery, Newcomen, and the early history of the steam engine", p. 129; Flinn, *History of the British coal industry*, p. 117; Allen, "Some early Newcomen engines", pp. 181–2; Rowlands, "Stonier Parrott and the Newcomen engine", p. 50; Musson, "Introduction"; Harris, "The employment of steam power", p. 139; Stewart, *The rise of public science*, pp. 341–3.

19 The frustration was particularly keen for those who happened to be in the midst of financial difficulties. A good case in point is Griff colliery in which Parrott and his partners had a stake. Two engines were installed (1714, 1718) proving successful from a technical point of view but the colliery did not meet the expectations of high profits and thus the partners decided to surrender the remainder of their 29–year lease to Richard Newdigate in 1720. The latter erected two more engines in 1725 but the colliery closed down two years later and the engines were dismantled and sold in 1731. The main reason for the demise of the colliery was that the more accessible seams were getting exhausted, making it impossible to compete effectively with the neighboring colliery at Hawkesbury. But the premium payments were another factor, in fact, re-opening the colliery was contemplated in 1728 once the patent expired. See, Jenkins, "Savery, Newcomen, and the early history of the steam engine", pp. 122, 131; Rolt, *Thomas Newcomen*, p. 84.

20 The engine at Austhorpe (8 hp) carried an annual payment of £250 "for working and keeping the engine in order". If that refers to the premium payment then the charge per hp comes to £31.25; see Smiles, *Lives of the engineers, Vol. 4*, p. 62.

21 "Steam and the city", p. 12.

22 Stevenston colliery spent £26 on repairs in 1723 but it is not clear whether this figure includes the cost of parts. Major replacement costs would refer to items such as boilers. Howgill colliery spent £18.78 in 1719 on "mending" its copper boiler with the expectation that it would last for a good many years, in contrast to iron boilers that would need replacement after one or two years depending on whether "day" or "coal" water was used. See Allen, "The 1715 and other Newcomen engines at Whitehaven", pp. 253–4; Whatley, "The introduction of the Newcomen engine to Ayrshire", p. 72.

23 This sort of arrangement, however, was not universal. The keeper's wage at Stevenston in 1723 was £52. For sources on the labor cost see: Whatley, "The introduction of the Newcomen engine to Ayrshire", p. 72; Bald, *General view of the coal trade of Scotland*, pp. 22–3; Allen, "The introduction of the Newcomen engine", p. 189; Rhodes, "Early steam engines in Flintshire", pp. 219, 223; Rolt and Allen, *The steam engine of Thomas Newcomen*, p. 153; Raistrick, "The steam engine on Tyneside", p. 139.

24 The engines whose data are taken as representative are: regarding *Engine I*, I take a weighted average of the labor and capital operating cost for the Howgill engine which was £301 for the period 1718–23, i.e., c. £60 annually, on average; and for four engines at Heaton colliery during the period 1734–39 at £143.3/engine. For *Engine II* I rely on data for six Heaton engines during two weeks in July 1741, the respective cost on an annual basis being c. £69. The latter figure is certainly an underestimate in light of economies of scale realized at Heaton when it comes to labor cost but not in collieries with a single engine. Kanefsky cites a figure of £1/week or more just for the wage of the engineman. Hence it was decided to assign the same value to *Engine II* for capital and labor operating cost borrowing the figure from *Engine I*. For Scotland, I rely on data of the weekly operating cost, minus fuel, of the engine at the Earl of Dunmore's coalworks in 1769; the respective figure comes to c. £231. For sources, see: Allen, "The 1715 and other Newcomen engines at Whitehaven", p. 254; Raistrick, "The steam engine on Tyneside", p. 139; Hamilton, *Economic history of Scotland*, p. 208; Tann, "The steam engine on Tyneside", p. 55; Kanefsky, *Diffusion of power technology*, pp. 172–3.

25 All references to the fuel consumption of individual engines and the operating time are based on evidence cited in the next chapter.

26 An indication that the estimated annual fuel bill is of the right order of magnitude is the evidence from Stevenston colliery where the respective figure was £39 in 1723; and the engine at Bagillt colliery also had a fairly low fuel bill in 1735 because it used sleck. See Whatley, "The introduction of the Newcomen engine to Ayrshire", p. 72; Rhodes, "Early steam engines in Flintshire", p. 221. The quote is from Stuart, *Historical and descriptive anecdotes*, p. 19.

27 Indicative of the high cost of fuel in London was the Newcomen engine that was installed in 1726, but discontinued in 1731, at the York Buildings running an annual bill of £1,000. According to the *London Daily Post* (April 18th, 1741), "the charge of working it, and some other reasons concurring, made its proprietors . . . lay aside the design"; cited in Rolt, *Thomas Newcomen*, p. 89. See also Rolt and Allen, *The steam engine of Thomas Newcomen*, p. 84; Rhodes, "Early steam engines in Flintshire", p. 219. Two other engines installed by the company beginning in the 1750s did run for 20 years at a time when fuel consumption had improved. See Watkins, *The steam engine in industry*, p. 11; Stowers, "Thomas Newcomen's first steam engine", p. 148.

28 Flinn stated that there were probably some similarities in the movement of prices overtime between coalfields though the absolute levels may have differed substantially; see his *History of the British coal industry, Vol. 2*, p. 306.

29 According to Pole, the duty added £350/annum to the annual fuel bill, though he does not specify the power of the engine he has in mind. Barton believed it added £600 in the case of larger engines. Barton, *Cornish beam engine*, pp. 17–18, 20; Kanefsky, *Diffusion of power technology*, p. 172; Pole, *Treatise on the Cornish pumping engine*, p. 13.

30 Replying to an inquiry in 1752, Brown pointed out that an engine with a 42-inch diameter would burn 20 bolls in 24 hours. Assuming 28 bolls = 1 Newcastle chaldron then this engine would burn 176.6 lbs per hour. Such cylinder diameter was *supposed* to correspond to a 25 hp engine but that would translate to a rate of 7 lbs/hp/hour, an unrealistically low figure. The only explanation is that Brown had in mind engines of much lower hp at this cylinder diameter. See, Raistrick, "The steam engine on Tyneside", p. 162; Raistrick, *Dynasty of ironfounders*, p. 145.

31 The fact that the Jarrow colliery engine, which was probably somewhat less powerful (40 inch diameter), had an annual bill of c. £250 in 1743 and that two engines at Elswick and the Earl of Dunmore's collieries (of unknown hp) had bills of £281 and £266 respectively in c. 1740 and 1769 indicates that the adopted figure is of the right order of magnitude. See Raistrick, "The steam engine on Tyneside", p. 142; Hamilton, *Economic history of Scotland*, p. 208.

32 During trials in 1768–70 one of the two Tresavean engines consumed 1,294 tons/year, i.e., similar to the figure adopted here. Indicative of the fairness of my fuel cost figure regarding Cornwall is that Barton's estimates for the annual bill of a somewhat larger Cornish engine (47 inch diameter) revolved around £1,500–2,000. There are references by Wilson to a number of other Cornish engines with considerably higher daily rates of fuel consumption compared to *Engine II*: two engines at Wheal Rose and Wheal Busy (c. 13 tons each), two engines at Chasewater (16.8 tons in winter, 12 in the summer), and one at Godolphin (6 tons). But it is not clear which specific engines he refers to (there were several in these mines) and the hp is often not known; but, given such figures, these engines were probably very large ones. See Wilson, *A comparative statement*, pp. 3–4; also Barton, *Cornish beam engine*, p. 20; Smiles, *Lives of the engineers*, p. 66.

33 Desaguliers argued that the operating cost of the Griff engine, installed in 1714, never exceeded £150 and data from Oct. 1728 to Oct. 1729, a "wet year", show that this and another engine at Griff installed in 1718 had a combined operating cost (but excluding the cost of new parts) which came to £94.6 per engine. In contrast, the operating cost of *Engine I/collieries* is estimated at £177.7. The latter figure appears quite plausible in light of the fact that one of the Griff engines was very small at 3 hp (the power of the second being unknown). The quote from Desaguliers is cited in Stuart,

Historical and descriptive anecdotes, p. 619; see also White, "Early Newcomen engines", pp. 209, 211–12.

34 Raistrick, "The steam engine on Tyneside", pp. 146, 153; Stowers, "The development of the atmospheric steam engine", p. 88; Dickinson, *Short history of the steam engine*, p. 61. The only figure I could find which is out of sync with my estimates is the one cited for the engine at Griff colliery at £208 (1770); see White, "Early Newcomen engines", p. 209.

35 Crafts, "Steam as a general purpose technology", pp. 342–3. My estimates on earlier engines also seem to be on firm ground. Dickinson cited the water-lifting performance of a colliery engine in 1752 based on a detailed contemporary account; its effective hp can be calculated as 11 hp, raised to 12.5 hp to get its nominal hp, i.e., to allow for friction. In other words, the power of this engine was very similar to that of *Engine I*. The author of this account estimated its annual cost at £365 but there was no mention of depreciation. If we assume that his cost breakdown was, more or less, applicable to earlier decades (a reasonable expectation); and if we add to his figure the rates I have adopted for *Engine I* regarding depreciation and the premium then its cost per hp was virtually identical to my figure for *Engine I/collieries*. See Dickinson, *Short history of the steam engine*, pp. 56–7.

36 Atack, "Fact or fiction?" also noted a gradual decline in the cost of steam in the case of the US driven by lower fuel costs but with water power persisting in locations where the cost of fuel was high and water power was available.

37 My comments on Allen's figures are based on a more refined analysis of the data which is not reproduced here due to space limitations, though easily deduced from the figures of Table 4.2. See Allen, *British Industrial Revolution*, pp. 172–5.

38 Flinn, *History of the British coal industry*, p. 113; Briggs, *Power of steam*, p. 35; Duckham, *History of the Scottish coal industry*, p. 81; Galloway, *The steam engine and its inventors*, p. 102 (where the quote comes from); Nef, *Rise of the British coal industry*, p. 358; White, "Early Newcomen engines", p. 209; Band, "The steam engines of Gregory mine", pp. 269–70.

39 Two teams of ponies at Wet Earth colliery (1752) raised 133,280 ft lbs/minute. The number of horses per team is not specified but if they were a total of six horses, each of them raised 22,213.33 ft lbs. Other experts, however, defined their lifting capacity as a range; according to one account, a horse working a gin on a circular track can exert 16,000–26,000 ft lbs per minute. See Flinn, *History of the British coal industry*, p. 114; Farey, *Treatise on the steam engine*, p. 439; Science Museum, *Catalogue of the collections in the Science Museum*, p. 8; Burn, *The steam-engine*, pp. 39–40.

40 Flinn, *History of the British coal industry*, p. 116.

41 Horses worked 20.4 hours a day while I made the assumption that the steam engine worked 12.26 hours/day. I have taken into account the annual cost of *Engine I/collieries*. The report of the mining agent refers also to the annual operating cost of horses once the reclaiming of the mine was complete but not enough information is given to engage in the same exercise. See Allen, "The 1715 and other Newcomen engines," pp. 242, 244, 261–3. Interest and depreciation charges were calculated based on a presumed purchase price of £10/horse. Horses used in mining cost at least £6–7 c. 1700, "and to pay any less was a false economy", while by 1775 they would cost Lumley colliery £12 per horse. The working life of horses was taken as 12 years. This may be somewhat of an overestimate, given that poor-quality horses had a life expectancy of 10–12 years, but I am assuming better-quality horses were used in mining, as Hatcher seems to imply. See Flinn, *History of the British coal industry*, p. 113; von Tunzelmann, *Steam power*, p. 118; Hatcher, *History of the British coal industry*, p. 227 (quote from this source).

42 I have assumed that there were 52 horses with three of them in each team, that a driver got paid 12d and that there was a tubman for every two teams getting 12d based on evidence from Gregory lead mine and Howgill colliery. See Stuart, *Historical and descriptive anecdotes*, p. 619; White, "Early Newcomen engines", pp. 208–9; Band, "The steam engines of Gregory mine", pp. 269–70.

43 Dickinson, *Short history of the steam engine*, pp. 56–7; Pacey, *The maze of ingenuity*, p. 159.

44 Wrigley, *Energy*, pp. 30–2.

45 I have assumed a 12.26 hours work day, that four horses used one pump, and the same operating cost for horses as in the unnamed colliery of 1752 to which I added estimates for interest and depreciation charges. See Scott, "Smeaton's engine of 1767 at New River Head", pp. 119–20.

46 Cited in Farey, *Treatise on the steam engine*, p. 228.

47 Duckham, *History of the Scottish coal industry*, p. 80; Kanefsky, *Diffusion of power technology*, pp. 139–40, 161–4.

48 Tann, *The development of the factory*, p. 65; quote from Duckham, *History of the Scottish coal industry*, p. 110.

49 The lifting capacity of such a "typical" wheel was conditioned by morphological factors, varying widely. The rule used to finding the power provided by a water stream is given in Allen, *Science of mechanics*, pp. 198–9 and Kanefsky, *Diffusion of power technology*, pp. 21–2. But to apply the rule we have to have precise information on water flows and heights for specific sites, something that is rarely the case.

50 Allen, "Some early Newcomen engines", p. 199; Flinn, *History of the British coal industry*, p. 111; Nef, *Rise of the British coal industry*, pp. 354–7; Band, "The steam engines of Gregory mine", p. 269.

51 Duckham, *History of the Scottish coal industry*, pp. 77–8; Kanefsky, *Diffusion of power technology*, pp. 226–7.

52 The references to the actual diffusion of the various methods in collieries and elsewhere are drawn from Chapter 3.

53 One of several examples being Elswick colliery in which traditional drainage methods failed to win in the late seventeenth century based on an affidavit given by William Cotesworth in 1722; see Galloway, *The steam engine and its inventors*, p. 102. For a more detailed description of such methods and their cost, see Nef, *The rise of the British coal industry*, pp. 353–9.

54 A single Savery engine did not raise water more than 15 yards, based on a sample of five observations, though it has been claimed that it had the ability to draw from double that length. Given the typical depths of contemporary mines (see below), five of those engines would have to be installed one on top of each other to achieve the same task as one Newcomen engine. Not only would fuel consumption be an issue, especially in regions far from coal mines, but the erection cost would be substantial and the risk of accidents and flooding would endanger the integrity of the engines. See Savery, *The miner's friend*, pp. 28, 50; Galloway, *The steam engine and its inventors*, pp. 67–8; Hills, *Power from steam*, p. 35; Clark, *An elementary treatise on steam*, p. 33; Jenkins, "Savery, Newcomen, and the early history of the steam engine", pp. 116–17.

55 In rare cases the depth of mines and the quantity of water to be lifted proved beyond the capabilities of Newcomen engines, as was the case with the 8 hp Park colliery engine in 1718. For sources, see Allen, "Introduction", p. 3; Fletcher and Crowe, *An early steam engine in Wednesbury*, p. 6; Rolt and Allen, *The steam engine of Thomas Newcomen*, pp. 61, 63, 146–7, 149; Galloway, *The steam engine and its inventors*, pp. 125–6; Stowers, "The development of the atmospheric steam engine", p. 88; Pacey, *The maze of ingenuity*, p. 159; Allen, "Some early Newcomen engines," p. 199; Harris, "The early steam engine on Merseyside", p. 112; Flinn, *The history of the British coal industry*, p. 125; Band, "The steam engines of Gregory mine, Ashover", p. 270; Science Museum, *Catalogue of the mechanical engineering collection*, p. 30. Two figures are cited in the literature for a couple of the sample's engines, the higher of the two being adopted. Engines which raised water from a well or a pond to a reservoir to power water wheels were not taken into account since the depths involved were not reflective of their capabilities.

56 The problem was exacerbated as time went by. In 1738 a grievance petition was brought to the House of Commons by members of professions utilizing large quantities of coal complaining about the high prices of Newcastle coal. In their response colliery owners noted their high operating cost and pointed out that without Newcomen engines many mines could not be won; see Raistrick, "The steam engine on Tyneside, p. 137. Flinn also echoes such views though the author finds his statement that the depth limit of sources alternative to steam was 30–50 yards a bit conservative, at least in relation to water wheels (see below); see his *The history of the British coal industry*, pp. 114.

57 The parish minister of Scoonie, Fife lamented the fact that local collieries could not reach deeper with water wheels; Duckham, *A history of the Scottish coal industry*, p. 80. See also Rolt and Allen, *The steam engine of Thomas Newcomen*, pp. 55–6; Fordyce, *A history of coal, coke, coal fields*, p. 16; Kanefsky, *The diffusion of power technology*, pp. 139–40.

58 Duckham, *A history of the Scottish coal industry*, pp. 77–8.

59 Allen, "Some early Newcomen engines", p. 199; Nef, *The rise of the British coal industry*, pp. 354–5; Flinn, *The history of the British coal industry*, p. 111.

60 Duckham, *A history of the Scottish coal industry*, p. 81; Kanefsky, *The diffusion of power technology*, p. 138.

61 Cited in Thurston, *Stationary steam engines*, p. 5.

62 The figures are from Wrigley, *Energy*, p. 94, Table 4.2.

63 The transportation network was of paramount importance not only on the demand side but also in conditioning the operating cost of steam engines through its impact on the price of coal as well as potentially causing information and logistical delays regarding the installation of engines.

64 Nuvolari, et al., "The diffusion of the steam engine", p. 195.

65 On the expenses of particular engine components, see Bald, *General view of the coal trade of Scotland*, pp. 160–5; Jenkins, "Savery, Newcomen, and the early history of the steam engine", p. 131; Fletcher and Crowe, *An early steam engine in Wednesbury*, pp. 7–8; Rogers, *The Newcomen engine*, p. 18; Allen, "The 1715 and other Newcomen engines," pp. 263–5, 267–8; Allen, "The 1712 and other Newcomen engines", pp. 60, 68, 70, 75–80; Raistrick, "The steam engine on Tyneside", pp. 139, 156–8.

66 The skills to make boilers were transferred by craftsmen who made them for breweries or sugar refineries; they were known as haystack or balloon from their shape and they kept evolving with different designs by John Payne, James Blakey, and others. For sources, see Science Museum, *Catalogue of the collections in the Science Museum . . . Stationary engines*, pp. 70, 116–17; Bald, *General view of the coal trade of Scotland* , pp. 20–1; Rogers, *The Newcomen engine*, p. 15; Burstall, *History of mechanical engineering*, p. 265; Kanefsky, *Diffusion of power technology*, pp. 150–1; Allen, "Some early Newcomen engines", p. 198; Allen, "The Newcomen engine and coalworks at the Hayes", p. 155; Dickinson, *Short history of the steam engine*, pp. 59–60; Allen, "The 1715 and other Newcomen engines", p. 255; Raistrick, "The steam engine on Tyneside", p. 146; Stowers, "The development of the atmospheric steam engine", p. 88; Allen, "The introduction of the Newcomen engine", p. 170.

67 Raistrick, *Dynasty of ironfounders*, pp. 128–9; Hart, *James Watt*, p. 145; Flinn, *History of the British coal industry*, pp. 119–21; Raistrick, "The steam engine on Tyneside", pp. 145, 156–8, 162; Dickinson, "The predecessors of Watt's engine", p. 1762; Stuart, *Historical and descriptive anecdotes*, p. 303; Dickinson, *Short history of the steam engine*, p. 61; Barton, *Cornish beam engine*, p. 19; Allen, "The introduction of the Newcomen engine", p. 170; Allen, "Some early Newcomen engines", p. 199; Crowley, *The beam engine*, p. 11; Briggs, *The power of steam*, p. 35; Kanefsky, *Diffusion of power technology*, p. 261; Rolt, *Thomas Newcomen*, pp. 81, 118–19; Rogers, *The Newcomen engine*, p. 11; Rolt and Allen, *The steam engine of Thomas Newcomen*, pp. 48–9, 67, 106.

68 Stuart, *Historical and descriptive anecdotes*, p. 303.

69 An illustration of such machinery can be found in Chaloner and Musson, *Industry and technology*, n. p., illustration # 59.

70 Desaguliers installed an engine in his garden in 1728 which cost him £80 and, despite the fact that the figure does not include the cost of piping that would have added several pounds, it was adopted because the purchase cost may have been lower in other instances; the 1712 engine installed at Kensington cost £50. See Switzer, *Introduction to a general system of hydrostatics and hydraulicks*, p. 328; von Tunzelmann, *Steam power*, pp. 47–8; Hills, *Power from steam*, p. 35; Thurston, *History of the growth of the steam engine*, p. 44.

71 Wrigley modified the design of the original model by relying on only one cylinder, as opposed to two in Savery's design. Steam was condensed in the cylinder having atmospheric pressure forcing up water from below; and then instead of expelling the water by steam, as in Savery's design, the water flowed out by gravity on to a cistern which stood above a water wheel. This modification reduced the necessary amount of steam to a bit higher than atmospheric pressure thereby reducing substantially the risk of boiler explosions as well as fuel consumption. He also incorporated some changes brought by Blakey who focused on introducing self-acting valve gear and using oil on the surface of the water in the cylinder to reduce steam condensation. These modifications, however, did not prove satisfactory. See Musson and Robinson, *Science and technology*, pp. 397–8; Thurston, *History of the growth of the steam engine*, pp. 44–5. On Savery's comments on the issue of fuel consumption see his *The miner's friend*, p. 28.

72 Farey, *Treatise on the steam engine*, p. 125; Goodeve, *Text-book on the steam engine*, p. 9; Thurston, *Manual of the steam-engine*, pp. 11–12. There are also two other accounts regarding fuel consumption of Savery engines; the Kensington engine of 1712 and one erected by Wrigley at the works of Mr. Kiers at St. Pancras, London towards the end of my period, or a bit beyond. But the references are not precise enough to allow the calculation of the rate. See Switzer, *Introduction to a general system of hydrostatics and hydraulicks*, p. 328; Farey, *Treatise on the steam engine*, p. 125; Stuart, *Historical and descriptive anecdotes* pp. 158–9; Stuart, *Descriptive history of the steam engine*, pp. 42–3; Thurston, *History of the growth of the steam engine*, p. 45. The recorded rates of the two Manchester engines are virtually identical to the estimates provided by Hills (31 lbs/hp/hour) and Thurston (33.26 lbs/hp/hour). See Hills, *Power from steam*, p. 242 and Thurston, "On the maximum contemporary economy of the high-pressure multiple-expansion steam-engine", pp. 313, 315.

73 Desaguliers noted that the Newcomen model was not the optimal choice in small sizes because its extra gearing rendered it too expensive per hp and the energy wasted to deal with friction was way too high in the context of such sizes; on the other hand, the Savery model was very cheap because it had few parts. Von Tunzelmann echoed this assessment: "In the eighteenth century the Savery engine remained economic but only for very low horsepower ratings (probably under 6 horsepower). The reasons were essentially the high fixed costs per horsepower of the Newcomen engine for these small engines." See von Tunzelmann, *Steam power*, p. 91. Desaguliers's comments are cited in Farey, *A treatise on the steam engine*, pp. 116–17.

74 Assuming a 12.26 hour work day. For *Engine I* the sample was comprised of the engines at Dudley Castle, Griff, Park, and Alan Flats; for *Engine II* from an unnamed colliery, and two engines installed at Warmley Brass. To find these figures one has to take the number of gallons lifted and multiply by 8.33 (translating it to lbs) and by the height in feet. The product should be divided by 60 to find the foot lbs/minute. To find the hp of an engine needed to drain this quantity, the final product should be divided by 33,000. See Michell, *Mine drainage*, p. 359; Anon., *Power catechism*, pp. 132–3; Allen, "Introduction"; Rolt and Allen, *The steam engine of Thomas Newcomen*, pp. 61,

146–7, 149; Rogers, *The Newcomen engine*, pp. 28–9; Allen, "Some early Newcomen engines", p. 199.

75 Galloway, *The steam engine and its inventors*, pp. 67–68; Hills, *Power from steam*, p. 35; Farey, *Treatise on the steam engine*, p. 125; Goodeve, *Text-book on the steam engine*, p. 9. For some additional comments and estimates on their lifting capacity, see Switzer, *Introduction to a general system of hydrostatics and hydraulicks*, p. 328; Clark, *Elementary treatise on steam*, p. 33.

Bibliography

Allen, J. S., "John Fidoe's 1727 Newcomen engine at Wednesbury, Staffs", *Transactions of the Newcomen Society*, 36 (1963–4), pp. 149–52.

Allen, J. S., "The Newcomen engine and coalworks at the Hayes, Lye, Stourbridge, 1760–69", *Transactions of the Newcomen Society*, 36 (1963–4), pp. 153–7.

Allen, J. S., "The 1712 and other Newcomen engines of the earls of Dudley", *Transactions of the Newcomen Society*, 37 (1964–5), pp. 57–84.

Allen, J. S., "Introduction", in J. M. Fletcher, and A. J. Crowe, *An early steam engine in Wednesbury: some papers relating to the coal mines of the Fidoe family, 1727–9*, (1966) pp. 1–4.

Allen, J. S., "Some early Newcomen engines and the legal disputes surrounding them", *Transactions of the Newcomen Society*, 41 (1968–9), pp. 181–201.

Allen, J. S., "The introduction of the Newcomen engine from 1710 to 1733", *Transactions of the Newcomen Society*, 42 (1969–70), pp. 169–90.

Allen, J. S., "Addendum to the introduction of the Newcomen engine from 1710–1733", *Transactions of the Newcomen Society*, 43 (1970–1), pp. 199–202.

Allen, J. S., "The 1715 and other Newcomen engines at Whitehaven, Cumberland", *Transactions of the Newcomen Society*, 45, 1972–3, pp. 237–68.

Allen, J. S., and M. H. Elton, "Edward Short and the 1714 Newcomen engine at Bilston, Staffs", *Transactions of the Newcomen Society*, 74 (2004), pp. 281–91.

Allen, R., *The British Industrial Revolution in global perspective* (Cambridge: Cambridge University Press, 2009).

Allen, Z., *The science of mechanics* (Providence: Hutchens & Cory, 1829).

Anonymous, *The power catechism: correct answers to direct questions covering the main principles of steam engineering and the transmission of power* (New York: McGraw-Hill Book Co., n. d.).

Ashton, T. S., and J. Sykes, *The coal industry of the eighteenth century* (New York: Augustus M. Kelley, 1967).

Atack, J., "Fact or fiction? Relative costs of steam and water power: a simulation approach", *Explorations in Economic History*, 16, 10 (1979), pp. 409–37.

Baines, T., and W. Fairbairn, *Lancashire and Cheshire, past and present. With an account of the rise and progress of manufactures and commerce . . .* 2 vols. (London: William Mackenzie, n. d.).

Bald, R., *A general view of the coal trade of Scotland* (Edinburgh: Oliphant & Brown, 1808).

Band, S., "The steam engines of Gregory mine, Ashover", *Bulletin of the Peak District Mines Historical Society*, 8, 5 (Summer 1983), pp. 269–95.

Barker, T. C., and J. R. Harris, *A Merseyside town in the industrial revolution, St. Helens, 1750–1900* (Liverpool: At the University Press, 1954).

Barton, D. B., *The Cornish beam engine* (Exeter: Cornwall Books, 1989).

Beveridge, W., *Prices and wages in England from the twelfth to the nineteenth century: Vol. I. Price tables: mercantile era* (London: Cass, 1965).

Briggs, A., *The power of steam: an illustrated history of the world's steam age* (Chicago: University of Chicago Press, 1982).

Burn, R. S., *The steam-engine, its history and mechanism: being descriptions and illustrations of the stationary, locomotive, and marine engine, for the use of schools and students*, 6th ed. (London: H. Ingram, 1854).

Burstall, A., *A history of mechanical engineering* (Cambridge, MA: MIT Press, 1965).

Chaloner, W. H., and A. E. Musson, *Industry and technology* (London: Vista Books, 1963).

Clark, D. K., *An elementary treatise on steam and the steam-engine, stationary and portable* (London: Lockwood & Co., 1875).

Crafts, N. F. R., "Steam as a general purpose technology: a growth accounting perspective", *Economic Journal*, 114 (2004), pp. 338–51.

Croft, T., *Steam-engine principles and practice*, 2nd ed. revised by E. J. Tangerman (New York and London: McGraw-Hill, 1939).

Crowley, T. E., *The beam engine: a massive chapter in the history of steam* (Oxford: Senecio, 1982).

Davey, H., "The Newcomen engine", *Proceedings of the Institute of Mechanical Engineers*, Oct. 1903, pp. 655–704.

Dickinson, H. W., "The predecessors of Watt's engine", *Power and the Engineer*, Oct. 4, 1910, pp. 1760–62.

Dickinson, H. W., with a new intro by A. E. Musson, *A short history of the steam engine* (New York: Augustus M. Kelley, 1965).

Duckham, Baron F., *A history of the Scottish coal industry, Vol. I: 1700–1815* (Newton Abbot: David & Charles, 1970).

Farey, J., *A treatise on the steam engine, historical, practical and descriptive* (London: Longman, Rees, Orme, Brown, and Green, 1827).

Fletcher, J. M., and A. J. Crowe, *An early steam engine in Wednesbury: some papers relating to the coal mines of the Fidoe family, 1727–9* (Wednesbury: Central Library, 1966).

Flinn, M. W., *The history of the British coal industry, Vol. 2, 1700–1830: The Industrial Revolution* (Oxford: Clarendon Press, 1984).

Fordyce, W., *A history of coal, coke, coal fields . . .* (London: S. Low, Son, and Co.; New York: Scribner & Co, 1860).

Galloway, R. L., *The steam engine and its inventors; a historical sketch* (London: Macmillan, 1881).

Goodeve, T. M., *Text-book on the steam engine*, 2nd ed. (London: C. Lockwood, 1879).

Hamilton, H., *An economic history of Scotland in the eighteenth century* (Oxford: Clarendon Press, 1963).

Harris, J. R., "The early steam engine on Merseyside", *Transactions of the Historical Society of Lancashire and Cheshire*, CVI (1954), pp. 109–16.

Harris, J. R., "The employment of steam power in the eighteenth century", *History*, LII (1967), pp. 133–48.

Hart, I. B., *James Watt and the history of steam power* (New York: Henry Schuman, 1949).

Hatcher, J., *The history of the British coal industry, Vol. 1, Before 1700: towards the age of coal* (Oxford: Clarendon Press, 1993).

Hills, R. L., *Power from steam: a history of the stationary steam engine* (Cambridge and New York: Cambridge University Press, 1989).

Jackman, W. T., *The development of transportation in modern England* (New York: A.M. Kelley, 1965), reprint, originally published in 1916.

Jenkins, R., "Savery, Newcomen, and the early history of the steam engine", *Transactions of the Newcomen Society*, 3 (1922–23), pp. 96–118.

Kander, A., P. Malanima, and P. Warde, *Power to the people: energy in Europe over the last five centuries* (Princeton: Princeton University Press, 2013).

Kanefsky, J. W., *The diffusion of power technology in British industry 1760–1870* (Ph. D. thesis, University of Exeter, 1979).

Levine, D., and K. Wrightson, *The making of an industrial society: Whickham, 1560–1765* (Oxford: Clarendon Press; New York: Oxford University Press, 1991).

Michell, S., *Mine drainage: being a complete practical treatise on direct-acting underground steam pumping machinery*, 2nd ed. (London: Crosby, Lockwood and Son; New York: Van Nostrand, 1899).

Musson, A. E., "Introduction", in Dickinson, *A short history of the steam engine*, n. p.

Musson, A. E., and E. Robinson, *Science and technology in the industrial revolution* (Manchester: Manchester University Press, 1969).

Nef, J., *The rise of the British coal industry, 2 vols.* (London: George Routledge & Sons, 1932).

Nixon, F., "The early steam engine in Derbyshire", *Transactions of the Newcomen Society*, 31 (1957–9), pp. 1–28.

Nuvolari, A., B. Verspagen, and G. N. von Tunzelmann, "The early diffusion of the steam engine in Britain, 1700–1800. A reappraisal", *Cliometrica*, 5 (2011), pp. 291–321.

Nuvolari, A., B. Verspagen, and G. N. von Tunzlemann, "The diffusion of the steam engine in the eighteenth century", in A. Pyka and H. Hanush, eds., *Applied evolutionary economics*, pp. 166–200.

Pacey, A., *The maze of ingenuity: ideas and idealism in the development of technology*, 2nd ed. (Cambridge, MA, and London: MIT Press, 1992).

Pole, W., *A treatise on the Cornish pumping engine*, (London: John Weale, 1844).

Pyka, A., and H. Hanusch, *Applied evolutionary economics and the knowledge-based economy* (Cheltenham, UK and Northampton, MA: Edward Elgar, 2006).

Raistrick, A., "The steam engine on Tyneside, 1715–1778", *Transactions of the Newcomen Society*, 17 (1936–7), pp. 131–63.

Raistrick, A., *Dynasty of ironfounders: the Darbys and Coalbrookdale* (London, New York and Toronto: Longmans, Green & Company, 1953).

Rhodes, J. N., "Early steam engines in Flintshire", *Transactions of the Newcomen Society*, 41 (1968–9), pp. 217–25.

Robinson, E., and A. E. Musson, *James Watt and the steam revolution* (New York: A. M. Kelley, 1969).

Rogers, K. H., *The Newcomen engine in the west of England* (Bradford-on-Avon: Moonraker Press, 1976).

Rolt, L. T. C., *Thomas Newcomen: the prehistory of the steam engine* (Dawlish, Eng.: David and Charles, 1963).

Rolt, L. T. C., and J. S. Allen, *The steam engine of Thomas Newcomen* (New York: Science History Publications, 1977).

Rosenberg, N., *Inside the black box* (Cambridge: Cambridge University Press, 1982).

Rowlands, M. B., "Stonier Parrott and the Newcomen engine", *Transactions of the Newcomen Society*, 41 (1968–9), pp. 49–67.

Savery, T., *The miner's friend, or an engine to raise water by fire described and of the manner of fixing it in mines* (London, 1702, reprinted 1827 for S. Crouch).

Science Museum, *Catalogue of Watt centenary exhibition* (London, 1919).

Science Museum, *Catalogue of the mechanical engineering collection in the Science Museum, South Kensington, with descriptive and historical notes*, 6th ed. (London, 1919).

Science Museum, *Catalogue of the collections in the Science Museum South Kensington* *with descriptive and historical notes and illustrations. Stationary engines*, comp. by H. W. Dickinson (London, 1925).

Kilburn, S. E., "Smeaton's engine of 1767 at New River Head, London", *Transactions of the Newcomen Society*, XIX (1938–9), pp. 119–26.

Smiles, S., *Lives of the engineers, Vol. 4* (London: John Murray, 1874).

Smith, A., "Steam and the city: the committee of proprietors of the invention for raising water by fire, 1715–1735", *Transactions of the Newcomen Society*, 49 (1977–78) pp. 5–20.

Stewart, L., *The rise of public science: rhetoric, technology, and natural philosophy in Newtonian Britain, 1660–1750* (Cambridge: Cambridge University Press, 1992).

Stowers, A., "The development of the atmospheric steam engine after Newcomen's death in 1729", *Transactions of the Newcomen Society, 35* (1962–3), pp. 87–96.

Stuart (Meikleham), R., *A descriptive history of the steam engine* (London: John Knight and Henry Lacey, 1824).

Stuart (Meikleham), R., *Historical and descriptive anecdotes of steam engines* (London John Knight and Henry Lacey, 1829).

Switzer, S., *An introduction to a general system of hydrostatics and hydraulicks, philo sophical and practical, Vol. 2* (London: T. Astley, 1729).

Szostak, R., *The role of transportation in the industrial revolution: a comparison of France and England* (Montreal and Kingston: McGill-Queen's University Press, 1991)

Tann, J., *The development of the factory* (London: Cornmarket Press, 1970).

Tann, J., "The steam engine on Tyneside in the Industrial Revolution", *Transactions of the Newcomen Society, 64* (1992–3), pp. 53–75.

Thurston, R. H., "On the maximum contemporary economy of the high-pressure multiple expansion steam-engine", *Transactions of the American Society of Mechanical Engineers*, XV (1893), pp. 313–437.

Thurston, R. H., *A history of the growth of the steam engine* (New York: D. Appleton and Company, 1897).

Thurston, R. H., *A manual of the steam-engine. For engineers and technical schools advanced courses, Part I, Structure and theory* (New York: John Wiley, 1907).

Thurston, R. H., *Stationary steam engines, simple and compound; especially as adapted to light and power plants*, 7th ed. (New York: J. Wiley & Sons; London: Chapman & Hall, 1902).

Trevithick, F., *Life of Richard Trevithick, with an account of his inventions, 2 vols* (London and New York: E. & F. N. Spon, 1872).

Turnbull, G., "Canals, coal and regional growth during the industrial revolution" *Economic History Review*, 2nd ser., XL (1987), pp. 537–60.

Von Tunzelmann, G. N., *Steam power and British industrialization to 1860* (Oxford Clarendon Press, 1978).

Whatley, C. A., "The introduction of the Newcomen engine to Ayrshire", *Industrial Archaeology Review* 2 (1965), pp. 69–77.

White, A. W. A., "Early Newcomen engines on the Warwickshire coalfield, 1714–1736" *Transactions of the Newcomen Society*, 41 (1968–69), pp. 203–16.

Willies, L., J. Rieuwerts, and R. B. Flindall, "Wind, water and steam power on Derbyshir lead mines: a list", *Bulletin of the Peak District Mines Historical Society*, 6, (December 1977), pp. 303–20.

Wilson, T., *A comparative statement of the effects of Messrs. Boulton and Watt's steam engines with Newcomen's and Mr. Hornblower's* (Truro: Printed by W. Harry, 1792).

Wrigley, E. A., *Energy and the English Industrial Revolution* (Cambridge: Cambridge University Press, 2010).

5 The role of British engineering skills in driving the diffusion of Newcomen engines, 1706–73

The development of engineering skills in Britain was one of the key factors shaping the diffusion trajectory of steam power, as has been pointed out by several historians.[1] Improving such skills would have had positive spillover effects in both the construction and management of such engines affecting virtually every component of total cost, but especially fuel consumption. At the dawn of the steam era the availability of skills relevant to the construction and management of engines was limited to the inventors of the first two functioning models, Savery and Newcomen. A remarkable diffusion of the relevant knowledge, however, took place between that time and 1773 in light of the adoption of nearly 570 engines. But how does one measure the spread of a particular skill? This can only be done through the specification of a proxy which reflects the improvement of such skills. The method adopted in this chapter will focus on how fuel consumption evolved; it will use anecdotal evidence and figures referring to this variable in order to outline the time frame in which such skills reached a critical mass.

The first section of this chapter will describe the status of engineering skills during the early phase of their development through the 1730s; the latter decade was the time when a major breakthrough took place with the construction of larger engines which offered the potential of achieving a level of fuel consumption which was significantly lower compared to earlier decades. The second section will focus on the process of learning-by-doing, a critical factor in driving improvements through the management of engines, which resulted in closing the gap between fuel consumption levels achieved by actual engines in relation to the "ideal" or potential levels of fuel consumption offered by the larger engines.

The early engineers

Skills relevant to the construction of the steam engine were virtually absent during the first dozen years or so (1706–18), while the aggregate diffusion line was barely distinguishable from the horizontal axis (see Figure 3.2). Despite the fact that not every engineer involved is known, it is fairly clear that Newcomen himself was mainly responsible for the erection of the engine through 1715, i.e., through the time the syndicate took over and he became a mere member of it; Savery was involved in only a couple of installations. The first recorded appearance of the

Parrotts and Sparrow, three major figures who eventually played a substantial role in the erection of engines, comes in 1715; however, their contribution remained fairly small through the next three years and even more so in the case of a couple of additional engineers (e.g., Beighton). All in all, there were no much more than half a dozen engineers who had the skills to erect the engine during the first twelve years. Concerns regarding the safety of the engine also existed. Writing in 1708, and presumably reflecting a more widespread perception, J. C. stated that among colliery owners "are not many dare Venture of it".[2] However, since the burden of installations relied almost exclusively on Newcomen's shoulders these fears were largely immaterial; even in their absence Newcomen could not have erected much more engines than he did. These problems were compounded by the inelastic supply of component parts, a fact which in itself reflects the lack of widespread engineering skills.[3]

Numerically speaking, the number of engineers possessing such skills gradually expanded from the late 1710s through 1745, right before the first structural break in the diffusion curve. It was the outcome of the "invisible hand" being in action, i.e., the relative scarcity of relevant engineering skills raised wages for the erection and management of engines to more than satisfactory levels; in turn, the latter acted as signals or price stimuli inducing the response of individuals with similar skills who decided to cross from other labor markets. The leading figures were the Parrotts/Sparrow trio, responsible for over a third (17) of the installations whose engineer is known (based on data from the revised Kanefsky database). But they were joined by at least half a dozen other engineers (e.g., Hornblower, Potter, and Beech) in addition to the contributions of Newcomen, the syndicate, and those engines constructed by Coalbrookdale.

Nevertheless, there were still major obstacles preventing the diffusion figures from becoming more robust. To begin with, setting up as an engine maker required a substantial sum of money. According to a mid-century account, it was a minimum of £500 and could not have been much lower earlier.[4] In addition, long delays persisted in pulling together the resources necessary to install an engine. A Newcastle colliery had to wait for months to get timber to London and from thence to Newcastle, as well as coping with the delayed arrival of workmen and advisers; and, once resources were pulled together, considerable time would elapse before the engine was constructed, twenty weeks in the case of Edmonstone colliery (1726). Personal communications were also painfully slow, creating a breeding ground for friction and disputes. Weeks would go by trying to solicit responses from engine makers or in dealing with the proprietors of the patent.[5] These problems, along with the slow growth of competent engineers, explain the lack of a structural break prior to the mid-1740s.

The critical factor that led to the latter lay mainly in a key development in the field of engineering, i.e., the construction of larger steam engines which created the potential of reducing their cost. The very first cylinders, made by bell-founders, were characterized by high cost and faulty workmanship. In some cases the piston was very tight, in many others too loose, causing condensation on top of the piston and thus the failure of the latter to travel the full distance at a considerable waste of steam. These technical flaws where bound to have the largest impact in places where fuel bills ran to high figures.[6] Instead of addressing this and other mechanical and thermal inefficiencies, engineers sought to compensate by attempting to construct larger cylinders which, in theory at least, entailed the prospect of aggravating the problem. However, boring equipment fell short of the task, with boring bars breaking in the effort to come up with larger cylinders. The pressures generated by this demand led the Coalbrookdale company to install in 1734 a mill with a larger boring bar. It seems to have been successful because a second one was ordered in 1745.[7] This was a crucial development because it allowed the mean size of engines to jump from c. 10 hp through the 1730s to c. 25 hp thereafter.

There is no question that the rise in the size of cylinders did not always lead to a proportional increase in the power of engines as Smeaton confirmed in 1769 by examining 15 engines in the Newcastle region and another 18 in Cornwall.[8] However, it certainly offered the *potential* of reducing fuel consumption per hp since, in theory, more powerful engines are more efficient. Smeaton compiled a table correlating engines of different hp with what their fuel consumption ought to have been. Based on it, for instance, an engine of 10 hp should have consumed c. 20–21 lbs of coal per hp/hour whereas the respective figure for a 25 hp engine should have been c. 16 lbs.[9]

The less-than-impeccable rationale which led to the invention of more powerful boring equipment is reflective of technological developments in an age which predates the institutionalization of science. The outcome, however, established a real opportunity in that the larger engines defined an envelope of superior potential possibilities when it comes to fuel consumption. But the extent to which the decline of fuel consumption of actual engines and the narrowing of the gap from ideal values could materialize was more a reflection of the evolution of engineering skills in terms of operating the engines through learning-by-doing.

Fuel consumption, 'ideal' and actual figures

Rolt questioned the notion that these larger engines were more efficient compared to the smaller ones constructed during Newcomen's lifetime, arguing, instead, that they may have been markedly inferior since they were constructed by less experienced engineers.[10] The secondary literature has decidedly rejected this view, favoring the assertion of a substantial decline in fuel consumption by the time the Watt engine came into the scene. However, there is a dazzling variation in the cited figures producing a sense of confusion. Figures referring to average practice prior to Smeaton's improvements are in the range of 20–45 lbs/hp/hour and a similar gap applies to best practice (25.5–51.5). The figures cited, referring to engines incorporating Smeaton's improvements, range from c. 14 to 35, interestingly enough made by the same author (Thurston). Regarding the proportional decline of fuel consumption due to Smeaton's work, Hodge claimed it was up to one-third. But according to an inscription on an engine erected by Boulton & Watt in 1785 it was "one-half" and Scott went as far as arguing that Smeaton's Long Benton engine (1772) reduced it by two-thirds.[11]

Table 5.1 Fuel consumption (lbs/hp/hour) of conventional Newcomen engines and those modified by Smeaton (in italics); estimates indicated by an *

Early group

Year	Name	Power	Location	Sector	Fuel consumption
1723	Stevenston [1]	? (25 inches)	Ayrshire	Colliery	43.5*
1725	Alan Flats	5	Durham	Colliery	45.3
1726	York Buildings	20	London	Waterworks	12.41
1729	Griff [2]	3	Warwickshire	Colliery	52.9
1732	Trelogan [3]	20	Flintshire	Colliery	22.52*

Late group

Year	Name	Power	Location	Sector	Fuel consumption
1756	York	5	N. Yorkshire	Waterworks	50.9
Post 1767	*"*	*5.86*	*"*	*"*	*34.4*
"	*" 4*	*"*	*"*	*"*	*39.5*
"	*" 5*	*8.45*	*"*	*"*	*24.6*
"	*" 6*	*6.29*	*"*	*"*	*29.3*
"	*" 7*	*"*	*"*	*"*	*34.1*
1759	Mill Close [8]	47	Derbyshire	Lead mine	9
1763	Walker [9]	98	Northumberland	Colliery	12.35/14*
1765	Experimental [10]	4			24.37
1768	Long Benton [11]	32	Northumberland	Colliery	21.8*
1769	Unknown	?	Cornwall	Metal mine	33.33
1769	New River Head	5	London	Waterworks	28
"	*" 12*	*"*	*"*	*"*	*22.3*
"	*" 13*	*"*	*"*	*"*	*23*
1769	Unknown	? (75 inches)	?	?	37.2
1769	Unknown	? (60 inches)	?	?	29
1769	Unknown	?	?	?	22.8
1769	Experimental [14]	1	Austhorpe		55
1769–70	Sample of 33 engines [15]	?	Newcastle and Cornwall	Collieries and metal mines	29.76 (mean)
1772	Unknown	?	Cornwall	Metal mine	19.7
1772	Long Benton	41	Northumberland	Colliery	26.14
1773	Kingston-upon-Hull	2.25	E. Yorkshire	Waterworks	32.2

Additional information: (1) Used small coal; (2) Mean of two engines; (3) Built using parts of one of the two 1726 York Buildings engines; (4) Used small coal; (5) Replaced boiler, increased length of the stroke; (6) Reduced number of strokes, used regular coal; (7) Used sleck; (8) Based on a trial right before sold to Delafield mine; (9) There are two estimates; the highest taken into account based on the credibility of the source (Stowers); (10) Designed by Smeaton based on standard practices; (11) Its hp was adjusted to take into account power wasted in friction; (12) Alterations made at the fulcrum of the great lever; (13) Increased the number of strokes; (14) Designed by Smeaton; (15) Some authors claim the figure came from a sample of 15 Newcastle engines based on information provided by William Brown but I have adopted Stower's claim that it included 18 additional large Cornish engines, for a total of 33.

Notes: To calculate fuel consumption per hp/hour it was necessary to know the number of hours per day engines worked but this information is missing in few cases. The evidence indicates that some engines worked in three 8-hour shifts, like the ones at Trelogan; or for every single week during the year, like the two Griff engines in 1729. But even in such cases there was bound to be intermittent interruption. Kanefsky assumes that engines worked, on average, for 12.26 hours a day and this figure was adopted where this information was missing. Also, for the Stevenston engine it was necessary to make an assumption on its hp which was taken to be 13.5, the mean value for hp of engines in the 1720s. See Kanefsky, *The diffusion of power technology*, p. 172; Rhodes, "Early steam engines in Flintshire," p. 223; White, "Early Newcomen engines", pp. 211–2; chapter 3 in this book.

Sources: Whatley, "The introduction of the Newcomen engine to Ayrshire", p. 72; Clayton, "The Newcomen-type engine at Elsecar," p. 108; Stuart, *Historical and descriptive anecdotes*, pp. 294–5, 322; White, "Early Newcomen engines", pp. 211–2; Allen, "The introduction of the Newcomen engine", p. 189; Farey, *A treatise on the steam engine*, pp. 235, 256–7, 262; Band, "The steam engines of Gregory mine, Ashover", p. 270; Stowers, "The development of the atmospheric steam engine," pp. 88, 90; Hodge, *The steam engine*, pp. 43–4, 120; von Tunzelmann, *Steam power*, pp. 18, 69; Fairbairn, *Treatise on mills*, p. 255; Allen, *The British industrial revolution*, pp. 165–6; Galloway, *The steam engine and its inventors*, pp. 129–30; Bourne, *A treatise on the steam engine*, p. 7; Russell, *A treatise on the steam engine*, p. 54.

The discrepancies of the figures stem from the fact that the various authors rely on limited evidence on which they base broad generalizations. This issue can be settled and more refined conclusions can be derived on the basis of a larger sample of engines and observations gathered by the author (Table 5.1).

The chronological distribution of engines in the sample is such as to allow their classification into two groups, encompassing an "early" (1723–32) and a "late" (1756–73) period. The "early" group is comprised of six engines and produces a mean of 38.25 lbs/hp/hour. This figure is very high judged with the hindsight of later developments and it was the outcome of faulty practices both in the construction and management of engines. There were numerous flaws in managing the early engines which have been pointed out extensively in the more technically oriented literature on the subject and thus reviewing them here would be redundant.[12] Some of these flaws, relating for instance to the careful tending of the fire, were easy to correct by spreading the coals evenly over the grate as opposed to placing them in the middle of it. But others were addressed through a gradual improvement in the learning-by-doing process.

The "late" group is comprised of 54 observations from 47 engines, both of the conventional Newcomen design and engines altered or constructed by Smeaton. The weighted mean of the entire "late" group is 29.5 lbs/hp/hour. The decline in fuel consumption is substantial (c. 23 percent) leaving no doubt that the increase in the size of engines did offer the potential of boosting fuel efficiency, an expectation that was abundantly clear in the minds of contemporary engineers.

Noting, however, the absolute decline of fuel consumption by contrasting mean figures on the basis of two samples put together by lumping engines of very diverse powers is not the most sophisticated way of measuring efficiency gains. Instead, the question which ought to be addressed is: given this potential for lower fuel consumption, to what degree were the practices of engineers managing these engines able to achieve the realization of this potential? In other words, what was the extent to which actual fuel consumption levels deviated from Smeaton's "ideal" figures?

Figure 5.1a addresses these questions by incorporating the figures of various engines and contrasting them to Smeaton's "ideal" curve; this figure captures the extent to which fuel consumption deviated from the "ideal" irrespective of the installation year. Figure 5.1b, on the other hand, measures the deviation by focusing on the chronology of installations; points falling above the horizontal axis denote engines with fuel consumption exceeding the "ideal", the reverse for those falling below the axis. Two caveats should be noted. First, there is a sizeable gap in the data between the early 1730s and the mid-1750s. Second, we have to rely on a fairly limited sample of 18 observations, notwithstanding the fact this is still

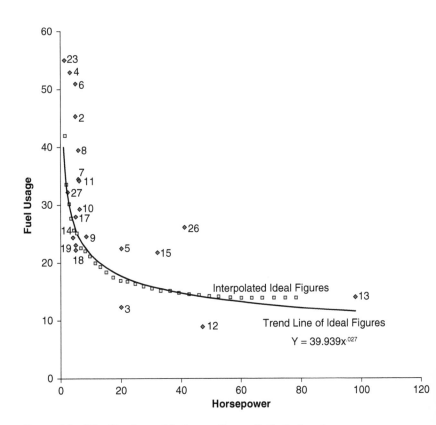

Figure 5.1a "Ideal" and actual fuel usage figures (in lbs/hp/hour)

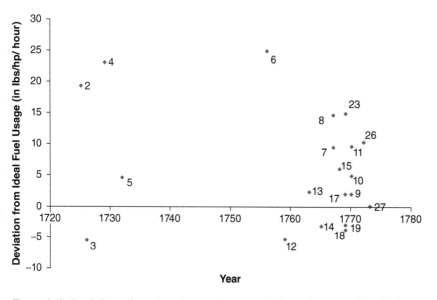

Figure 5.1b Deviations of actual fuel usage from "ideal" figures by year of installation

Sources and explanations: The figures next to the bullet points correspond to the enumeration of the relevant engines in Table 5.1. The sources are cited in the latter table.

a greater amount of evidence compared to the ones other historians have relied on in the past.[13] Notwithstanding these issues, two conclusions, of somewhat different levels of confidence, can be drawn from the regression analysis described in Appendix 5A. First, the more robust results show an inverse relationship between hp and fuel consumption, thereby reinforcing Smeaton's expectations. Second, the reduction in the fuel consumption values is not continuous but presents a somewhat erratic pattern, though this instability is eliminated by 1761–2, thereafter indicating a consistently downward trend and a narrowing gap between "ideal" and actual fuel consumption levels.

Newcomen engines did not go through major improvements until the very end of the period, notwithstanding the enlargement of cylinders and a few other minor exceptions.[14] Additional breakthroughs in addressing the inefficiencies of the engine had to await the appearance of Smeaton. He combined an understanding of scientific principles with empirical acumen, unlike engineers such as Brown and the Hornblowers who could tinker empirically but could not explain why things worked the way they did; or Desaguliers who would pontificate on scientific principles but could not suggest practical solutions. Smeaton relied on observations of conventional Newcomen engines, particularly a sample of 33 of them installed in the Newcastle region and Cornwall. By using sophisticated mathematical inferences, he was able to specify the right proportions of different parts of the engine and to implement certain micro-improvements.[15] Smeaton's alterations were not always sound nor had he progressed far enough by 1773 to make a major contribution to the decline of fuel consumption;[16] the mean value of fuel consumption in the engines he engaged in was virtually identical with the mean value in the rest of the sample (see Table 5.1). Part of the explanation lies with the main structural deficiency of the Newcomen engine, the alternate heating and cooling of the cylinder which, according to one account, resulted in wasting 3/8 of the fuel used for an engine with a 52-inch cylinder.[17] Most importantly, his "innovations do not seem to have been widely copied," or, I would add, refined.[18]

In the absence of major improvements in terms of design and the failure to adopt Smeaton's alterations to a large number of engines, it would not be far-fetched to argue that the more skillful management of engines on a day-to-day basis was a factor of crucial importance. While the ability to construct more powerful engines offered the *potential* of achieving decreases in fuel consumption, it was the distribution of competent managing engineers at the local level that was crucial in realizing this potential. However, as the econometric analysis suggests, the improvement of engineering skills was a long-drawn process which started producing consistent results towards the end of the period. A major factor behind this delay was the asymmetry of skills across regions conditioned by the spatial dispersion of sectors pertinent to the adoption of the engine and the degree to which they offered employment opportunities.

The regions of the country which attracted the largest number of engineers were obviously the coal mining centers of the northeast and the Midlands, the latter area having already a longstanding tradition emanating from the presence of the metal trades. The case of Cornwall exemplifies perhaps best that a region with a limited availability of engineering skills could catch up fairly quickly, particularly once the Hornblowers moved in during the 1740s. Pole convincingly speculated that there was a stronger incentive to improve fuel efficiency in Cornwall than in collieries, the latter having access to very cheap fuel. The literature is peppered with references to numerous attempts to make improvements, mostly regarding the function of the boiler. But better efficiency came about from better attendance of these engines as opposed to technical improvements.[19]

At the other end of the spectrum, engineering skills were the least developed in Scotland which looked right across the border, at the northeastern coalfield, for transfer of technical know-how.[20] The order for the first steam engine at Stevenston colliery was placed in 1719 by the partners leasing the colliery but the installation was delayed for a year because Meres, the leading figure of the syndicate controlling the patent, could not persuade skilled English engineers to go to work in "wet and slavish" Scotland; even the iron boiler had to be supplied by Stonier Parrott from his base in Staffordshire. Such scarcity of skills was bound to be reflected on the level of wages. When eventually Peter Walker was persuaded to move to Ayrshire from Whitehaven he was offered a salary of £1/week, an offer that was extended to managing the engine at a salary of £60/year; nevertheless, he moved back to Whitehaven in December 1720 leaving the construction of the engine unfinished.[21] It was perhaps the dissemination of stories like this which convinced other colliery owners to offer way more generous compensation packages later on. When Andrew Wauchope entered an agreement for the installation of an engine at Edmonstone colliery in 1726 he offered an annual salary of £200/year and half of the net profits of the colliery after all expenses were deducted. The exact same deal was offered a year later to the two engineers who came from Durham to erect the Whitehill engine. What is even more remarkable is that often the price of failure rested exclusively on the shoulders of Scottish colliery owners. In the case of the Edmonstone and Whitehill engines the agreements provided that if the engines failed to work properly, they were to be dismantled, the materials to be taken back to England by the engineers, along with the payment of compensation for their efforts. Such generous compensation packages indicated, according to Bald, "that these engines were very little understood".[22]

Engineering skills and the cost of steam power

The *potential* of reducing fuel consumption was in place in the years following the installation of the more powerful boring mill by Coalbrookdale (1734) and it became even more pronounced when the second mill was installed in 1745. That is not to say that the full potential of the savings offered by more powerful engines was realized the moment these engines entered the market. The Newcomen engine was not constructed on the basis of a plate supplied by a single maker. Instead, parts came from a diverse range of suppliers based on convenience or price; it employed various craftsmen such as carpenters, masons, plumbers, blacksmiths, as well as engineers. Such diversity was bound to produce an asymmetry of skills both in terms of constructing and managing it. But according to Barton, with sufficient time allowed, the engine was simple enough to make it work tolerably well given the existing skills of craftsmen and engineers, assuming a constant supervision by an experienced engineer.[23]

The fact that we witness the first structural break the year after the installation of the second powerful boring mill by Coalbrookdale indicates that the transmission of skills in managing the engines and realizing a significant reduction in cost had gained momentum by then. Reinforcing the validity of this statement is the wider regional and sectoral dispersion of the diffusion pattern achieved by that time.[24] According to the regression results of Appendix 5A, notwithstanding some degree of caution stemming from the limitations of the sample, the realization of potential savings continued to exhibit an erratic pattern but the trend became irreversible by the early 1760s presumably because the improvements in terms of managing the engine hit a critical mass point by that time. By the end of the period fuel consumption was reduced by nearly a quarter (23 percent) which in places like Cornwall would translate to annual savings well exceeding £300 and in London well over £400.[25]

The spread and deepening of engineering skills were of paramount importance in reducing the cost of steam power and, in conjunction with the technical and geographical limitations of other power sources, were a major factor in driving the diffusion process.

Appendix 5A: Engine efficiency evaluation

By Lawrence Costa

We regress a time trend and engine size (size in horsepower that is) on engine efficiency, which is measured in coal usage per horsepower. There is a caveat here in that horsepower and fuel usage values are available for only 18 engines. Given such a small sample size, we must exercise care in interpreting results. By this, we mean that the statistical results here should not be interpreted alone; rather they must be considered in conjunction with anecdotal, non-quantifiable evidence.

With that noted, we may proceed with the analysis. The regression in question is modeled as *Fuel Usage* $= \alpha + \beta_1(Trend) + \beta_2(Horsepower) + \beta_3(Trend^2) + \beta_4(Horsepower^2) + \beta_5(Horsepower\ Trend\ Interaction)$. Standard OLS results are reported in the table below.

We have included several specifications of the regression in Table 5A.1 by excluding certain regressors. However, Wald tests reject the null hypotheses that any coefficients are zero.

As interpretation goes, let us begin by considering the effect of the time trend. This appears to have an overall negative influence (*i.e.*, fuel usage falls as time goes on) but the impact is nonlinear. Notice that the level trend variable has a negative coefficient where it is the only trend variable. But, whenever a squared

Table 5A.1 Engine efficiency regressions

Regression		Constant	Trend	HP	Trend²	HP²	HP*Trend	R²
1	Coefficient	46.146	1.062	−3.377	−0.019	0.006	0.044	0.723
	SE	23.848	1.300	0.790	0.015	0.003	0.013	
	95% upper	57.163	1.663	−3.012	−0.013	0.007	0.050	
	95% lower	35.129	0.462	−3.741	−0.026	0.004	0.037	
2	Coefficient	30.575	0.798	−0.919	−0.011	0.007		0.471
	SE	31.015	1.722	0.348	0.020	0.004		
	95% upper	44.903	1.593	−0.758	−0.002	0.008		
	95% lower	16.247	0.002	−1.080	−0.020	0.005		
3	Coefficient	46.715	−0.141	−0.903		0.007		0.459
	SE	9.420	0.156	0.338		0.004		
	95% upper	51.066	−0.069	−0.747		0.009		
	95% lower	42.363	−0.213	−1.059		0.005		
4	Coefficient	22.062	0.962	−0.331	−0.012			0.339
	SE	33.027	1.852	0.130	−0.021			
	95% upper	37.319	1.818	−0.271	−0.002			
	95% lower	6.804	0.107	−0.391	−0.023			
5	Coefficient	40.362	−0.107	−0.304				0.323
	SE	9.499	0.167	0.119				
	95% upper	44.750	−0.030	−0.249				
	95% lower	35.974	−0.184	−0.359				

trend term is included, the level variable takes a positive sign. Taken in concert with the negative term on the squared trend variable, this could indicate that fuel efficiency worsened for a time before beginning to improve. If we consider the marginal effect of the time trend from regression one, we have

$$\frac{\partial(Fuel\ Usage)}{\partial(Trend)} = \beta_1 + \beta_3(Trend) + \beta_5(Horsepower)$$

$$= 1.062 - 0.019(Trend) + 0.044(Horsepower)$$

where, if we ignore the effect of the interaction term, the trend begins to impact negatively after 55 periods, or around 1761 in our sample. The interaction term, if we use the simple average horsepower of the sample, serves to push this out about one period, or to 1762. However, given the small sample size, it is perhaps best to simply note that fuel efficiency seemed to improve as time went on (though it is possible that things got worse before getting better).

Turning to the horsepower figures, we see a somewhat more straightforward relationship. The level terms are negative throughout the different regression specifications. When included, squared terms take a positive coefficient. Using a similar marginal analysis to the one above, we may write

$$\frac{\partial(Fuel\ Usage)}{\partial(Horsepower)} = \beta_2 + \beta_4(Horsepower) + \beta_5(Trend)$$

$$= -3.337 + 0.006(Horsepower) + 0.044(Trend)$$

where, again ignoring the interaction effect, an increase in horsepower would begin to be correlated with an increase in fuel usage after 556 periods. As this is significantly larger than the sample period, it is safe to conclude that horsepower appears inversely related to fuel usage throughout.

Notes

1 E.g., Nuvolari, et al., "The diffusion of the steam engine in eighteenth century Britain"; idem, "The early diffusion of the steam engine."
2 "The compleat collier", p. 10.
3 As an illustration, an agreement was signed on 10 November 1715 for the installation of an engine at Howgill colliery (Whitehaven) but the working of the engine was delayed until 1717. One of the problems was the delivery of parts. Whitehaven not having much of direct trade with London or Bristol, the construction of the boiler and barrels was consigned to a William Nicholson, formerly a shipmaster and at that time the owner of a public house in Dublin. In another case recorded in 1718, Meres, the most active member of the patent syndicate, offered a prospective buyer a cast iron cylinder up to 24 inch diameter but noted that anything of a larger size would take six months to deliver. See Allen, "The 1715 and other Newcomen engines", p. 245; idem, "Some early Newcomen engines", p. 199.
4 Armytage, *A social history of engineering*, pp. 81–2; see also Lord, *Capital and steam-power*, p. 58.

5 Rolt, *Thomas Newcomen*, p. 83; Rowlands, "Stonier Parrott and the Newcomen engine", pp. 57–8.
6 The engine at Wheal Rose (Cornwall) is said to have been so expensive to run by 1725 that the adventurers drove a mile-and-a-half adit in order to discontinue it despite the fact the mine was very rich; Rogers, *The Newcomen engine*, pp. 16, 18. This alarming attitude was echoed in the writings both of contemporaries and later historians: "The great expense of fuel was still a heavy tax upon the use of the engine, for every one of magnitude consumed £3000 worth of coal per annum; and as the mines were worked lower, and more power became requisite, the expense was frequently so great as to balance the profits of many mines. If therefore new improvements had not arisen, the use of the engine must soon have been limited to those works whose produce was so rich, or profits so great, as to enable them to bear this heavy expense of drainage". Pole, *A treatise on the Cornish pumping engine*, p. 18. The same statement, almost verbatim, can be found In Pryce's appendix to his *Mineralogia Cornubiensis* published in 1778; cited in *The Notched Ingot*, July 1966, p. 19.
7 Bourne, *A treatise on the steam engine*, p. 9; Rolt, *Thomas Newcomen*, pp. 121, 125; Stuart, *Historical and descriptive anecdotes*, p. 303.
8 One 60 inch cylinder engine developed more hp compared to five engines with larger cylinders. See Farey, *A treatise on the steam engine*, p. 234; Mott, "The Newcomen engine in the eighteenth century", pp. 82–3.
9 The table is cited in Farey, *A treatise on the steam engine*, p. 183. It should stressed that Smeaton's figures should not be taken to denote absolute minimum levels of fuel consumption. Instead, they refer to figures corresponding to what he felt was satisfactory efficiency at different levels of hp.
10 *Thomas Newcomen*, p. 125.
11 Smeaton erected engines during the period 1767–84; Stowers, "The development of the atmospheric steam engine", p. 90. See also Scott, *Matthew Murray*, p. 73; Scott "Smeaton's engine of 1767", p. 122; Hodge, *The steam engine*, p. 44; von Tunzelmann *Steam power*, pp. 68–9; Kanefsky, *The diffusion of power technology*, pp. 172–3; Law *The steam engine*, p. 28; Allen, *The British Industrial Revolution*, pp. 164–5, 170–1 Hills, *Power from steam*, pp. 36–7, 131; Crafts, "Steam as a general purpose technology", p. 342; Thurston, "On the maximum contemporary economy of the high-pressure multiple-expansion steam-engine", pp. 313, 315; Thurston, *A manual of the steam engine*, p. 32; Science Museum, *Catalogue of the mechanical engineering collection* p. 29. Some of the figures cited by various authors are expressed in duty which was converted to fuel consumption. This is done by dividing the number 1,980,000 by the duty figure. If the duty is expressed in units other than lbs the conversion has to be made first from that unit (e.g., cwt) to lbs. Or, divide 166.32 by the duty in millions of lbs to find fuel consumption in lbs/hp/hour. See Clark, *The steam engine*, pp. 3–4 Bourne, *A catechism of the steam engine*, p. 109.
12 Some of them were the following: boilers were often small, badly constructed, and placed too far from the fire; the injection cistern was often placed too low and thus water was inadequately dispersed within the cylinder; the amount of water required for condensation was underestimated; the valve gearing was poorly constructed causing the steam admission valve to not open fully. See Bourne, *A treatise on the steam engine*, p. 9; Rolt, *Thomas Newcomen*, p. 127; Mott, "The Newcomen engine in the eighteenth century", pp. 82–3.
13 In order to incorporate engines in Figures 5.1a and 5.1b their hp has to be known. However, that is not always the case (see Table 5.1).
14 Savery engines were operated with simple plug valves, turned by hand four times minute, and the very early Newcomen engines worked by the same method. But by 1719, perhaps as early as 1712, an automatic plug valve gear worked by a plug rod connected to the beam was in place. The names of Henry Beighton and Humphrey

Potter have been discussed in relation to this improvement. See Science Museum, *Catalogue of the collections*, p. 70; Science Museum, *Catalogue of the mechanical engineering collection*, p. 28.

15 Among the alterations he implemented, for instance, in the New River Head engine (1769) were the following: he increased the piston load; shifted the pivot on the working beam a bit off-center; used larger pumps; wrapped the cylinder and piston with cloth to minimize heat loss; and made the cylinder tall and smaller in diameter hoping to achieve easier condensation. The combined result was to increase the speed of the engine, raising more water with less fuel. Some other changes he brought in included sheathing the under side of the piston with water which prevented condensation by the water lying on top of it. He also discovered that, surprisingly, some of the steam in the cylinder should be left uncondensed in each cycle. It was a matter of a cost-benefit analysis, so to speak. There was the benefit of achieving complete condensation by having the atmosphere exert its full 15 lbs per square inch force. But cooling the engine down to a perfect vacuum would require so much heat to warm it up again that the net effect in terms of fuel economy would be negative. He also discovered that allowing a slight leakage of air into the cylinder allowed this air to act as an effective insulating layer between the working steam and cool metal and thus reduced the loss of steam due to excessive steam condensation. See Cardwell, *Turning points*, p. 83; Bourne, *A treatise on the steam engine*, pp. 7, 9; Farey, *A treatise on the steam engine*, p. 233–4; von Tunzelmann, *Steam power*, pp. 17–8; Rolt, *Thomas Newcomen*, p. 125–7; Stowers, "The development of the atmospheric steam engine", p. 90; Halsey, "The choice between high-pressure and low-pressure steam power", p. 734.

16 Contrary to one of his alterations, some authors have argued that it is better to have a larger piston and a smaller stroke because it decreases the amount of friction in proportion to the area of the cylinder. See Partington, *A course of lectures*, p. 41; Hodge, *The steam engine*, p. 40.

17 Farey, *A treatise on the steam engine*, p. 308.

18 Tann, "The steam engine on Tyneside", p. 56.

19 Pole, *A treatise on the Cornish pumping engine*, pp. 17–18; Rolt, *Thomas Newcomen*, pp. 60–1; Rogers, *The Newcomen engine*, p. 16.

20 For instance, when John Earl of Mar developed an interest in improving his collieries in Clackmannanshire he sent his manager to the Newcastle region in 1709 to inspect water-draining machinery; see Fordyce, *A history of coal, coke, coal fields*, p. 16.

21 His hiring caused an alarm to coal masters in Whitehaven due to the intense competition between them and their counterparts in Ayrshire for the Dublin market which the former had dominated up to that point. See Flinn, *The history of the British coal industry*, p. 118 (where the quote is cited); Rolt and Allen, *The steam engine of Thomas Newcomen*, p. 68; Whatley, "The introduction of the Newcomen engine in Ayrshire", p. 71. In a letter written by John Spedding, agent of Howgill colliery (Whitehaven) in 1719 or 1720 the following remark was made: "in all the time our engine has bin at work [since 1717] there is nobody that can undertake the management or is in the least capable of putting any thing to rights when out of order except P. Walker and my Brother [Carlisle]"; cited in Allen, "The 1715 and other Newcomen engines," p. 253.

22 Bald, *A general view of the coal trade of Scotland*, pp. 20, 22–3, 167–9, 171 (quote from p. 22). On the other hand, Stuart suggested that the proprietors entered into these onerous terms because they were desperate since the quantity of water to be drained was often so large as to render mines inoperative; see *Historical and descriptive anecdotes*, p. 621. This factor, however, could simply exacerbate the problem posed by the scarcity of engineering skills.

23 Barton, *The Cornish beam engine*, p. 19; see also Raistrick, *Dynasty of ironfounders*, p. 128.

24 See Nuvolari et al., "Early diffusion."

25 See the figures of fuel bills in such locations cited in Chapter 4.

Bibliography

Allen, J. S., "Some early Newcomen engines and the legal disputes surrounding them", *Transactions of the Newcomen Society*, 41 (1968–9), pp. 181–201.

Allen, J. S., "The introduction of the Newcomen engine from 1710 to 1733: second addendum", *Transactions of the Newcomen Society*, 45 (1972–3), pp. 223–6.

Allen, J. S., "The 1715 and other Newcomen engines at Whitehaven, Cumberland", *Transactions of the Newcomen Society*, 45 (1972–3), pp. 237–68.

Allen, R., *The British Industrial Revolution in global perspective* (Cambridge: Cambridge University Press, 2009).

Armytage, W. H. G., *A social history of engineering*, 4th ed. (London: Faber and Faber, 1976).

Bald, R., *A general view of the coal trade of Scotland* (Edinburgh: Oliphant & Brown, 1808).

Band, S., "The steam engines of Gregory mine, Ashover", *Bulletin of the Peak District Mines Historical Society*, 8, 5 (Summer 1983), pp. 269–95.

Barton, D. B., *The Cornish beam engine* (Exeter: Cornwall Books, 1989).

Bourne, J., *A catechism of the steam engine,* 5th ed. (New York: D. Appleton & Co., 1864).

Bourne, J., *A treatise on the steam engine in its application to mines, mills, steam navigation,and railways* (London: Longman Brown Green & Longmans, 1846).

Cardwell D. S. L., *Turning points in western technology* (New York: Science History Publications, 1972).

Clark, D. K., *The steam engine: a treatise on steam engines and boilers* (London, Glasgow, Edinburgh, and New York: Blackie & Son, 1891).

Clayton, A. K., "The Newcomen–type engine at Elsecar, West Riding", *Transactions of the Newcomen Society*, 35 (1962–3), pp. 97–108.

Crafts, N. F. R., "Steam as a general purpose technology: a growth accounting perspective", *Economic Journal*, 114 (2004), pp. 338–51.

Fairbairn, W., *Treatise on mills and millwork, Part I: On the principles of mechanism and on prime movers* (London: Longman, Green, 1864).

Farey, J., *A treatise on the steam engine, historical, practical and descriptive* (London: Longman, Rees, Orme, Brown, and Green, 1827).

Flinn, M. W., *The history of the British coal industry, Vol. 2, 1700–1830: The Industrial Revolution* (Oxford: Clarendon Press, 1984).

Fordyce, W., *A history of coal, coke, coal fields* . . . (London: S. Low, Son, and Co.; New York, Scribner & Co, 1860).

Galloway, R. L., *The steam engine and its inventors; a historical sketch* (London: Macmillan, 1881).

Halsey, H. I., "The choice between high–pressure and low-pressure steam power in America in the early nineteenth century", *Journal of Economic History*, 41, 4 (1981), pp. 723–44.

Harris, J. R., "The employment of steam power in the eighteenth century", *History*, 70 (1967), pp. 133–48.

Hills, R. L., *Power from steam: a history of the stationary steam engine* (Cambridge; New York: Cambridge University Press, 1989).

Hodge, P. R., *The steam engine; its origin and gradual improvement, from the time of Hero to the present day* (New York: D. Appleton, 1840).

J. C., *The compleat collier or the whole art of sinking, getting, and working coal-mines as is now used in the northern parts, especially about Sunderland and Newcastle* (London: Printed for George Conyers, 1708).

Kanefsky, J. W., *The diffusion of power technology in British industry 1760–1870* (Ph. D. thesis, University of Exeter, 1979).

Law, R. J., *The steam engine; a brief history of the reciprocating engine* (London: H.M. Stationery Office, 1965).

Lord, J., *Capital and steam-power, 1750–1800*, 2nd ed. (London: Cass, 1966).

Mott, R. A., "The Newcomen engine in the eighteenth century", *Transactions of the Newcomen Society*, 35 (1962–3), pp. 69–86.

Notched Ingot, The, "After Newcomen" (July 1966), pp. 17–19.

Nuvolari, A., B. Verspagen, and G. N. von Tunzelmann, "The diffusion of the steam engine in eighteenth century Britain", in Pyka and Hanusch, eds., *Applied evolutionary economics*, pp. 166–200.

Nuvolari, A., B. Verspagen, and G. N. von Tunzelmann, "The early diffusion of the steam engine in Britain, 1700–1800. A reappraisal", *Cliometrica*, 5 (2011), pp. 291–321.

Partington, C. F., *A course of lectures on the steam engine* (London: G. Virtue, 1826).

Pole, W., *A treatise on the Cornish pumping engine* (London: John Weale, 1844).

Pyka, A., and H. Hanusch, eds., *Applied evolutionary economics and the knowledge-based economy* (Cheltenham, UK: Edward Elgar, 2006).

Raistrick, A., *Dynasty of ironfounders: the Darbys and Coalbrookdale* (London, New York and Toronto: Longmans, Green & Company, 1953).

Rhodes, J. N., "Early steam engines in Flintshire", *Transactions of the Newcomen Society*, 41 (1968–9), pp. 217–25.

Rogers, K. H., *The Newcomen engine in the west of England* (Bradford-on-Avon: Moonraker Press, 1976).

Rolt, L. T. C., *Thomas Newcomen: the prehistory of the steam engine* (Dawlish, Eng.: David and Charles, 1963).

Rolt, L. T. C., and J. S. Allen, *The steam engine of Thomas Newcomen* (New York: Science History Publications, 1977).

Rowlands, M. B., "Stonier Parrott and the Newcomen engine", *Transactions of the Newcomen Society*, 41 (1968–9), pp. 49–67.

Russell, J. S., *A treatise on the steam engine: from the seventh edition of the Encyclopaedia Britannica* (Edinburgh: A. and C. Black, 1846).

Science Museum, *Catalogue of the collections in the Science Museum South Kensington, with descriptive and historical notes and illustrations. Stationary engines*, comp. By H. W. Dickinson (London, 1925).

Science Museum, *Catalogue of the mechanical engineering collection in the Science Museum, South Kensington, with descriptive and historical notes*, 6th ed. (London, 1919–).

Kilburn, S. E., *Matthew Murray: pioneer engineer, records from 1765 to 1826* (Leeds: Jowett Ltd., 1928).

Kilburn, S. E., "Smeaton's engine of 1767 at New River Head, London", *Transactions of the Newcomen Society*, 19, 1938–9, pp. 119–26.

Stowers, A., "The development of the atmospheric steam engine after Newcomen's death in 1729", *Transactions of the Newcomen Society*, 35 (1962–3), pp. 87–96.

Stuart (Meikleham), R., *Historical and descriptive anecdotes of steam engines* (London: John Knight and Henry Lacey, 1829).

Tann, J., "The steam engine on Tyneside in the Industrial Revolution", *Transactions of the Newcomen Society*, 64 (1992–3), pp. 53–75.

Thurston, R. H., *A manual of the steam-engine. For engineers and technical schools; advanced courses, Part I, Structure and theory* (New York: John Wiley, 1907).

Thurston, R. H., "On the maximum contemporary economy of the high-pressure multiple-expansion steam-engine", *Transactions of the American Society of Mechanical Engineers*, XV (1983), pp. 313 et seq.

Von Tunzelmann, G. N., *Steam power and British industrialization to 1860* (Oxford: Clarendon Press, 1978).

Whatley, C. A., "The introduction of the Newcomen engine to Ayrshire", *Industrial Archaeology Review*, 2 (1965), pp. 69–77.

White, A. W. A., "Early Newcomen engines on the Warwickshire coalfield, 1714–1736", *Transactions of the Newcomen Society*, 41 (1968–69), pp. 203–16.

6 Firm size and market demand as determinants of diffusion

The role of the threshold (minimum) level of output

The behavior of the cost of steam power, conditioned by factors such as the improvement of engineering skills and the presence of the premium, was one of the primary determinants of the diffusion process on the supply side. But demand considerations were also of paramount importance. The installation of a Newcomen engine, along with the ancillary costs it entailed, was an expensive affair. It raised the fixed cost of investment projects as well as the productive capacity of firms and, by doing so, it defined a threshold level of output at which marginal cost and marginal revenues became equal. This threshold level of output specified the minimum scale of operation that would justify investment on a steam engine. Getting there, however, was not a straightforward process. Existing transportation networks created market fragmentation in product markets; hence the geographical location of firms in the context of particular markets played a crucial role by justifying (or not) the attainment of the threshold level of output. It will be argued that while the expiration of the patent and the radical reduction of cost due to the appearance of larger engines moved the diffusion process forward, the impediments posed by market configurations proved to be a more intractable problem holding back the adoption rate of engines.

Despite the obvious relevance of demand factors, the literature has largely neglected this issue. One may come across references to market conditions becoming a matter of consideration for the adoption of particular engines. But there is not a single prior attempt to outline a comprehensive theoretical framework in which the role of market fragmentation and the constraints it imposed on the size of firms conditioned their ability to adopt steam engines. This chapter will attempt to fill this void by considering the top two sectors in terms of steam power diffusion: mining, with particular emphasis on collieries, as well as the iron industry in relation to the adoption of engines in the production process of blast furnaces.

The mining sector

Once steam power became available in collieries allowing extraction from greater depths, cost shot up substantially because of not only the purchase of engines but also the installation of more powerful winding machinery, underground haulage equipment, and better ventilation. Flinn estimated, from a small sample of engines installed during the period 1729–65, that their purchase cost was a mere 35.7 percent of the total capital cost for the creation of pits they served.[1] Following Flinn's estimate and given the purchase price of an engine in the 1740s onwards (£1,750), the desire to expand output by sinking into greater depths translated to an initial fixed cost of £4,900. The subsequent operating cost of extraction per 1,000 tons of coal was calculated by Pollard at £22.6 for the largest collieries (which he defines as those producing in the range of 15–25,000 tons/year or above); the cost was somewhat smaller for medium-sized collieries producing below that range of output, at £20.3 per 1,000 tons.[2] Figure 6.1 draws the marginal cost (MC) lines for both types of collieries based on the above information. I also adds the marginal revenue (MR) lines based on coal price data provided by Ashton and Sykes. The mean price per ton was £0.23 during the period 1740–71 but the range of deviations from this figure are also taken into account by drawing the MRmax and MRmin lines.

The threshold point where MR = MC corresponds to an annual output of nearly 23,000 tons.[3] Proper sensitivity analysis would dictate the specification of upper and lower-bound limits; however, it is not feasible given the data limitations. For

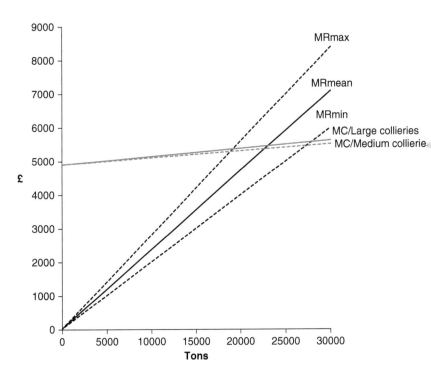

Figure 6.1 Marginal cost and marginal revenue for large and medium collieries following the installation of an engine

Sources: Ashton and Sykes, *The coal industry*, p. 252; Pollard, "Coal mining," pp. 37–49.

instance, we do have a good sense of the purchase price of engines prior to the 1740s but not estimates on marginal cost. Nor do we have plentiful data, regardless of the time period, on how much ancillary costs (e.g., sinking of shafts) added to the cost of an engine. However, these caveats, particularly those relating to the lack of plentiful data, should not be overstated. After all, Pollard's figures regarding the dividing range between large and medium-sized collieries (15–25,000 tons/year) encompasses the figure of the threshold level of output specified here.

The specification of the threshold level of output should not be viewed as a rigid dividing line. The prospect of increasing output precisely due to this capital investment by reaching deeper seams meant that the undertaking was justified even for collieries that achieved an annual output which approached the threshold point prior to the investment and/or because of high levels of profitability. The ability of collieries to reach and/or approach the threshold level of output hinged on three factors: first, on the presence of a low-cost transportation network; second, whether this network linked a colliery with industries or households generating a high level of demand; and, third, the degree of competition within particular markets. Two broad categories can be discerned based on the first of these factors, i.e., whether the colliery had access to low-cost water routes as opposed to overland transportation; but significant variation existed within each category depending on the configuration of the other two factors.

The first category in which these factors converged in the most favorable way encompasses the northeastern collieries with their access to low-cost sea routes linking them with the lucrative London market.[4] Such collieries were ranked among the most highly capitalized businesses at the time, reaching output levels well beyond the threshold. At the top of the pyramid were collieries such as Long Benton whose output from just one pit (Lane) was c. 45,000 tons per annum, on average, during the period 1748–50.[5] While the vast majority of the largest collieries were located in the northeast, few outliers could be found elsewhere. One such instance was collieries in the Halkyn mountains of Flintshire (e.g., Trelogan, Pant Vein) which were exceptionally rich in coal.[6]

In some other cases the critical factors that determined the level of output were not all quite as favorable. For instance, three collieries (Broseley, Benthall, and Barr) dominated coal traffic along the Severn, taking advantage of a low transportation route and dealing with a robust level of demand but not quite comparable to that of collieries in the northeast. In such cases, reaching the threshold level of output, and therefore justifying the purchase of an engine, was a more ambivalent affair.[7] Such mines comprised the bottom layer in this category of large collieries.

A second broad category refers to landlocked collieries without access to sea routes facing a fairly high transportation cost but variable levels of demand depending on their location. In this case a critical factor was whether the existing transportation network created a localized market that resembled a pocket, insulating collieries from outside competition. A very well documented case in point is the collieries owned by the family of Jonathan Case in Merseyside. Their location near the chief regional markets of Liverpool and the saltfields, the insulation provided by poor communication channels precluding penetration by collieries from the eastern edge of the coalfield, and the ability to attract outside capital, all contributed to the installation of an engine at Whiston colliery in 1719. The transportation parameters, however, changed once the Prescott–St. Helens turn-pike (1746) and the Sankey canal (1755) were constructed. Competition became intense and, coupled with the creation of a debt whose settlement forced the sale of some collieries by Thomas Case, the son of Jonathan, it marked the end of the brief period of prosperity. According to Harris, the experience of this family reflects the precariousness of business affairs in the eighteenth century and the potential of the purchase of the steam engine contributing to high indebtedness. Such lessons were quickly learned by others thereby explaining the failure of the engine to be widely adopted until thirty years after the erection of the Whiston engine in the context of the

> smaller scale and poorer markets of the industry on Merseyside . . . The pull of the market, the ability of the industry to attract capital, and the incentives to deeper working were here not sufficient to call for the employment of the costly engine in anything like the same degree [as in the Newcastle coalfield]. Even after the Savery patent expired in the 1730s, and the premium was no longer an issue, there was a delay before it became extensively adopted.[8]

The more widespread adoption of the engine was fostered when commercial conditions expanded in relation to the coal markets of Liverpool and Cheshire. This expansion started at the Prescott end of the coalfield with an engine installed in 1740 at Prescott Hall colliery and a second one in 1753.[9] The adoption of the engine at the St Helens section of the coalfield came after the turnpiking of the road to Prescott but prior to the construction of the canal. The first one was probably at Eccleston colliery in 1751 but it was a short-lived affair; but soon others followed especially after the opening of the canal.

A similar case was Bedworth colliery, located near the junction of two heavily traveled roads and 5–6 miles from Coventry, achieving an output in the range of 20–30,000 tons at the dawn of the steam era; this was considered the most important colliery in the area at that time. But even in this case "the primitive road system which existed in the first part of the eighteenth century imposed its own limits on the market for coal produced in the Bedworth-Nuneaton area"; however, it eventually did install an engine with some delay, in 1726.[10]

These two examples illustrate conditions that would allow some landlocked collieries to reach the threshold level of output. However, for the majority of landlocked collieries the attainment of such a scale of operations was not feasible, primarily because of the more considerable distances involved in relation to urban centers and/or low population densities. One such illustration is Elland colliery, located south of Halifax. The price of carriage to places like Wakefield, Leeds, or Bradford, at distances of 10 miles or more, would have raised the price at levels double or triple what could be offered from collieries located nearer these towns, hence forcing it to operate at a low scale. Similarly, statistics referring to 35 inland collieries in Durham reveal that their average output was

5,600 tons/year. The same principle applied to collieries at Beaudesert or Dudley in the context of Staffordshire or collieries at Wigan, St Helens, or Bolton in the context of Lancashire. In all these locations, the ability to sell was determined by distance and not by how low the pithead price was. According to Nef, there were scores of inland collieries all through Yorkshire, Lancashire, and the Midlands following the restoration whose output was 2,000–5,000 tons.[11]

The crucial role of demand factors and transportation cost is revealed in a much starker and more dramatic fashion in the case of Scotland.[12] Scotland was a poor country though living standards were improving in the course of the eighteenth century. Coal sales for household consumption would be mainly directed to Glasgow and Edinburgh, both well placed near collieries (4 and 5.5 miles away respectively) and to a lesser extent to places like Dundee, Aberdeen, and Inverness. Part of the demand would be satisfied by the Newcastle coalfield up as far as the Forth but the presence of the 3s 6d per ton tax on all sea-coal depressed the level of sales to the point that even by 1775, according to a parliamentary committee, no more than £3,000 was collected from taxes. Peat remained the favorite choice, although intense use created a growing scarcity. The level of demand was such that scores of colliery owners abandoned the idea of installing an engine. John Gray, the owner of Westmuir colliery, opted instead to erect a windmill in 1737. Sir John Clerk II wrote in his journal enthusiastically about the Newcomen engine following an inspection of Richard Ridley's collieries in Newcastle; however, he was also dissuaded due to the low scale of his operations imposed by market limitations. The owners of Bo'ness colliery contemplated the purchase of a steam engine in 1734 after getting an estimate for £1,500 but they opted out.[13]

But the case of Ayrshire, and particularly of Stevenston colliery, was radically different.[14] The region possessed rich seams, and this persuaded the owners (the Cunninghames) to engage, as early as 1678, in sophisticated mineral surveys, drainage projects, and the construction of a harbor at Saltcoats. The investment proved very costly, forcing the sale of a large part of the estate in order to focus on mineral resources, despite aid received by the government and local landowners. Ayrshire was predominantly rural and, despite some signs of industrialization during the eighteenth century, local demand was trivial due to high transportation cost; in a typical week during the 1720s, Stevenston colliery sold only 2.5 loads (8 loads = 1 ton) at the county level. Instead, it was demand from Ireland that drove the aforementioned capital formation, at times being three times higher compared to supply, driving prices to high levels. Whitehaven across the border contributed substantially to the supply. Ayrshire and Cumberland are the same distance from Ireland but Whitehaven interests dominated the market, though Ayrshire managed occasionally to worry their rivals, at one point capturing 16 percent of the market.

By 1720 demand was high enough to justify the installation of the first engine at Stevenston colliery, erected by John Potter of Durham who was the northern agent of the patent proprietors. The hope was to reach a very thick seam of 7 ft (Parrot coal) found at a depth of 20 fathoms. However, the engine proved ineffective in reaching depths beyond 16 fathoms. Such depth was not remarkable but it has to be borne in mind that the pits were very near sea water and thus prone to excessive flooding. The problems with the engine and financial difficulties of the lessees led them to give up the management of the seams and the latter was taken over by Potter and Daniel Peck. The new partners invested heavily, £1,670 by 1723, and built a larger engine in 1721 that was capable of reaching the rich seam at 20 fathoms. Shortly thereafter trade with Ireland took off, the number of ships increased from 20 to 33, with their capacity also increasing, and exports reached 21–25,000 tons (compared to 1,400 tons in 1691). In January 1723, one of their main rivals on the English side (Spedding) revealed in a letter that he was alarmed by the progress made by Ayrshire, reflecting a widespread feeling that Whitehaven might be overshadowed. All in all, five engines were installed during the period 1720–47. Exports slackened a bit by the middle of the century and engine installation came to a halt; but they picked up again and three more engines were installed between 1768 and 1771; Cumberland, on the other hand, had installed nine engines during this time. The story of the Stevenston colliery proves that despite the lack of a local engineering tradition, if market conditions were robust and the flooding problem was serious enough, though manageable, capitalists involved in this sector were prepared to spend large sums of money to seize opportunities. Most importantly, it illustrates that the figure specified as the threshold level of output is roughly accurate. The second, more effective, engine was installed on the expectation that the expansion of output would lead to reaching the threshold figure, as it did.

"Coal-mining was generally a very profitable business for those fortunate enough to occupy coal-bearing land or willing to risk the relatively large sums of capital essential for successful enterprise." But scattered profit rates and figures cited by Flinn suggest that there were plenty of collieries for which the purchase of an engine and contingent equipment was out of the question due to their limited operating scale.[15] And Barker and Harris capture the importance of these factors by noting that the engine's "arrival on any coalfield was essentially depended on the market value of the coal and on the degree of capital available for investment".[16] Transportation networks were such as to create market fragmentation and the level of demand within each pocket was critical in determining the scale of operation and thus the ability to install an engine.

The cost of the engine and related expenses acted as an entry barrier elsewhere in the mining sector, such as the lead mines of Derbyshire. Rich veins had been discovered from the seventeenth century onwards but the problem of water drainage was often a recurrent and difficult one. Various pumping devices and adits were used, the latter proving effective when it came to draining the upper strata. The Newcomen engine had the potential of making a significant dent in solving the problem, particularly in light of the fact that lead mine operators had access to good coal supplies, allowing them to keep operating costs fairly low. The decision to install an engine would become clearly justified by the discovery of rich seams; the used engine that was purchased from Mill Close mine in 1768 and erected at Gregory mine was the direct result of coming across some rich deposits generating substantial profits.[17]

But the ownership structure of these mines was such as to render investment in a steam engine a difficult task. The mines adopted the book system of 24 shares which were often purchased by men of limited financial means such as smelters and lead merchants. "The [installation] cost of a pumping engine was often so crippling that even when much rich ore was mined and sold, there was little profit."[18] However, local businessmen proved quite innovative in dealing with such matters. An interesting arrangement was struck regarding the erection of the Maeslygan engine in 1735. The mines were owned by the London Lead Company which, in an effort to cope with the high cost of installation, came to an agreement with another lead company to its west in order to share the fixed and operating cost of the engine. The neighbors agreed to pay £600 towards the cost of sinking the shaft and building the engine and to pay another £350 per quarter for having the right to work the engine; or pay £60 annually in the event that the London Lead Company ceased its operations there.[19] In light of such schemes, it is not surprising that Derbyshire became the county with the sixth-highest rate of diffusion by 1773.

The cost of the engine was also an issue in Cornwall in the context of the local metal mining industry which presented wide variations in the rate of capitalization of local companies and also having to contend with the high cost of fuel coming from Wales as well as the duty on coal which was in place until 1741.[20] In a petition to Parliament seeking to abolish the latter, the signatories noted that copper and tin mining would virtually disappear in the absence of new lodes, hence the need to work the old ones economically.[21] Cornwall was one of the pioneering counties at the dawn of the steam era but adoption quickly came to a halt because of the problems posed by the small scale of many mines and the high cost of fuel; being unable to afford an engine, they reverted to water power and adits to deal with drainage problems.

But there were obviously exceptions on the other side of the spectrum. According to a statement by Watson, a "very old" mine (the North Downs copper mine) in Redruth made a profit upwards of £100,000 during the period 1718–58.[22] It is not specified whether the figure refers to gross or net profits but it amounts to an annual average of £2,500. Given such figures, it is not surprising that this mine erected an engine in 1747, a second one in 1756, and a third one in 1763. According to Barton, it was the abolition of the duty in 1741 and the growth of demand for Cornish copper due to the onset of widespread European war that led to a resurgence in the exploitation of Cornish mines and renewed interest in the erection of engines made evident by Hornblower coming to the county (with his two sons) in 1745, as well as John Wise, John Nancarrow and others.[23]

Blast furnaces

A similar issue of entry barriers existed in the iron industry where the diffusion of steam power was closely connected with the introduction of new coke blast furnaces and revolved around the cost of producing pig iron by using steam power as opposed to doing so in charcoal furnaces.

The average total cost (ATC) of producing a ton of pig iron in charcoal furnaces in the first half of the century ranged from a little over £4 to c. £6.50–7, with selling prices in the range of £5–6; the former sometimes exceeded the latter but pig iron was an intermediate product and hence what mattered was the profitability of bar iron.[24]

These figures can only be compared with those at Coalbrookdale, the only firm working with coke at the time. The company worked its two furnaces (named New and Old) with water wheels. Production was characterized by the usual volatility with peaks in the winter and troughs in the summer. With an annual output of 202 tons per furnace, ATC oscillated in the range of £7.66–10.81 in 1709–32 with a mean of £8.50, well above comparable figures for charcoal furnaces. During the years 1733–4 the company faced a decline of power to the furnaces due to severe drought. At the same time, there was an expansion of demand for pig iron in Bristol and the building up of the trade for engine and pipe castings. In the face of this increased demand and power shortages, the company was forced to engage in efficiency improvements that came about through learning-by-doing, better organization, and an improved device for pumping water using horses.[25] As a result, output per furnace rose to c. 300 tons per year during the period 1735–8 and ATC dropped to £6.70. By the late 1730s the ATC of coke furnaces approached the upper end of the cost range of charcoal furnaces but remained clearly higher compared to their variable cost.[26] The sole reason Coalbrookdale was able to stay in business in the first half of the century despite its higher prices is because of its patented innovation of thin-walled castings.[27]

The event that turned the tide was the installation of the first water-returning steam engine in the early 1740s and the erection of four larger furnaces at Kettley and Horsehay during the years 1754–8, all operated with steam engines. Output figures per furnace went up in the range of 600–800 tons in the period 1755–61 leading to another precipitous decline of ATC, down to £4.16 (selling price at £6.53), mainly due to the economizing of coal and labor. Output per furnace witnessed a decline during 1767–73, though the figures were still quite substantial at c. 540 to over 600 tons; ATC stood at £3.91 in 1767–74 (selling price at £6.14).[28]

In contrast, in the years following 1750 the unit variable cost of charcoal furnaces became higher compared to the ATC of coke furnaces and the gap was quite substantial by the end of the decade. Charcoal furnaces had a variable unit cost of £4.50 or higher in the 1750s, rising to £5.50 or higher in the 1760s. The most likely reason was a sharp increase in the demand for iron, leading producers to try to meet that demand but in the process driving up the prices of inputs with an inelastic supply such as charcoal whose price increased by 50 percent between the 1740s and 1760s. The combination of a stagnant technology and rising input prices led to the increase in charcoal pig iron prices.[29]

Figure 6.2 provides a visual impression of how the cost trajectories of the two types of furnaces evolved. By the 1750s the ATC of coke iron was below the variable cost of charcoal iron; and in the case of very efficient producers, such as some Welsh furnaces, the gap was more than £2.[30] The cost scissors between the two types of furnaces became increasingly wider. The productivity gains scored

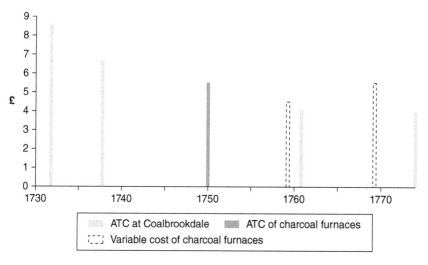

Figure 6.2 Variable and average total cost per ton of pig iron in charcoal furnaces vs. Coalbrookdale

For sources, see text. Notes: Some of the values are means of a wider range. The figures for the variable unit cost of charcoal furnaces are minimum values whereas the ATC of certain, more efficient, coke blast furnaces towards the end of the period was lower compared to Coalbrookdale; hence the bars from c. 1760 onwards underestimate the widening cost differential of the two methods.

by coke furnaces stemmed from steam providing a stronger blast in the context of larger furnaces, reducing seasonal interruptions, increasing output, savings in the use of inputs and, in the end, reducing unit cost. On the other hand, the use of charcoal could not support a heavier "charge" due to its lower internal temperature compared to coke. Output increases were far more modest and were more than counterbalanced by the rise in the price of charcoal.[31] The cost trajectories of the two methods conditioned construction activity. While there were only three coke furnaces c. 1750, the figure rose to 14 a decade later and 30 by c. 1775.[32]

There is no doubt that the use of Newcomen engines became closely connected with the erection of coke furnaces; the latter "served to speed diffusion of the new technique".[33] Despite the gains, however, the proportion of steam engines utilized in this sector approached, but did not quite reach, one-third of the total number of installed furnaces by the end of the period.[34] In other words, the question to be addressed is why the diffusion of steam power in the iron industry was not faster. Part of the explanation lies in the high demand for pig iron which "dragged" the prices of charcoal pig to levels which still allowed profits to be made, albeit shrinking. But another factor of great importance was that the investment cost involved in the installation of a coke furnace operated by steam power must have loomed large in the minds of business owners.

The two Horsehay coke furnaces cost £3,810 each while their counterparts at Dowlais and Plymouth each bore a figure of £4,000.[35] If we take the latter figure as representative of the installation cost c. 1770 and add the cost of what was a typical steam engine at the time (c. 25 hp), then the total comes to £5,750. This figure is certainly an underestimate. Extra cost may have been involved in extending the road and track network as well as other appurtenances. Moreover, the power of steam engines installed in blast furnaces was more likely higher than 25 hp. The two engines installed at Horsehay in the 1750s were of 30 and 45 hp and, judging from the size of cylinders of other engines installed, their power was also, by and large, higher than the figure on which I am relying; by implication their purchase and installation costs would have been more than £1,750.[36]

Figure 6.3 provides a visual impression of the levels of output that had to be reached in three coke furnaces in order to get MR equal to MC. The respective threshold output levels ranged from 2,578 to 3,285 tons. When divided by the annual output of these furnaces, the time it would take to defray the cost of the original investment in a coke blast furnace and a steam engine is virtually identical, almost 4.5 years in each case; and, given the underestimation bias regarding the original cost, the amount of time involved was very likely higher.[37]

The cost of the original investment could be financed by means of one of two possible methods. One way was through the profits generated by charcoal furnaces. Scattered data from throughout the period indicate that such a task would have been quite difficult. The book profit of Leighton furnace during the year November 1717 to October 1718 was £1,965, while in 1716 the profits of the company "from all sources", including forges, was £3,850. This, however, was an exceptional period of growth coinciding with the interruption of trade with Sweden which led to a boost in the production levels of domestic iron. The annual profits of Chapell furnace seem to have been more typical; they stood at over £200 in the late 1740s but became feeble and more variable in the period 1755–62 averaging c. £90. The profit/loss account of Bank furnace also exhibited wide variability in the period 1706–43, ranging from –£259 to £827 but with a mean figure at c. £198. Furnaces were part of integrated concerns, with forges most likely generating more substantial profits; it was out of the latter that large investments had to be financed.[38]

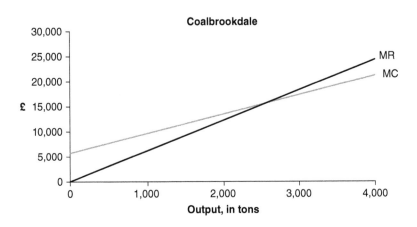

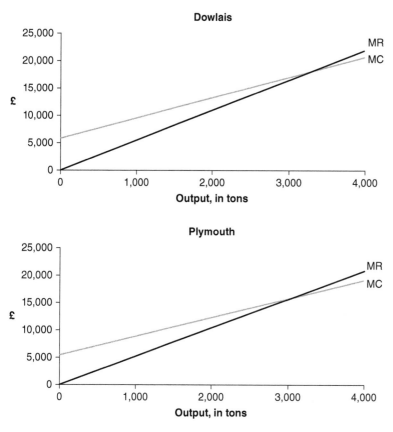

Figure 6.3 The threshold output level at which MR = MC following construction of a coke
    blast furnace and the installation of a steam engine c. 1770

Source: See text. The Coalbrookdale figures refer to 1767–73, for Dowlais to 1770–5, and for Plymouth
to 1766.

The second way was by the partners of the firm digging into their pockets;
and the digging had to be deep. Most coke smelting businesses involved less than
eight partners, in many cases requiring a contribution of c. £1,000 from each one
to undertake an investment of such scale, a very substantial amount for the time.

In the end, "the size of the investment needed to build and operate a coke furnace was another significant barrier to entry" which "slowed the flow of resources
into the coke-smelting sector" and, in conjunction with it, the adoption of steam
power.[39] This factor carried more weight in the iron industry than in collieries. In
the latter case a medium-sized colliery would be able to get to the threshold level
of output within a year; in contrast, in the case of blast furnaces the amount of
time involved was nearly fivefold. These differences were crucial in explaining
why the diffusion of steam power reached by the early 1770s approximately half

of the potential rate of adoption in the mining sector, in fact more so in collieries, but not quite one-third in the case of the iron industry.

Notes

1   The engine at North Wood colliery cost £1,000 (1753) but the inclusion of the cost of just sinking shafts raised the figure to £1,614. The cost of the Tanfield Lea engine (1755) was £1,200 but if we add the sinking costs of three shafts and the cost of drainage with the engine during the process (£2,160), "laying and leveling" two tracks of waggonway a distance of 2,178 yards with necessary bridges which cost another £748, then the total figure was £4,108. See Flinn, *The history of the British coal industry,* pp. 192–3, 200, 294.

2   Pollard's figures on MC refer to the period 1750–1850. Flinn and Pollard are in agreement that the cost of pumping, by including all kinds of "engines and pumps," was c. 10 percent, though the latter author raises this figure to nearly a quarter for medium-sized collieries. The biggest items of expenditure were the underground labor cost (about half of total cost), and rents and waggonway operation accounting for about a quarter. See Flinn, *The history of the British coal industry,* pp. 291–2, 294; Pollard, "Coal mining", pp. 37–49.

3   The threshold level of output would certainly be lower during earlier decades since steam engines were cheaper. Griff colliery, one of the pioneering firms in the installation of steam power having adopted four engines by 1730, had achieved by the latter time an annual output of 18,000 tons. See Flinn, *The history of the British coal industry*, p. 201

4   In referring to Tanfield Lea colliery, Flinn suggested that the "extreme limit of workable transport distances from the staithes of the Tyne" was c. 7 miles. See his *The history of the British coal industry*, p. 294.

5   Louis, "Early steam engines in the north of England", p. 527. Entry cost for a typical colliery in the northeast, raising an output of c. 25,000 chaldrons (66,250 tons) and extracting a net profit of c. £5,000, was estimated at £10–20,000. And in some extreme cases the cost of the initial investment was even more extravagant. During a parliamentary inquiry during the late 1730s, the testimony of a certain George Cloughton revealed that Heaton colliery cost £40,000 to win. See Raistrick, "The steam engine on Tyneside", p. 137; Farey, *A treatise on the steam engine*, p. 228; Pollard, "Coal mining", pp. 58–9.

6   These collieries generated high profits particularly since the crown was willing to provide easy leasing terms plus a 25 percent reduction in royalties in order to facilitate the installation of engines. See Rhodes, "Early steam engines in Flintshire", pp. 219–20, 223.

7   Broseley installed an engine in 1715 but the other two collieries failed to do so. Nef, *The rise of the British coal industry*, pp. 359–60.

8   Harris, "The early steam engine on Merseyside", pp. 110–13, quote from p. 112. Harris's assessment is that the expiration of the patent was less significant compared to the ability of collieries to reach the threshold level of output. This assessment is shared by the author based on the analysis laid out in the Epilogue.

9   The lessee of the colliery was forced to raise the price of coal by the heavy expense of the engine, passing on the hike to Liverpool industrialists, salt rock refiners, and households, and in turn creating an outrage and providing the incentive for the promotion of the Sankey canal. See ibid; Barker and Harris, *A Merseyside town*, p. 65.

10   White, "Early Newcomen engine", p. 209.

11   Nef, *The rise of the British coal industry*, pp. 359–60. Although his comments refer to the latter part of the seventeenth century, such conditions persisted in many locations for several decades thereafter.

12 Duckham, *A history of the Scottish coal industry*, pp. 78, 81; Hamilton, *An economic history of Scotland*, p. 207.

13 While considering it, they asked workers to accept a reduction of wages and lay offs in order to save money since they deemed the cost of the engine fairly steep. Nef, *The rise of the British coal industry, vol. 2*, p. 191.

There are multiple instances of estate papers from Scotland showing that there were small collieries up to the 1760s and beyond that could be won with as little as £60–75. Working on the shallow crops meant that water drainage was not a problem; when water accumulation became an issue, they would be abandoned. Duckham, *A history of the Scottish coal industry*, p. 87.

14 Whatley, "The introduction of the Newcomen engine to Ayrshire", pp. 69–70, 72, 74; Lebon, "Development of the Ayrshire coalfield", pp. 138–40.

15 *The history of the British coal industry*, pp. 317–20, 322–4, 326, quote from p. 326. Such profit figures exhibited considerable fluctuations. Business cycles, according to Flinn, had nothing to do with it. Instead, it was access to new seams that brought a temporary uptick in profitability followed by a decline once they were exhausted. Sheer luck, determined by location, was the primary factor.

16 Barker and Harris, *A Merseyside town*, p. 65.

17 Profits reached £2,497.61 in 1770, £7,577.85 in 1771, and £15,024.44 for 1772. However, "with the available evidence it is unclear whether the later rich deposits encountered were the direct result of pumping"; that raises the possibility that the *ex ante* decision to purchase the engine was marred by ambivalence. See Band, "The steam engines of Gregory mine", pp. 270, 272.

18 Kirkham, "Steam engines in Derbyshire lead mines", pp. 81–2, quote from latter page.

19 Rhodes, "Early steam engines in Flintshire", p. 220.

20 Barton, *The Cornish beam engine*, pp. 17–8.

21 It also pointed out that a depression of the local mining industry will result in the king losing duty revenues due to the lower level of exports that will ensue as well as by the loss of duties imposed on other items used in the operation of mines. The text of the petition submitted to the Parliament, along with the latter's decision on abolishing the duty, are reproduced in Pole, *A treatise on the Cornish pumping engine*, pp. 14–16.

22 Watson, *A compendium of British mining*, p. 32.

23 This assertion ties in well with the evidence on diffusion which restarts in 1746 after a 20-year absence of installations. Barton, *The Cornish beam engine,* p. 18. According to Rogers, 11 cylinders were sent to Cornwall during the period 1744–50 compared to only five during 1751–60, suggesting to him that the abolition of the duty was the critical factor. That contrasts with an opinion by Rowe, that Rogers discusses but dismisses, according to which the expansion of installed engines came a decade after the abolition of the duty because of the peace of 1748 making it more safe to import coal into Cornwall and export ores free from the risk posed by privateers. Rogers, *The Newcomen engine in the west of England*, p. 16.

24 Variable cost was by far the biggest component of ATC. The respective figures stood at £3.6 at Pontypool furnace in 1704 (selling at a price of £6/ton); Leighton furnace (Furness) had a variable cost of £4 in November 1717–October 1718, selling at a price of £6.7; Backbarrow furnace operated at a slightly higher figure, £4.26/ton in 1747. On the other hand, Bank and Barnby furnaces had a variable cost of £6/ton in 1720–37. See Hyde, *Technological change*, p. 32; Allen, *The British Industrial Revolution*, p. 225; Raistrick, "The South Yorkshire iron industry", pp. 68–9; Marshall, *Furness and the Industrial Revolution*, pp. 22, 250; Rees, *Industry before the Industrial Revolution*, p. 216.

25 However, it is worth noting that company records from July 1735 report that despite the new pumping device there was an insufficiency of water for three-quarters of the 46 weeks the furnaces were blown. All references to Coalbrookdale are from Raistrick,

Dynasty of ironfounders, pp. 107–13, 115–18, 144; Allen, *The British Industria. Revolution,* pp. 224, 226.

26 The comparison of the two costs is not entirely adequate because it does not take into account regional differences in factor prices that may have resulted in costs o: coke pig iron lower than that of Coalbrookdale in the hypothetical event coke fur- naces were installed elsewhere. But that is unlikely because the costs of coal and ore in other regions were higher, hence the cost differential probably understates the gap in terms of using the two types of furnaces. See Hyde, "The adoption of coke smelting", p. 405.

27 Ibid., pp. 406–7.

28 Two Welsh coke furnaces had even lower costs. The one at Dowlais stood at £2.52 in 1764 (selling price at £5.87) and £3.73 in 1770–5 (selling price at £5.48); in the forme: year annual output was 732 tons. The cost figure at Plymouth was £3.35 in 1766 (selling price at £5.20) producing an output of 700 tons. See Hyde, pp. 411–14.

29 Nevertheless, the high level of demand kept prices above costs and thus slowed the exit of charcoal furnaces from this sector. Prices at the furnace of charcoal pig iron (based on data from Backbarrow and Bringwood furnaces) during the period 1750–7: fluctuated between £7 and £8. See Hyde, "The adoption of coke smelting", pp. 401 407–8; idem, *Technological change,* p. 205.

30 Coke pig iron prices had to be lower than charcoal pig prices because there was a quality difference; the higher silicon content of the former made it more difficult and costlier for the forgemaster to convert it into bar iron. Nevertheless profit margin remained quite substantial towards the end of the period; by the 1760s profit margin per ton exceeded £2. See Hyde, "The adoption of coke smelting", p. 414; idem *Technological change,* p. 63.

31 The estimated typical output of a charcoal furnace increased between c. 1750 and c. 1775 from 375 to 450 tons; that of coke furnaces from 500 to 800 tons. The latter accounted for a little over half of the industry's output. See Hyde, "The adoption of coke smelting", p. 408.

32 During the same period the number of charcoal furnaces declined from 71 to 44. Se ibid., p. 408

33 Hyde, *Technological change,* pp. 71, 73, quote from the former page.

34 See Chapter 3.

35 Hyde, "The adoption of coke smelting", pp. 411–12; Davies and Pollard, "The iro: industry," pp. 96, 98.

36 For the purchase cost of a typical engine towards the end of the period and the technica features of these engines, see Chapter 4.

37 The annual output of Coalbrookdale was taken as 580 tons; for Dowlais the 176 figure of 732 tons was utilized in the absence of data for 1770–5; for Plymouth it wa 700 tons.

38 Raistrick and Allen, "The South Yorkshire ironmasters", pp. 180–1; Marshall, *Furnes and the Industrial Revolution,* p. 22.

39 Hyde, "The adoption of coke smelting", p. 415.

Bibliography

Allen, R., *The British Industrial Revolution in global perspective* (Cambridge: Cambridg University Press, 2009).

Ashton, T. S., and J. Sykes, *The coal industry of the eighteenth century* (New Yorl Augustus M. Kelley, 1967).

Band, S., "The steam engines of Gregory mine, Ashover", *Bulletin of the Peak Distri Mines Historical Society,* 8, 5 (Summer 1983), pp. 269–95.

Barker, T. C., and J. R. Harris, *A Merseyside town in the industrial revolution, St. Helens, 1750–1900* (Liverpool: Liverpool University Press, 1954).

Barton, D. B., *The Cornish beam engine* (Exeter: Cornwall Books, 1989).

Clark, D. K., *An elementary treatise on steam and the steam-engine, stationary and portable* (London: Lockwood & Co., 1875).

Davies, R. S. W., and S. Pollard, "The iron industry, 1750–1850", in Feinstein and Pollard, eds., *Studies in capital formation*, pp. 73–104.

Duckham, Baron F., *A history of the Scottish coal industry, volume I: 1700–1815* (Newton Abbot: David & Charles, 1970).

Farey, J., *A treatise on the steam engine, historical, practical and descriptive* (London: Longman, Rees, Orme, Brown, and Green, 1827).

Feinstein, C. H., and S. Pollard, eds., *Studies in capital formation in the United Kingdom, 1750–1920,* (Oxford: Clarendon Press, 1988).

Fletcher, J. M., and A. J. Crowe, *An early steam engine in Wednesbury: some papers relating to the coal mines of the Fidoe family, 1727–9* (Wednesbury: Central Library, 1966).

Flinn, M. W., *The history of the British coal industry, Vol. 2, 1700–1830: The Industrial Revolution* (Oxford: Clarendon Press, 1984).

Hamilton, H., *An economic history of Scotland in the eighteenth century* (Oxford: Clarendon Press, 1963).

Harris, J. R., "The early steam engine on Merseyside", *Transactions of the Historical Society of Lancashire and Cheshire*, CVI (1954), pp. 109–16.

Hyde, C. K., *Technological change and the British iron industry, 1700–1870* (Princeton: Princeton University Press, 1977).

Hyde, C. K., "The adoption of coke smelting by the British iron industry, 1709–1790", *Explorations in Economic History*, 2nd ser., X (1973), pp. 397–418.

Jenkins, R., "Savery, Newcomen, and the early history of the steam engine", *Transactions of the Newcomen Society*, 3 (1922–3), pp. 96–118.

Kirkham, N., "Steam engines in Derbyshire lead mines", *Transactions of the Newcomen Society*, 38 (1965–6), pp. 69–88.

Lebon, J. H. G., "Development of the Ayrshire coalfield", *Scottish Geographical Magazine*, XLIX (1933), pp. 138–54.

Louis, H., "Early steam engines in the north of England", *Transactions of the Institute of Mining Engineers* 82 (1931–2), pp. 526–30.

Marshall, J. D., *Furness and the Industrial Revolution: an economic history of Furness (1711–1900) and the town of Barrow (1757–1897)* (Barrow-in-Furness: Barrow-in-Furness Library and Museum Committee, 1958).

Nef, J., *The rise of the British coal industry*, 2 vols. (London: George Routledge & Sons, 1932).

Pacey, A., *The maze of ingenuity: ideas and idealism in the development of technology*, 2nd ed. (Cambridge, MA, and London: MIT Press, 1992).

Pole, W., *A treatise on the Cornish pumping engine* (London: John Weale, 1844).

Pollard, S., "Coal mining, 1750–1850", in Feinstein and Pollard, eds., *Studies in capital formation*, pp. 35–72.

Raistrick, A., "The steam engine on Tyneside, 1715–1778", *Transactions of the Newcomen Society*, 17 (1936–7), pp. 131–63.

Raistrick, A., "The south Yorkshire iron industry", *Transactions of the Newcomen Society*, 19 (1938–9), pp. 51–86.

Raistrick, A., *Dynasty of ironfounders: the Darbys and Coalbrookdale* (London, New York and Toronto: Longmans, Green & Company, 1953).

Raistrick, A., and E. Allen, "The South Yorkshire ironmasters, 1690–1750", *Economic History Review*, IX (1939), pp. 168–85.

Rees, W., *Industry before the Industrial Revolution, Vols. I and II* (Cardiff: University of Wales Press, 1968).

Rhodes, J. N., "Early steam engines in Flintshire", *Transactions of the Newcomen Society*, 41 (1968–9), pp. 217–25.

Rogers, K. H., *The Newcomen engine in the west of England* (Bradford-on-Avon: Moonraker Press, 1976).

Savery, T., *The miner's friend, or an engine to raise water by fire described and of the manner of fixing it in mines* (London, 1702, reprinted 1827 for S. Crouch).

Thurston, R. H., *Stationary steam engines, simple and compound; especially as adapted to light and power plants*, 7th ed. (New York: J. Wiley & Sons; London: Chapman & Hall, 1902).

Watson, J. Y., *A compendium of British mining, with statistical notices of the principal mines in Cornwall* (London: Munro and Congreve Printers, 1843).

Whatley, C. A., "The introduction of the Newcomen engine to Ayrshire", *Industrial Archaeology Review* 2 (1965), pp. 69–77.

White, A. W. A., "Early Newcomen engines on the Warwickshire coalfield, 1714–1736", *Transactions of the Newcomen Society*, 41 (1968–9), pp. 203–16.

Epilogue

This study has considered the role of two key factors driving the diffusion of Newcomen engines through 1773. On the supply side was the evolution of the cost of steam power broken down to its constituent components in relation to the cost, technical capabilities, and geographical dispersion of alternative techniques. The decline of cost of steam power was driven by the presence (or absence) of the patent premium and the improvement of engineering skills over time. On the demand side, it considered the impact of market fragmentation, imposed by an imperfect transportation network, on the level of demand and size of output at the firm level.

The first, fairly obvious, conclusion to draw is that the expiration of the premium failed to make a significant impact when we consider diffusion at the aggregate level, contrary to what has been argued so often by the existing literature but without much evidence to support such statements; simply put, there is no structural break prior to the 1740s. This statement cries out for some kind of explanation. The premium ranged within a wide span, occasionally being set at exorbitant levels. A sample of such premium values gave a mean of £138 for the entire period it was in place, accounting for c. one-tenth of the annual cost of steam power in places with high fuel costs (e.g., London) to as high as c. one-third in English collieries where the latter cost was far less dramatic.[1]

There is no question that the payment of the premium acted as an impediment to diffusion, as several writers have suggested.[2] But the fact lost in the literature is that the amounts charged either declined sharply or turned to modest lump sums beginning c. 1726 (see Figure 4.1): perhaps caused by a sense of defensiveness on the part of the proprietors following the petition to the Parliament initiated by Sparrow asking to render the patent void, capitalizing on the frustration of business owners. The sharp decline of the premiums c. 1726 meant that this factor became less burdensome prior to the formal expiration of the patent; and it explains why there is no radical upturn of the aggregate diffusion curve right after 1733. It was not a matter of having exorbitant premiums up to that year followed by no premiums. Instead, it was a matter of alleviation of this type of cost in a two-step process, contributing to sustaining the mild increase of the diffusion curve's slope.[3] This fact has been largely lost in the modern literature which views 1733 as the critical breaking point in the diffusion of steam power during the pre-Watt era.

In order to make sense of the trajectory of the aggregate diffusion curve, one has to focus on patterns observed at the sectoral level. It is adoption at the level of individual sectors which conditioned regional patterns of diffusion and converged in determining the aggregate adoption of hp. Two types of visual aids will be utilized to delve into this type of analysis. First, Figure E.1 presents graphs with the diffusion curves in four different sectors/locations, in each case accompanied by tables which break down the evolution of the different types of cost. The period up to 1740, characterized by small engines of c. 10 hp, is divided into three sub-periods: 1706–25 when the premiums were at the highest levels; 1726–33 when the premiums declined drastically, down to mean values that were about half of what they used to be; and 1734–9 when there was no premium while the typical engine was still small. The period 1740–73 represents the time when more powerful engines come to the fore. The analysis of these four periods will utilize the results of Bai-Perron tests undertaken in order to find structural breaks in all four sectors/locations examined (see Appendix E.1). In addition, Figure E.5 provides a visual impression of the regional dispersion of the diffusion process. The maps showing the relative significance of each county, based on which quartile they belong to, are reproduced for three years: 1718, in order to capture the pioneers of the diffusion process; 1745, the year prior to the first structural break at the aggregate level; and 1773, the end of the period.

Let us start with the mining sector, accounting for 87 percent of the total hp adopted by 1773, the lion's share going to collieries. Figure E.1 presents the diffusion of hp in English collieries. Bai-Perron tests reveal the presence of structural breaks, the top two in the post-1740 period, but all values are strikingly weak compared to other sectors/regions justifying the visual impression one gets from the smoothness of the diffusion curve. The evolution of cost per hp seems to have no significant impact on the diffusion process. The premium declined by about £10 c. 1726 and that much more when it expired in 1733; however, the weakest structural break comes at a time (1720) when none of these cost reductions kicked in. That is not to say the role of the premium was irrelevant. But while its two-step reduction fueled diffusion, it failed to produce a strong structural break because the alleviation of the monetary burden it imposed was gradual.

On the other hand, the top two structural breaks come at moments (1746 and 1764) when the reduction of cost per hp due to the larger engines is very modest. The improvement of engineering skills, reflected in the construction of more powerful engines and the better management of them, also does not seem to have made a sizeable impact since fuel efficiency in this sector was not of paramount importance.

However, the more modest cost reduction of the post-1740 period coincided with the initial phase of improvement of the transportation infrastructure. The latter determined regional variations in the level of demand which, in turn, conditioned the size of collieries, and hence whether they could achieve the threshold level of output at c. 23,000 tons.[4] Through 1740 or so the collieries whose output rose well above the threshold were mainly in the northeastern coalfield (Northumberland and Durham). There were a few outliers in the Midlands (Staffordshire and

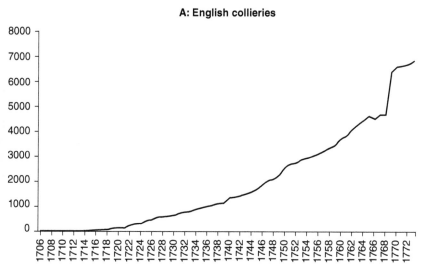

	1706–25	1726–33	1734–9	1740–73
Interest	5.5	5.5	5.5	3.5
Depreciation	8.25	8.25	8.25	5.25
Premium	20.6	10.31	0	0
Labor, parts, repairs	12.67	12.67	12.67	5.06
Coal	5.1	5.1	5.1	13.9
Cost per hp	52.12	41.83	31.52	27.71

Figure E.1 English collieries: cumulative hp installed and cost per hp

Warwickshire) as well as the isolated case of Flintshire but the impression is that in most cases current or anticipated output in these collieries exceeded the threshold to a more modest extent compared to the northeast. This statement is visually confirmed by the first two maps of Figure E.5 focusing on the counties at the top two quartiles. But once this first batch of large collieries drove the initial phase of the diffusion process, the rate of adoption hinged on transportation improvements and the expansion of market demand. Progress made in both respects was driven by the favorable conditions still facing the northeastern coalfield coupled with improvements in other regions brought by the construction of turnpikes and the initial phase of the canal era. However, favorable developments beyond the northeastern coalfield were slow and came by very gradually, hence failing to overturn the relative dominance of the latter; this is evident from the fact that the only coal-bearing counties in the top two quartiles during the period 1746–73 were Durham and Northumberland. In the end, neither the cost reductions brought by larger engines nor the expansion of the transportation network were dramatic enough in themselves to make a radical dent in the diffusion process. But their combined effect was significant enough to bring about the two modest structural breaks during the post-1740 period.

These assertions are also applicable, by and large, to the case of Scotland. In fact, in this case the role of demand was probably even more powerful. There was a structural break, of a fairly weak value, in 1720 but once again it comes at such time that it fails to produce a correlation with the behavior of the premium values (see Figure E.2). Instead, it coincided with the time Stevenston colliery initiated a wave of installations in an effort to capture a larger share of the Irish market. But unlike England, Scottish figures of steam power diffusion do produce a structural

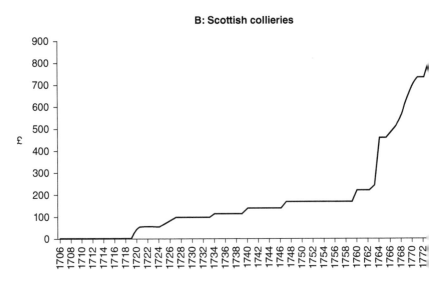

Cost per hp (£)

	1706–25	1726–33	1734–9	1740–73
Interest	5.5	5.5	5.5	3.5
Depreciation	8.25	8.25	8.25	5.25
Premium	20.6	10.31	0	0
Labor, parts, repairs	23.1	23.1	23.1	9.24
Coal	5.1	5.1	5.1	13.9
Cost per hp	62.55	52.26	41.95	31.89

Figure E.2 Scottish collieries: cumulative hp installed and cost per hp break of a very high value in 1764. Part of it is explained on the basis of cost reductions brought by the introduction of larger engines. But the role of market expansion, exemplified (among others) in the resurgence of exports from Ayrshire to Ireland after a brief period of slackening, must have been also quite substantial.

The so-called "microbiology" of the diffusion process was different in other segments of the mining sector. Cornwall, for instance, was one of the pioneers in the diffusion process in the early part of the century but the effort quickly came to a halt due to the heavy burden imposed by fuel prices coupled with the presence of fairly abundant water supplies offering a cheaper alternative. The two-step reduction of the premium knocked off c. £20 from the very large cost per hp but failed to make any difference in the diffusion pattern; the rate of installations was very anemic through the mid-1720s and entirely absent through the mid-1740s (Figure E.3); as a result, the relative position of the county dropped from the second to the

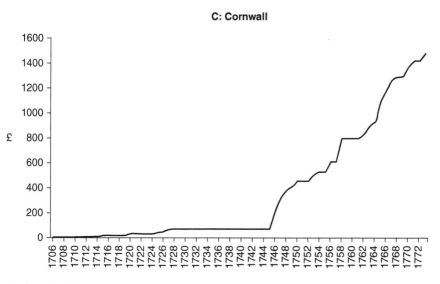

C: Cornwall

Cost per hp (£)

	1706–25	1726–33	1734–9	1740–73
Interest	5.5	5.5	5.5	3.5
Depreciation	8.25	8.25	8.25	5.25
Premium	20.6	10.31	0	0
Labor, parts, repairs	12.67	12.67	12.67	5.06
Coal	73.54	73.54	73.54	58.92
Cost per hp	120.56	110.27	99.96	72.73

Figure E.3 Cornwall: cumulative hp installed and cost per hp fourth quartile by 1745 (Figure E.5). What turned the tide, producing a structural break with a very robust value in 1746, was the combination of the resurgence of European demand for Cornish copper and the reduction of the cost per hp by over £27 due to the higher efficiencies achieved by the larger engines. These two events took place simultaneously in the early 1740s prompting the coming of the Hornblowers in 1745 (a year prior to the structural break) and other prominent engineers.

The "microbiology" was somewhat different in other segments of the mining industry such as the lead mines of Derbyshire. The price of coal was not a heavy burden and the expansion of output was feasible through the discovery of rich seams. The problem lay, instead, in the low capitalization rates of these mines which were caused by funds being drawn mainly from individuals of fairly limited financial means. But the favorable conditions were strong enough to take Derbyshire from the fourth quartile by 1718 to the second and third by 1745 and 1773 respectively (see Figure E.5).

All in all, the conditions which drove the diffusion process in the mining sector were either very favorable throughout this period, such as strong market demand and the substantial size of collieries in the northeast; or they were improving sharply in the case of Cornwall by the early 1740s or gradually (with the expansion of demand in collieries elsewhere). It comes as no surprise then that the mining sector was at the forefront of the diffusion process and achieved a rate of adoption which reached an estimated figure of approximately half of the ideal rate.[5]

But conditions in other sectors and locations were less favorable. In the iron industry the diffusion of steam power was tied to the installation of coke blast furnaces encountering two types of obstacles: first, coke furnaces gained a cost advantage over charcoal furnaces fairly late, beginning in the 1750s; and, second, defraying the initial combined cost of a coke blast furnace and of a steam engine required fivefold the amount of time it took in collieries. Progress was made, as shown by the fact that Shropshire moved from the fourth to the third quartile between 1718 and 1773 (see Figure E.5). But it was progress far less spectacular compared to the mining sector. Diffusion in the iron industry accounted for a little less than a third of the ideal rate and only 6 percent of the total amount of hp installed by 1773.

The configuration of circumstances was even less favorable in London. From the four sectors/regions examined closely, it was the only one where the cost of steam was high enough at the dawn of the steam era to match the cost of horses; this fact, coupled with obstacles imposed by the syndicate, kept diffusion at very low levels for the first decade (see Figure E.4). A structural break does take place in 1726 which can probably be attributed to the first radical reduction of the premiums; the latter declined by c. £10, an amount that may have proven sufficient at the margin to render, for the first time, steam power preferable to horses. The second, more robust, structural break takes place in 1743 coinciding with the higher fuel efficiency of the larger engines and highlights the beginning of a more steady progress in the diffusion path. But this was a location with very limited potential for the diffusion of steam power since it lacked the two sectors of the economy at the forefront of the process.

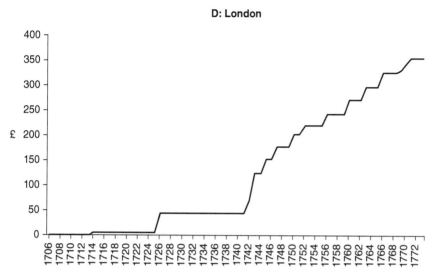

Cost per hp (£)

	1706–25	1726–33	1734–9	1740–73
Interest	5.5	5.5	5.5	3.5
Depreciation	8.25	8.25	8.25	5.25
Premium	20.6	10.31	0	0
Labor, parts, repairs	12.67	12.67	12.67	5.06
Coal	87.6	87.6	87.6	76.2
Cost per hp	134.6	124.3	114	90

Figure E.4 London: cumulative hp installed and cost per hp

John Farey, the most reputable expert on steam power at the beginning of the nineteenth century, remarked:

> This circumstance [high fuel consumption of Newcomen engines] limited the use of this kind of engine very much. To draw water from coal-pits, where they can be worked with unsaleable small coals, they are still universally employed; and they answered very well for draining valuable mines; or for supplying a great and wealthy city with water; also for some other purposes, where a great expense could be borne; but in a great number of cases, to which the unlimited powers of steam engines are now applied with advantage, the expense of fuel would have precluded the use of them, if a more economical system than Newcomen's had not been invented.[6]

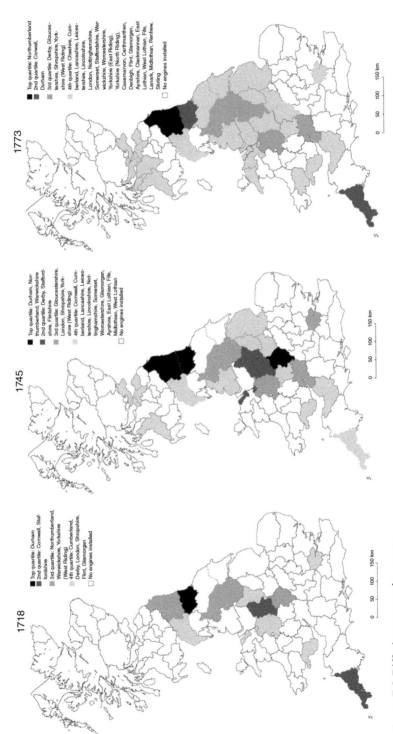

Figure E.5 Diffusion patterns by county

This quote encapsulates perfectly the main argument of this study. The installation of nearly 570 non-experimental engines by 1773 was indeed a "remarkable" feat that had to overcome a series of impediments to the diffusion process. The presence of the patent premium was one of them, stalling diffusion because of the erratic and restrictive policies of the syndicate. Its reduction and eventual elimination boosted the rate of adoption but failed to have a radical impact either because the cost of steam was not very substantial to begin with (e.g., in the case of collieries) or because other factors proved more important. These other factors were the more substantial cost reductions brought about by the larger engines in the form of better fuel efficiency and lower labor and capital cost per hp, developments that proved to be very important in regions some distance away from collieries. Achieving less market fragmentation through expansion of the transportation network was also very crucial because it would have allowed more firms to reach the shifting threshold levels of output "where a great expense could be borne". These improvements were under way by the 1740s but they did not go far enough by the early 1770s, hence leaving substantial gaps between the actual and potential levels of diffusion in the sectors relevant to the adoption of steam power. This incomplete process had to await further improvements which were ushered in during the next phase, the last quarter of the nineteenth century, an era marked by Watt's genius.

Appendix E.1: Sectoral/regional structural change evaluation
By Lawrence Costa

In this section, we use regional diffusion data to perform a simple OLS regression of the time period on cumulative horsepower. From there, we make use of Bai-Perron tests to evaluate structural breaks in the diffusion pattern. The structural break tests are listed below; all of them use a trimming percentage of 15 and report at the 95 percent confidence level. The years of potential breaks are listed by region (then by highest confidence level) in the rightmost column of the table. The software used for this test is Eviews 8.

Region	Break Test	F-Statistic	Scaled F-Statistic	Bai-Perron Critical Value	Break Date Indicated
Cornwall	0 vs. 1	809.18	1,618.35	11.47	1746
	1 vs. 2	33.33	66.67	12.95	1764
	2 vs. 3	1.89	3.78	14.03	
	3 vs. 4				
London	0 vs. 1	491.15	982.30	11.47	1743
	1 vs. 2	32.97	65.94	12.95	1726
	2 vs. 3	9.86	19.72	14.03	1754
	3 vs. 4	0.91	1.82	14.85	

(continued)

(continued)

Region	Break Test	F-Statistic	Scaled F-Statistic	Bai-Perron Critical Value	Break Date Indicated
English	0 vs. 1	147.30	294.60	11.47	1746
Collieries	1 vs. 2	35.24	70.47	12.95	1764
	2 vs. 3	10.55	21.10	14.03	1720
	3 vs. 4	0.51	1.03	14.85	
Scottish	0 vs. 1	1,285.53	2,571.06	11.47	1764
Collieries	1 vs. 2	19.73	39.46	12.95	1720
	2 vs. 3	7.71	15.42	14.03	1754
	3 vs. 4	2.08	4.16	14.85	

Notes

1 See Chapter 4.
2 Allen, "The introduction of the Newcomen engine", p. 170; Flinn, *The history of the British coal industry*, p. 121; Rhodes, "Early steam engines in Flintshire", p. 221 Harris, "The employment of steam power in the eighteenth century", p. 139.
3 The mean value of the premium up to 1726 was £206, declining to half this amount subsequently; see Chapter 4.
4 A reminder that the respective figure was lower prior to 1740. Once the threshold level of output was achieved, defraying the installation cost of an engine and its related appurtenances could come, more or less, within a year (see Chapter 6).
5 See Chapter 3.
6 Farey, *A treatise on the steam engine*, p. 307.

Bibliography

Allen, J. S., "The introduction of the Newcomen engine from 1710 to 1733", *Transaction of the Newcomen Society*, 42 (1969–70), pp. 169–90.

Farey, J. *A treatise on the steam engine, historical, practical and descriptive* (London Longman, Rees, Orme, Brown, and Green, 1827).

Flinn, M. W., *The history of the British coal industry, Vol. 2, 1700–1830: The Industrial Revolution* (Oxford: Clarendon Press, 1984).

Harris, J. R., "The employment of steam power in the eighteenth century", *History*, LII (1967), pp. 133–48.

Rhodes, J. N., "Early steam engines in Flintshire", *Transactions of the Newcomen Society*, 41 (1968–9), pp. 217–25.

Index

For Product Safety Concerns and Information please contact our EU
representative GPSR@taylorandfrancis.com
Taylor & Francis Verlag GmbH, Kaufingerstraße 24, 80331 München, Germany

www.ingramcontent.com/pod-product-compliance
Ingram Content Group UK Ltd.
Pitfield, Milton Keynes, MK11 3LW, UK
UKHW020952180425
457613UK00019B/649